the essential

seafood

cookbook

the essential
seafood
cookbook

This edition produced specially for Borders Group, Inc. by arrangement with
Murdoch Books Pty Limited. Printed 2005.

First published by Murdoch Books Pty Limited.

Chief Executive: Juliet Rogers
Publisher: Kay Scarlett

ISBN 1-74045-779-X

Printed by 1010 Printing International Limited.
PRINTED IN CHINA

IMPORTANT: Those who might be at risk from the effects of salmonella food poisoning
(the elderly, pregnant women, young children and those suffering from immune deficiency diseases)
should consult their GP with any concerns about eating raw eggs.

OUR STAR RATING: When we test recipes, we rate them for ease of preparation.
The following cookery ratings are used in this book:
☆ A single star indicates a recipe that is simple and generally quick to make—perfect for beginners.
☆☆ Two stars indicate the need for just a little more care, or perhaps a little more time.
☆☆☆ Three stars indicate special dishes that need more investment in time,
care and patience—but the results are worth it. Even beginners can make these
dishes as long as the recipe is followed carefully.

SEAFOOD

From crab cakes in a New York eatery, to moules marinière in a French bistro, or finger-stinging salty hot fish and chips on a windy seafront, seafood is deliciously at home just about anywhere. Today, with caviar the costliest food known to man and whole fish prepared in restaurants that wouldn't even dream of serving hamburgers, it is hard to imagine that until the nineteenth century seafood was poor man's fare. Lobster and oysters were cheap and cheerful and giving up meat on Fridays to make do with a humble fish supper was an exercise in religious humility. But our values have changed and now fresh seafood enjoys the respect and popularity it deserves, all around the world.

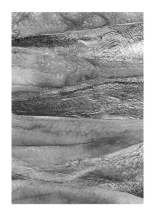

CONTENTS

SPECIAL FEATURES

ALL ABOUT SEAFOOD

This book is a comprehensive guide to preparing and cooking seafood. Seafood has unfairly earned the tag 'difficult to cook', partly because in some cases it can require varying amounts of preparation for cooking. The perception of seafood cookery being daunting has persisted in spite of the fact that seafood cooks relatively quickly. Although the cooking methods are the same as for meat, fish, for example, doesn't have as much connective tissue as meat, so it breaks down more quickly when heat is applied. To add further weight to the 'difficult' tag, many species of seafood, especially fish, have ended up with more than one common name, often leading to confusion. We try to address both of these problems and hope to inspire you to experiment in the kitchen and make use of the wonderful array of seafood that is readily available.

We have compiled an illustrated glossary of seafood. Obviously it is impossible to picture every species, so we have chosen a few of the most commonly available worldwide, listing their common as well as less common names. Within the glossary, we have also recommended the most suitable cooking methods for each species. Some cuts of fish are very versatile—fillets, for example, can be pan-fried, coated and deep-fried, poached, steamed, minced and used for pâtés, terrines or fish cakes. Some seafood, however, is more limited in the way it can be cooked, mainly because of flavour and texture.

On the preparation pages (24–31), we show how to clean and prepare seafood before cooking, as well as how to serve whole cooked fish. If filleting fish or cutting up squid still seems too daunting, talk to your fishmonger. Most are happy to carry out all preparation and offer advice, perhaps suggesting a local variety of fish or other seafood suitable for your chosen recipe.

Within the recipes themselves, we list some possible alternatives if your first choice of fish or other seafood is not available.

FIRM OR SOFT? OILY OR DRY?

Don't be put off by the descriptions used for seafood. There are many ways of differentiating between types of fish—saltwater and freshwater, cold and warm water, flat and round. But in relation to cookery, the descriptions you will usually hear are firm, soft, oily and dry.

FIRM FLESH Most fish have a relatively solid flesh that holds together during cooking. Fish with soft flesh require more gentle cooking methods.

COLOUR AND FLAVOUR Lighter-coloured flesh usually indicates a more delicate flavour. Freshwater fish are usually sweet, although some have a strong, sometimes slightly muddy flavour.

OILINESS Oily fish have the fat content dispersed throughout the flesh whereas most white fish have drier flesh because they store fat in their livers.

CHOOSING FRESH SEAFOOD

We all know seafood should be absolutely fresh when we buy it. But if it doesn't actually smell 'off', is there any way to tell just how fresh it is? Seafood is divided into three main categories (fish, crustaceans and molluscs) and each has characteristics of freshness:

WHOLE FISH:

- Eyes should be clear, bright and bulging (avoid fish that have dull, sunken and cloudy eyes)
- Skin and flesh should have a lustrous appearance and feel firm. If a fish can be bent so its mouth can kiss its tail, it is probably past its prime
- Fish tails should be moist and pliable, not dried out
- Fish with scales should have a good even coverage and if patchy-looking are best avoided. Scales should be firm and intact
- Gills should be bright (from bright to dark red, depending on species)

FISH FILLETS/CUTLETS:

- Flesh should look moist and lustrous, with no signs of discolouration. The fillets or cutlets should not be sitting in a pool of liquid
- Fish fillets should not be dried at the edges

CRUSTACEANS (prawns, crabs, lobsters, bugs, freshwater crayfish):
- No discolouration or 'blackness', particularly at the joints (claws, nippers, heads etc.)

● Bodies, claws, nippers etc. should be fully intact and not broken or missing
● Bodies should be free of water or liquid and should be heavy in relation to size

LIVE CRUSTACEANS (usually blue, black or green):
● Should be active and moving freely. Nippers and claws should be intact, not broken or loose
● Mud crabs should be tied up until after they have been cooked

All crustaceans should feel heavy for their size. Crustaceans shed their shells as they grow and after about 4 months, grow into a new shell. If they feel light, it may mean they are still growing and, if so, the flesh will be watery.

MOLLUSCS (invertebrates with soft unsegmented bodies and often a shell):
univalve (one shell) e.g. winkles, whelks, abalone;
bivalve (two shells) e.g. mussels, oysters, scallops:
● Shells should be tightly closed, or close quickly after a tap on the bench, be intact and look lustrous. Flesh should be firm and 'plump';
cephalopods (octopus, squid, cuttlefish):
● Flesh should be firm and resilient and spring back when touched
● Head, tentacles and body should be intact and not loose

STORING SEAFOOD IN THE REFRIGERATOR

FISH FILLETS AND CUTLETS: Prepare whole fish by scaling, gutting and cleaning, then rinsing under cold water. Pat dry to remove any traces of scales or intestinal lining (or ask your fishmonger to prepare the fish). Place in a covered container (or in a freezer bag on a plate) in the coldest part of the fridge and use within 2–3 days of purchase.

CRUSTACEANS AND MOLLUSCS: Wrap large crustaceans such as crayfish, lobsters and crabs in foil, then place in a container or on a plate. All other shellfish can be placed in a covered container or in a freezer bag on a plate. Store in the coldest part of the fridge and use within 2–3 days. Use raw crustaceans and molluscs (prawns, crabs, lobsters, oysters) within 1–2 days of purchase. To keep mussels, pipis and freshwater crayfish alive, store in a bucket of water in the coldest part of the house, covered loosely with a damp cloth, away from direct sunlight. They can be refrigerated in hot weather for up to 3 days.

STORING SEAFOOD IN THE FREEZER

Ideally, all seafood is best eaten fresh. However, if you have caught your own and had a lucky day, you can freeze it when it is very fresh.

If you are buying from the fishmonger, make sure the fish hasn't already been frozen and thawed. Clearly label and date for freezing. Don't defrost frozen seafood at room temperature: thaw in the fridge. Some seafood, such as crumbed fish fillets, calamari or prawns, can be cooked from frozen. Avoid refreezing seafood as this alters the flavour and texture and can lead to spoilage.

WHOLE FISH, FILLETS AND CUTLETS: Scale, clean and gut, rinse under cold water, pat dry with paper towel, then freeze in an airtight bag. Whole fish can be frozen for up to 6 months (oily fish such as tuna, mullet, Atlantic salmon, sardines, can be frozen for up to 3 months). Fillets and cutlets should be frozen in bags in smaller portions for up to 3 months.

PRAWNS: Do not peel. Place in a plastic container and cover with water—this forms a large ice block which insulates the prawns and prevents freezer burn. Freeze for up to 3 months. When required, thaw in the refrigerator overnight.

OTHER CRUSTACEANS AND MOLLUSCS: Freeze for up to 3 months. For ease of handling, wrap large crustaceans such as crayfish, lobsters and crabs in foil, then place in an airtight freezer bag before freezing. Octopus, squid and cuttlefish should be gutted before freezing and can be frozen for up to 3 months. Oysters shouldn't be frozen as the flavour will alter.

ABOVE: Dressed crab (page 95)

A WORD ABOUT COOKING SEAFOOD

Seafood should never be overcooked or it will be dry, tough or rubbery. It should be removed from the heat as soon as it is 'just done'—the internal heat will finish the cooking process. But how can we tell when the moment is right? Most seafood is cooked when it loses its translucent appearance and turns opaque. Fish starts to flake and separate from the bone. Some seafood, such as tuna and Atlantic salmon, is best served while it is still rare in the centre—just like a good steak.

Fish fillets are used extensively in the book because of their versatility. They should be cooked as soon as possible after preparation or purchase so they don't have time to dry out.

Molluscs are cooked briefly or eaten raw. The shells can be prised open—you may need to cut the muscle that holds each shell together, or they can be steamed open. It is very important not to overcook molluscs or they will toughen.

Small octopus can be fried, barbecued or grilled, but larger octopus need to be tenderized at the fishmongers, then need long simmering in liquid. When tenderized, the tentacles curl up.

Small cuttlefish and squid are delicious fried and the bodies are ideal for stuffing. Large cuttlefish and squid require long simmering.

COOKING METHODS FOR SEAFOOD

POACHING, or gentle simmering of food in a liquid, ensures fish or shellfish stay moist. It can be done on the stove or in the oven and is best for fish with firm flesh. Salted water is suitable but to add flavour, you can use a flavoured liquid such as court-bouillon, or fish stock. The liquid should be kept so that it is not boiling, but just slightly moving on top. Whole fish, cutlets or fillets can be poached. Fish such as whiting, with soft flesh, delicate texture and mild flavour, benefit from being poached in a court-bouillon

or fish stock. Special fish poachers are necessary for large whole fish such as salmon. Squid and shellfish such as lobster, crabs, yabbies, bugs, mussels, pipis, clams can also be poached.

STEAMING is another gentle cooking method, suitable for nearly all types of fish (white-fleshed fillets, cutlets, steaks and small whole fish) and shellfish (mussels, crabs, scallops, prawns) but is ideal for fish with delicate flesh, and shellfish, especially mussels. Bivalves such as mussels are cooked in a little wine or liquid in a tightly sealed pan over high heat. Other seafood should

be cooked over simmering liquid, not in it. The liquid can be water, stock, court-bouillon or white wine. Steaming requires no fat, making the food easily digestible. To add flavour, fish should be seasoned before steaming or placed on fresh herbs or vegetables whilst cooking. Fish should not overlap or be touching or it will not cook evenly.

BAKING whole fish in the oven is one of the simplest cooking methods. Fish can be baked in or over liquid as an alternative to poaching or steaming. The oven temperature is usually

170°–190°C (325°–375°F) and the fish can be placed on a vegetable that has a high water content, to help the fish keep its moisture. Haddock, sea bass, bream and snapper are especially suited to this cooking method.

GRILLING AND BARBECUING both involve intense sources of high heat. One of the most important factors is preheating. Cutlets or fish steaks from larger oily fish such as salmon or mackerel, or small whole fish such as red mullet are best suited, though any firm-fleshed fish can be used.

The fish should be no more than 5 cm (2 inches) thick or they will overcook on the outside before cooking through. To ensure even cooking, fish should be returned to room

temperature before grilling or barbecuing. With lean fish such as bream, it is a good idea to marinate it to prevent it drying out, or baste it with butter or oil during cooking. Or you can wrap fish in foil and let it steam in its own juices.

STEWING AND CASSEROLING Large chunks of fish or seafood are cooked for a short time in a lot of liquid. Most fish are suitable—delicate-fleshed fish such as John dory, whiting and red mullet

and firm-fleshed bream and sea bass. Avoid combining strongly flavoured, oily fish such as mackerel and herring in stews as the flavour might overpower other seafood. Mussels, prawns and lobster make delicious additions to stews.

DEEP-FRYING Battered or coated fish is fried in a saucepan one third full of oil that is heated to

180°–190°C (350°–375°F). Peanut or corn oil are best. The fish or seafood is exposed to a temperature nearly twice that of boiling water and this is why it requires a protective coating. The coating turns crisp and golden but the flesh remains moist and tender. If the fish isn't coated, moisture will escape and the fish will overcook and dry out. Small whole fish such as whitebait, sardines and thin fillets and firm-fleshed shellfish are most suitable. Thicker larger fish and fillets tend to dry out and overcook on the outside before cooking through.

PAN-FRYING The most popular method of pan-frying is to dust fish fillets with flour and cook in a layer of hot oil or butter, preferably clarified. The flour forms a golden crust and the fish stays

moist and doesn't stick to the pan. This is suited to firm white-fleshed fish and especially skinned fillets of flat fish such as sole. It is also suitable for medium whole fish, fish cutlets and steaks. Cook thicker fillets over high heat until a golden crust forms on both sides, then lower the heat so the centre cooks through.

STIR-FRYING is a simple quick method of cooking food in oil in a wok or large frying pan over high heat. Food is usually cooked in batches so the temperature of the wok or pan

does not drop, thus stewing the food. All the food is returned to the wok at the end to heat through. Firm-fleshed fish, prawns, squid and cuttlefish are well suited to stir-frying.

GLOSSARY

Shown here are a few common seafood varieties from the hundreds harvested worldwide. To help with menu planning, we have given an indication of flesh type and suitable cooking methods. Sizes are a rough guide.

ANCHOVIES (8–15 cm/3–6 in)
ALSO KNOWN AS smig
COOKING bake, barbecue, grill, pan-fry
FLESH soft, oily; strong flavour

BARRAMUNDI (60–120 cm/24–48 in)
ALSO KNOWN AS barra, giant perch
COOKING bake, barbecue, grill, pan-fry, poach, steam
FLESH firm, white, moist; mild flavour

BLUE-EYE (55–90 cm/22–36 in)
ALSO KNOWN AS blue-eye trevalla, blue-eye cod, deep-sea trevalla, sea trevally, deepsea trevally
COOKING bake, barbecue, pan-fry, poach, steam
FLESH firm, white, moist; mild flavour

BONITO (35–60 cm/14–24 in)
ALSO KNOWN AS horse mackerel
COOKING barbecue, grill, pan-fry
FLESH firm; mild flavour

BREAM, SILVER (20–40 cm/8–16 in)
ALSO KNOWN AS porgy, silver or black bream
COOKING bake, barbecue, grill, pan-fry, poach
FLESH soft, white, moist; mild flavour

CARP (35–60 cm/14–24 in)
ALSO KNOWN AS mirror, calico carp
COOKING bake, pan-fry, poach, steam
FLESH firm; sweet flavour, can be muddy

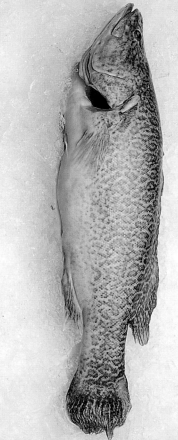

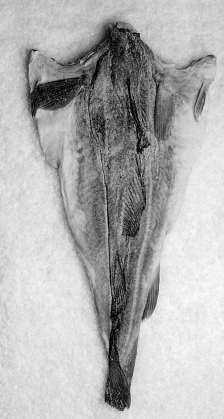

COD (40–90 cm/16–36 in)
COOKING bake, barbecue, grill, pan-fry,
poach, steam
FLESH firm, white; sweet flavour

COD, MURRAY (40–60 cm/16–24 in)
COOKING bake, barbecue, grill, pan-fry,
poach, steam
FLESH firm, white, moist; mild flavour

COD, SALT (30–40 cm/12–16 in)
ALSO KNOWN AS bacalao
COOKING soak overnight, then casserole,
stew, make into croquettes or dips
FLESH firm; distinct, salty flavour

COD, SMOKED (UNCOOKED)
(25–30 cm/10–12 in)
COOKING bake, grill, pan-fry,
poach, steam
FLESH firm, large flake; smoky flavour

COLEY (40–90 cm/16–36 in)
ALSO KNOWN AS coalfish, saithe
COOKING casserole, deep-fry, pan-fry, soup
FLESH soft, white

DAB (15 cm/6 in)
ALSO KNOWN AS dab sole, garve, sand dab
COOKING barbecue, grill, pan-fry, poach,
steam
FLESH white; sweet, delicate flavour

FLATHEAD (30–60 cm/12–24 in)
COOKING bake, barbecue, deep-fry,
grill, steam
FLESH firm, dry, white; mild, sweet flavour

GARFISH (30–35 cm/12–14 in)
ALSO KNOWN AS garpike, sea eel, needlefish

COOKING bake, barbecue, grill, pan-fry, poach
FLESH soft, fine, white; delicate, sweet flavo

FLOUNDER (25–30 cm/10–12 in)
COOKING bake, barbecue, grill, poach
FLESH white, soft, moist; delicate flavour

GEMFISH (60–90 cm/24–36 in)
ALSO KNOWN AS southern kingfish, hake

COOKING bake, barbecue, grill, pan-fry, poac
FLESH firm, moist; mild flavour

GROPER (80–120 cm/32–48 in)
ALSO KNOWN AS bass groper, hapuku
COOKING bake, barbecue, grill, pan-fry,
poach, steam
FLESH firm; mild flavour

HADDOCK (60 cm/24 in)
COOKING barbecue, grill, pan-fry, smoke, salt
FLESH soft, white; often smoked

HAKE (60 cm/24 in)
ALSO KNOWN AS blue whiting
COOKING bake, barbecue, grill, pan-fry,
poach, steam
FLESH white, moist, delicate texture;
mild flavour

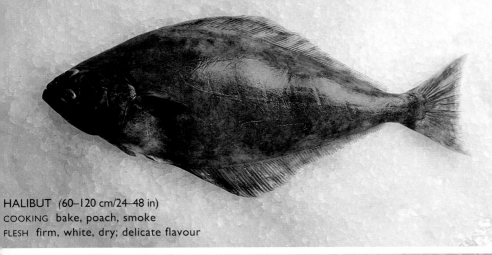

HALIBUT (60–120 cm/24–48 in)
COOKING bake, poach, smoke
FLESH firm, white, dry; delicate flavour

HERRING (18–40 cm/7–16 in)
COOKING bake, barbecue, casserole, grill, pan-fry
FLESH soft, oily; strong flavour

JEWFISH (30–120 cm/12–48 in)
ALSO KNOWN AS mulloway, butterfish, silver jew, jewie

COOKING moist methods: bake (covered), grill or barbecue (baste frequently)
FLESH firm, white, can be dry; mild flavour

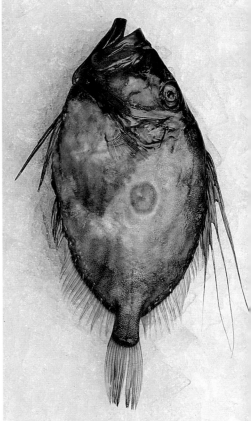

LEATHERJACKET (35 cm/14 in)
ALSO KNOWN AS file fish, ocean jacket, cream fish
COOKING bake, barbecue, grill, pan-fry, poach, steam
FLESH firm, white, moist; very mild flavour

JOHN DORY (30–45 cm/12–18 in)
ALSO KNOWN AS kuparu, St Peter's fish
COOKING bake, barbecue, deep-fry, grill, pan-fry, poach, steam
FLESH fine, firm, white, moist; sweet flavour

KINGFISH (60–120 cm/24–48 in)
ALSO KNOWN AS yellowtail kingfish, southern yellowfish
COOKING bake, casserole, pan-fry, poach, sashimi (raw), steam
FLESH oily, firm, white and dark, delicate texture; delicate flavour, larger kingfish have stronger flavour

LEMON SOLE (50 cm/20 in)
ALSO KNOWN AS lemon fish, lemon dab
COOKING barbecue, grill, pan-fry

FLESH white, delicate texture; sweet, delicate flavour

LING (90–100 cm/3–4 ft)
ALSO KNOWN AS rock ling
COOKING bake, barbecue, grill,
pan-fry, poach, steam

FLESH firm, white, moist, large flake;
mild flavour

MACKEREL, SPANISH
(55–120 cm/22–48 in)
ALSO KNOWN AS grey mackerel

COOKING bake, barbecue, pan-fry
FLESH firm, white and dark, oily;
strong, distinct flavour

MACKEREL, SMOKED (30–40 cm/12–16 in)
FLESH moist, pinkish; slightly smoky flavour

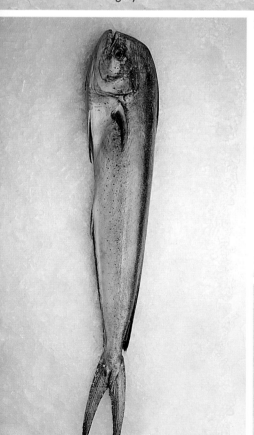

MONKFISH (30–120 cm/12–48 in)
ALSO KNOWN AS anglerfish, stargazer
COOKING bake, barbecue, grill, pan-fry, poach

FLESH firm, white, moist, meaty (usually only
the skinned tail sold); mild flavour

MAHI MAHI (1.5–1.8 m/5–6 ft)
ALSO KNOWN AS dolphinfish, dorado
COOKING bake, barbecue, grill,
pan-fry, poach
FLESH firm, white, moist; mild flavour

MULLET, SEA (30–45 cm/12–18 in)
ALSO KNOWN AS grey mullet
COOKING bake, barbecue, grill, pan-fry
FLESH pink, firm, moist, oily; strong flavour

ORANGE ROUGHY
(35–50 cm/14–20 in)
ALSO KNOWN AS red roughy,
sea perch, deepsea perch

PERCH, OCEAN (20–30 cm/8–12 in)
ALSO KNOWN AS coral perch

COOKING grill, pan-fry, poach, steam
FLESH firm, white; delicate flavour

PIKE (80–90 cm/32–36 in)
ALSO KNOWN AS shortfin pike, sea pike, snook
COOKING bake, barbecue, grill, pan-fry, poach, steam
FLESH fine, soft, white; sweet flavour

PLAICE (45 cm/18 in)
COOKING grill, pan-fry, poach, steam
FLESH white; delicate flavour

RED EMPEROR (60–100 cm/24–40 in)
COOKING bake, barbecue, deep-fry, grill, pan-fry, steam
FLESH firm, white, moist; delicate flavour

RED MULLET (20–40 cm/8–16 in)
ALSO KNOWN AS goatfish, barbounia, rouget
COOKING grill, bake, barbecue, pan-fry, poach, steam (whole)
FLESH firm, white; delicate flavour

RED ROCK COD (20–35 cm/8–14 in)
COOKING bake, barbecue, grill, poach, steam
FLESH firm, white, moist; mild flavour

COOKING bake, barbecue, deep-fry, grill, pan-fry, poach, steam
FLESH firm, white; mild flavour

REDFISH (20–30 cm/8–12 in)
ALSO KNOWN AS nannygai, red snapper
COOKING bake, barbecue, grill, poach, steam
FLESH firm, white to pinkish; mild flavour

ROE, COD (1–2 mm/$^1/_8$ in)
SUBSTITUTE tarama (grey mullet roe)
COOKING boiled whole roe can be fried or grilled, make into dips
FLESH salty flavour

ROE, LUMPFISH (2 mm/¹/8 in)
sometimes marketed as caviar
FLESH small red or black beads;
salty flavour

ROE, SALMON (4 mm/¹/4 in)
FLESH large, orange, glossy beads;
salty flavour

ROE, STURGEON (BELUGA CAVIAR)
(2 mm/¹/8 in)
FLESH dark grey, glossy beads;
salty flavour

SARDINE (12–20 cm/5–8 in)
ALSO KNOWN AS pilchards (when larger),
bluebait
COOKING bake, barbecue, grill, pan-fry
FLESH soft, fine, oily; strong flavour

SKATE (up to 2 m/80 in wide)
ALSO KNOWN AS ray
COOKING (remove skin before cooking)
bake, grill, pan-fry, poach
FLESH soft, pinkish white; sweet,
delicious flavour

SALMON, ATLANTIC
(65–75 cm/26–30 in)
COOKING barbecue, bake, grill, poach,
sashimi (raw), steam, pan-fry
FLESH firm, oily, moist, orangy-pink;
rich, distinctive flavour

SEA BASS (80–100 cm/32–40 in)
COOKING bake, barbecue, grill,
pan-fry, poach, steam
FLESH firm, white; delicate flavour

SNAPPER (45–75 cm/18–30 in)
ALSO KNOWN AS cockney bream,
red bream, squir, pinkies

COOKING bake, barbecue, grill, pan-fry, poac
sashimi (raw), smoke, steam
FLESH firm, white, moist, slightly oily;
mild flavour

SWORDFISH (1.5–3 m/5–10 ft)
COOKING grill, bake, barbecue, pan-fry
FLESH firm, meaty, tends to be dry;
mild flavour

TREVALLY (40–100 cm/16–40 in)
ALSO KNOWN AS skippy, jack
COOKING bake, barbecue, grill, casserole,
pan-fry, poach, sashimi (raw)

FLESH firm, pink, dry to slightly oily;
mild to strong flavour

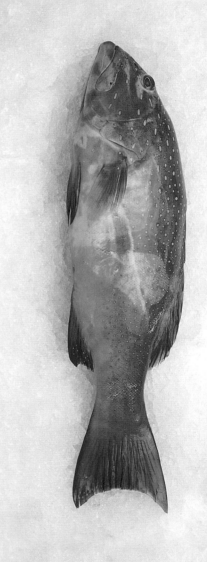

TROUT, CORAL (35–80 cm/14–32 in)
ALSO KNOWN AS leopard or
blue spot trout
COOKING bake, barbecue, pan-fry,
poach, steam
FLESH firm, white, moist; sweet,
mild flavour

TROUT, OCEAN (50–80 cm/20–32 in)
COOKING bake, barbecue, grill, pan-fry,
poach, steam
FLESH firm, moist, orangy-pink; delicate,
sweet flavour

TROUT, RAINBOW (20–30 cm/8–12 in)
ALSO KNOWN AS steel head trout, river trout
COOKING bake, barbecue, grill, poach, smoke,
FLESH oily, moist, soft, pink; mild, delicate
flavour, can be muddy

TROUT, SMOKED (30 cm/12 in)
COOKING salads, bake, soups
FLESH pale pink, firm, moist;
slightly smoky flavour

TUNA, YELLOWFIN (50–190 cm/20–60 in)
COOKING bake, barbecue, grill,
sashimi (raw), smoke
FLESH firm, deep red, oily; medium flavour

TURBOT (100 cm/40 in)
COOKING bake, barbecue, grill,
pan-fry, poach, steam
FLESH white; delicate flavour

WAREHOU, BLUE (35–55 cm/14–22 in)
ALSO KNOWN AS snotty-nose
trevalla, black trevally, snotgall trevally,
trevally
COOKING barbecue, grill, pan-fry,
patties, poach, smoke, steam
FLESH firm, white, slightly oily;
mild flavour

WHITEBAIT (6 cm/2¹/₂ in)
COOKING deep-fry, patties, fritters,
omelettes
FLESH delicate flavour (eaten whole)

WHITING, KING GEORGE
(20–30 cm/8–12 in)
COOKING bake, barbecue, grill,
pan-fry, poach
FLESH soft, white; delicate, sweet flavour

WHITING, SAND (20–30 cm/8–12 in)
COOKING bake, barbecue, grill,
pan-fry, poach
FLESH delicate texture, fine white, soft;
delicate flavour

ABALONE (12 cm/5 in diameter)
ALSO KNOWN AS mutton fish, ear shell,
paua, ormer
COOKING small ones marinated and eaten
raw; larger ones sliced and briefly fried or
casseroled
FLESH cream colour; mild flavour

BALMAIN BUGS (8 cm/3 in)
ALSO KNOWN AS shovel-nosed or slipper
lobster
COOKING bake, barbecue, grill, pan-fry
FLESH moist; sweet, distinct flavour

CLAMS/VONGOLE
(SHELL: 4 cm/1 1/2 in)
COOKING pan-fry, soup, steam
FLESH slightly chewy; salty flavour

COCKLES (SHELL: 6 cm/2 1/2 in)
ALSO KNOWN AS ark shell
COOKING bake, barbecue, pan-fry, poach,
steam
FLESH firm; distinct flavour

CRAB, BLUE SWIMMER (15 cm/6 in)
ALSO KNOWN AS blue manna, sand crab
COOKING boil, curry, pan-fry, soups,
stir-fry, steam
FLESH soft, moist; mild, sweet flavour

CRAB, BROWN (25 cm/10 in)
COOKING boil, poach, steam
FLESH soft, moist; medium,
distinct flavour

CRAB, MUD (18 cm/7 in)
ALSO KNOWN AS mangrove, black crab
COOKING deep-fry, pan-fry, poach, soup,
steam, stir-fry
FLESH firm, moist; distinct, sweet flavour

CUTTLEFISH (20–25 cm/8–10 in)
COOKING bake, barbecue, deep-fry,
pan-fry, steam
FLESH firm; sweet flavour

LANGOUSTINE (25 cm/10 in)
ALSO KNOWN AS Dublin Bay prawn,
Norway lobster
COOKING barbecue, grill, pan-fry
FLESH firm, moist; sweet flavour

LOBSTER (30 cm/12 in)
COOKING barbecue, grill, pan-fry, poach, steam

FLESH firm; sweet flavour

MARRON (27 cm/11 in)
ALSO KNOWN AS freshwater crayfish

COOKING barbecue, boil, grill, pan-fry, poach, steam
FLESH firm, moist; sweet flavour

LOBSTER, ROCK (30 cm/12 in)
ALSO KNOWN AS crayfish, cray, spiny lobster
COOKING barbecue, grill, pan-fry, poach, ste[a]
FLESH firm; sweet flavour

MORETON BAY BUGS (8 cm/3 in)
ALSO KNOWN AS bay or flat head lobster
COOKING bake, barbecue, grill, pan-fry
FLESH moist, firm; sweet flavour

MUSSELS, BLACK (SHELL: 6 cm/2 1/2 in)
ALSO KNOWN AS blue mussels,
poor man's oyster
COOKING barbecue, bake, pan-fry,
poach, steam, raw
FLESH moist; distinct flavour

MUSSELS, GREEN-LIP (SHELL: 8 cm/3 in)
COOKING barbecue, bake, pan-fry, poach,
steam, raw
FLESH moist; distinct flavour

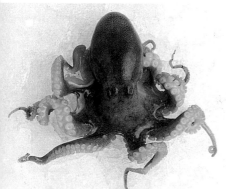

OCTOPUS (15–30 cm/6–12 in)
COOKING barbecue, casserole, grill,
pan-fry, steam
FLESH firm; mild, sweet flavour

OYSTERS, ANGASI (SHELL: 8 cm/3 in)
COOKING bake, deep-fry, grill, pan-fry,
steam; raw
FLESH soft, moist; very strong flavour

OYSTERS, PACIFIC (SHELL: 8 cm/3 in)
COOKING bake, deep-fry, grill, pan-fry,
steam; raw
FLESH soft, moist; strong salty flavour

OYSTERS, ROCK (SHELL: 8 cm/3 in)
COOKING bake, deep-fry, grill, pan-fry,
steam
FLESH soft, moist; sweet sea flavour

PIPIS (SHELL: 4–5 cm/1¹/2–2 in)
COOKING barbecue, poach, stir-fry, steam
FLESH slightly chewy; sweet flavour

PRAWNS, KING
(10–12 cm/4–5 in)
ALSO KNOWN AS jumbo shrimp
COOKING bake, barbecue, deep-fry,
grill, pan-fry, poach, steam
FLESH moist, firm; sweet flavour

PRAWNS, TIGER (8 cm/3 in)
COOKING bake, barbecue, deep-fry,
grill, pan-fry, poach, steam
FLESH moist, firm; sweet flavour

SCALLOPS, SAUCER (SHELL: 10 cm/4 in)
ALSO KNOWN AS Queen scallops
COOKING barbecue, grill, pan-fry,
poach, steam
FLESH moist, soft; distinct flavour

SCALLOPS, SOUTHERN
(SHELL: 8 cm/3 in)
ALSO KNOWN AS Tasmanian scallops
COOKING barbecue, grill, pan-fry,
poach, steam
FLESH moist; mild flavour

SCAMPI (15 cm/6 in)
COOKING barbecue, grill, pan-fry
FLESH firm, moist; sweet flavour

SEA URCHIN (5 cm/2 in diameter)
ALSO KNOWN AS oursin
COOKING cream sauces, raw, souffles
FLESH sweet salty flavour

SQUID (5–23 cm/2–9 in)
ALSO KNOWN AS calamari
COOKING bake, deep-fry, pan-fry,
poach, steam
FLESH sweet, mild flavour

WHELKS (SHELL: 8 cm/3 in)
COOKING steam
FLESH slightly chewy

WINKLES (SHELL: 2–3 cm/3/4–1 1/4 in)
ALSO KNOWN AS periwinkles
COOKING steam (remove from shell)
FLESH slightly chewy; distinct flavour

YABBIES (15 cm/6 in)
ALSO KNOWN AS lobby, crawbob,
freshwater crayfish
COOKING barbecue, grill, pan-fry
FLESH firm, moist; sweet flavour

PREPARATION

● Use a very sharp knife when preparing fish and dip your fingers in salt to help you grip.

● A fillet is a boneless piece of fish. It is produced by cutting the flesh from either side of the backbone of the fish. A cutlet (or steak) is a thick slice through the body of the fish.

● Round fish (salmon, trout, bream) have a round body and eyes on either side of the head. They yield two fillets, one from each side.

● Flat fish (flounder, plaice, sole) have both eyes on the top. They can yield four fillets, two from each side.

● Rinse gutted seafood very well—any residue can cause a bitter taste.

● Lobster and crabs bought live have the best flavour. The most humane method of killing is to submerge them in a slurry of ice and water for 20–30 minutes, or pierce them between the eyes with a sharp knife or skewer. To immobilize live crustaceans, place them in the freezer for 1 hour (don't leave for much longer or you will freeze the flesh).

● Soak clams and pipis in cold water to get rid of sand and grit (or buy them sand-free).

Fish scalers have a sharp ridged edge. The back of a knife or a spoon can also be used.

When handling raw fish, dip your fingertips in salt to make it easier to keep hold of the slippery skin.

CLEANING AND FILLETING ROUND FISH

1 Hold the fish firmly at the tail. Lifting it slightly, scrape against the direction of the scales with a fish scaler. Do it in the sink, or outdoors. Rinse.

2 Use a sharp knife to slit the belly, then remove the gut. Rinse under cold water, then pat dry with paper towel.

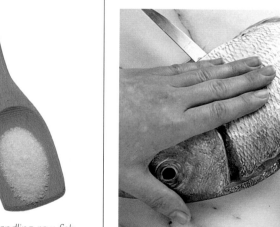

3 To fillet, slice horizontally along either side of the body. Keep the knife close to the bone. Use a sawing action, working towards the tail.

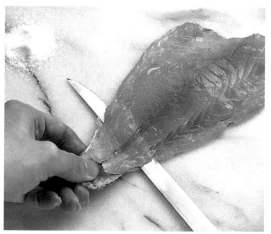

4 Place the fillet skin-side-down. Starting at the tail, run a sharp knife between the skin and flesh, pushing down firmly, cutting and lifting as you go.

CUTTING ROUND FISH CUTLETS

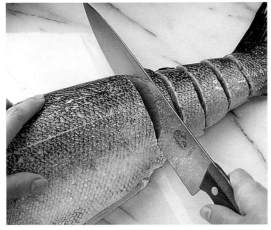

1 Use a large knife or, for large fish, a cleaver, to slice cutlets. Hold the fish firmly and cut through.

2 Separate the whole fish into fillets. If not using straight away, wrap individually and freeze.

FILLETING FLAT FISH

1 Cut down to the backbone. Use a sawing motion to remove two fillets from either side.

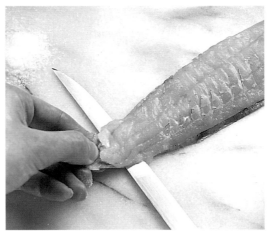

2 With the skin-side-down, run a knife between the skin and flesh, cutting and lifting as you go.

SERVING WHOLE BAKED FISH

1 Run a spoon or flat-bladed knife down the centre of the fish, then carefully pull the fish away from the bone.

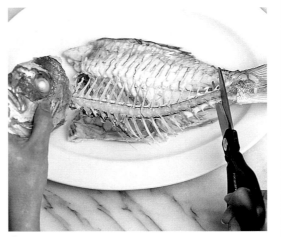

2 Lift out the backbone and rib bones and snip with scissors just before the tail. The fillets can be rearranged back on the fish for serving.

The long flexible blade on a filleting knife is ideal for preparing raw fish. Keep the blade sharp.

BONING GARFISH

1 Wash the insides of the gutted garfish well under cold running water to remove the dark lining which can cause a bitter taste. Pat dry.

2 Remove the head from the fish. With the fish out flat, run a knife along the bones on either side of the backbone. Don't cut right through.

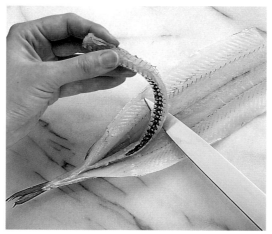

3 Ease the backbone out using a knife to cut through any connective tissue. Snip off the bone at the tail, with scissors, and discard.

PREPARING RAW LOBSTER

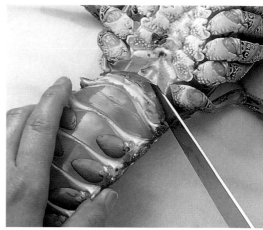

1 Cut into the membrane on the underside of the lobster, where the head and body join, to loosen. Twist or cut off to remove the tail.

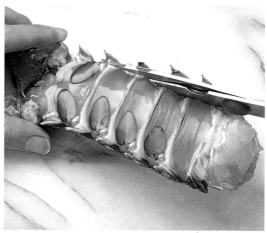

2 Cut down both sides of the shell on the underside, between the flesh and soft underside shell using a pair of scissors.

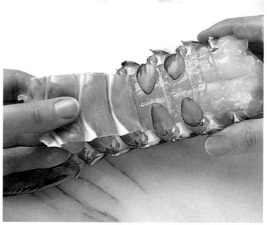

3 Peel back the soft undershell. Gently pull out the flesh in one piece. Pull out the vein from the back with your fingers, or when cutting.

Small sharp knives are used when it is necessary to have good control, and for smaller seafood.

PREPARING COOKED LOBSTER

1 Grasp the head and body with two hands and twist them firmly in opposite directions, to release the tail.

2 With scissors, cut down both sides of the shell on the underside, placing the scissors between the flesh and soft shell.

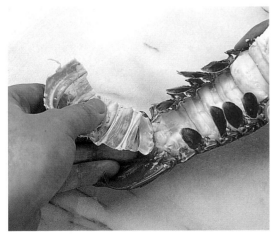

3 Peel back the soft undershell to reveal the flesh. Gently pull out the flesh in one piece. Scrape meat out of claws with a lobster pick.

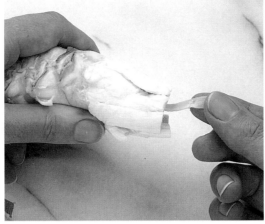

4 Gently pull out the vein, starting at the head end, or remove when cutting the lobster into medallions or pieces.

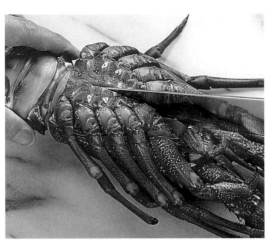

OR **1** Turn the lobster upside-down, insert a knife through the shell between the legs and cut through. Repeat, cutting through the tail.

2 Remove the meat from the tail and cut into slices or pieces. Wash the shell under cold water to remove any residue from the head.

A lobster pick is used to extract the sweet meat from the claws and other parts that are difficult to reach on lobster and crab.

A broad-bladed, strong knife is necessary to cut through hard shells and ensure neat slicing. A cleaver can also be used.

PREPARING CRAB

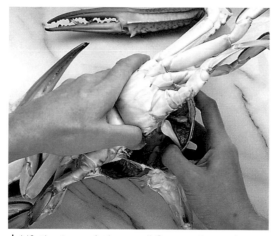 

1 Lift the 'apron', the small flap on the underside of the crab, and prise off the top hard shell.

2 Remove the soft internal organs and pull off the spongy grey fingers (the gills).

 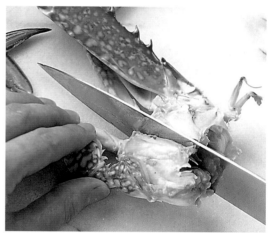

3 Using a large sharp knife, cut the crab lengthways through the centre of the body, to form two halves with the legs attached.

4 Cut each half of the crab in half again, crossways. Remove the meat with your fingers, a knife or lobster/crab pick.

Lobster/crab crackers have a ridged inner edge near the hinge, to provide grip when cracking the shells.

SHUCKING OYSTERS

 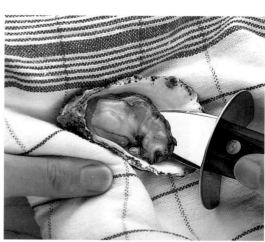

1 Wrap a tea towel around the unshucked oyster. Work the oyster shucker into the oyster and twist to break the hinge.

2 Remove the top shell, slip the shucker between the oyster and the shell to release. Rinse both to remove grit. Replace the oyster.

Shuckers are used to open oysters and other live molluscs. The guard protects your hands.

PREPARING BUGS

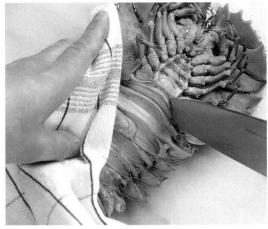

1 Cut into the membrane where head and body join, to loosen, then twist or cut off the tail.

2 Cut down both sides of the underside shell, placing the scissors between the flesh and shell.

3 Peel back the soft underside shell to reveal the flesh. Gently pull the flesh out in one piece. Discard the shell.

OR   Turn the bug upside-down. Insert a large knife through the shell between the legs and cut through. Repeat, cutting along the tail.

Strong kitchen scissors can be used for cutting through shells on crustaceans.

PEELING AND DEVEINING PRAWNS

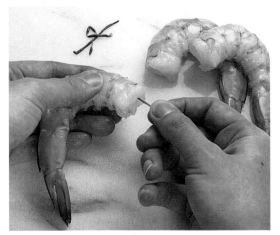

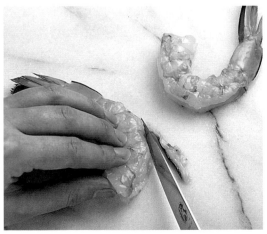

Peel the prawns, leaving the tails attached. Gently pull out the dark vein from each prawn back, starting at the head end.

OR   Cut a slit down the back of each peeled prawn with a sharp knife. Scrape away each dark vein along the back.

PREPARING MUSSELS

Choose a brush with stiff bristles for scrubbing the outside of mussels and other shells.

1 Clean fresh mussels by thoroughly scrubbing the shells with a stiff brush. This removes any grit or weed from the shells.

2 Pull out the hairy beards. Discard open mussels that don't close when tapped. Mussels that have been frozen won't close.

When shelling shellfish, a tea towel is useful for grasping shells and protecting your hand.

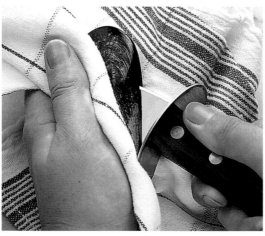

3 To open mussels for stuffing, wrap a tea towel around them, work an oyster shucker between the shells and twist to open. Release the mussel.

CLEANING SQUID

1 Grasp the body in one hand and the head and tentacles in the other. Pull firmly to separate. If using tentacles, cut the head away and discard.

2 Pull the quill, the transparent cartilage, from inside the body of the squid and discard. Remove and discard any white membrane.

3 Under cold water, pull away the skin. The flaps can also be used. Use the body, flap and tentacles whole, or cut the body into rings.

PREPARING OCTOPUS

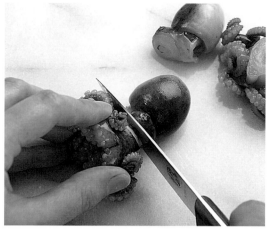

1 Using a small knife, carefully cut between the head and tentacles of the octopus, just below the eyes.

2 Grasp the body of the octopus and push the beak out and up through the centre of the tentacles with your finger.

3 Cut the eyes from the head of the octopus by slicing a small round off, with a small sharp knife. Discard the eye section.

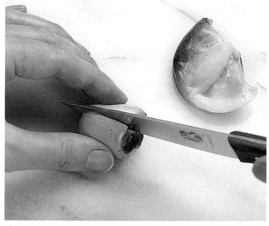

4 To clean the octopus head, carefully slit through one side, avoiding the ink sac, and scrape out any gut from inside.

5 When you have slit the head open, rinse under running water to remove any remaining gut.

CLEANING SCALLOPS

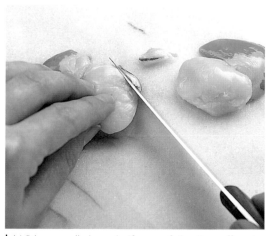

1 With a small sharp knife, carefully slice off and discard any vein, membrane or hard white muscle from each scallop.

These long thin metal skewers are excellent for threading scallops onto for grilling or barbecuing.

SOUPS & CHOWDERS

It is amazing just how many different fish soups there are in this world, and how many of them have become almost national dishes—clam chowder and bouillabaisse being probably the most popular examples. While most of us are familiar with the creamy New England clam chowder, how many know that there is another lesser-known but equally delicious chowder—the tomato-based Manhattan chowder? And that the word 'chowder' comes from the French *chaudière*, the large cauldron in which soup is traditionally cooked?

COURT-BOUILLON & FISH STOCK
Flavoursome home-made stock can make the difference between a good soup and a fabulous one.

Unlike other stock, fish stock is cooked over low heat for only a short time. If it is cooked too long, it will become bitter. The bones and trimmings must be clean of all blood and intestines or these will taint the flavour of the stock. Most fish bones are suitable, although bones from oily fish are not as good. It is important to remove any scum from the surface of

the stock during cooking, otherwise the liquid will be cloudy. Fish stock and court-bouillon can be refrigerated for up to 1 week or frozen for up to 6 months.

MAKING FISH STOCK
You will need a large, heavy-based saucepan or stockpot. To prepare fish trimmings for the stock, discard the eyes

and gills, then roughly chop the bones, heads and tails. Soak the bones and trimmings in cold salted water for about 10 minutes, to remove any blood. Drain and rinse under cold water. Place 2 kg (4 lb) of chopped fish trimmings, 1 roughly chopped celery stick, including the leaves, 1 chopped onion, 1 unpeeled chopped carrot, 1 sliced leek, 1 bouquet

garni, 12 black peppercorns and 2 litres (64 fl oz) of water in the saucepan. Bring the mixture slowly to the boil and carefully skim off any froth that forms on the surface using a sieve or a ladle. Reduce the heat to low and simmer very gently for 20 minutes. Skim the frothy scum from the surface regularly. Ladle the stock in batches into a sieve, lined with damp muslin, sitting over a bowl. To keep the fish stock clear, do not press the solids, but simply allow the stock to strain undisturbed. Allow to cool, then refrigerate for up to 1 week. Makes about 1.75 litres (56 fl oz).

MAKING COURT-BOUILLON

Court-bouillon is the flavoured liquid in which fish is traditionally poached. Fish that is to be served cold is left to cool in the liquid. To make court-bouillon, place 1 litre (32 fl oz) water, 1/2 cup (125 ml/4 fl oz) white wine, 1 onion, carrot and celery stalk, all sliced, 6 peppercorns and a bouquet garni in a large pan. Bring to the boil, reduce the heat and simmer for 30 minutes. Strain and chill. Spices and flavourings can be added, according to your taste. For a slight aniseed flavour, add some sliced fennel to the pan. For a hint of citrus, add a few pieces of lemon, lime or orange rind.

Generally, small fish pieces or fillets are poached in gently simmering court-bouillon, whereas large fish are added to cold court-bouillon which is then heated, to ensure even cooking.

MAKING A BOUQUET GARNI

To make a bouquet garni for the stock, bunch together a bay leaf, sprig of thyme and a few stalks of parsley, then wrap the green part of a leek loosely around the herbs. Tie together with string.

FREEZING STOCK

If you want to prepare stock and freeze it, simply cool the stock, then line a measuring jug with a plastic bag and ladle or pour the amount you want to freeze into the plastic bag. Remove the bag from the jug, label the bag, seal securely and freeze. Repeat until all the stock is used. Alternatively, reduce the stock by half, pour the cooled stock into ice cube trays and freeze. To use, dilute the stock with equal amounts of water.

MEDITERRANEAN FISH SOUP

Preparation time: 30 minutes
Total cooking time: 45 minutes
Serves 4

1/2 teaspoon saffron threads
3 teaspoons oil
2 large onions, thinly sliced
1 leek, white part only, chopped
4 cloves garlic, finely chopped
1 bay leaf, torn
1/2 teaspoon dried marjoram
1 teaspoon grated orange rind
2 tablespoons dry white wine
1 red pepper (capsicum), cut into bite-sized
  pieces
500 g (1 lb) ripe tomatoes, chopped
1/2 cup (125 ml/4 fl oz) tomato passata
2 cups (500 ml/16 fl oz) fish stock
2 tablespoons tomato paste
  (tomato purée)

2 teaspoons soft brown sugar
500 g (1 lb) skinless fish fillets (eg. snapper,
  red mullet, red rock cod, ocean perch),
  cut into bite-sized pieces
3 tablespoons chopped fresh parsley

1 In a small bowl, soak the saffron threads in
2 tablespoons boiling water.
2 Heat the oil in a large heavy-based pan, over
low heat. Add the onion, leek, garlic, bay leaf
and marjoram. Cover and cook for 10 minutes,
shaking the pan occasionally, until the onion is
soft. Add the rind, wine, pepper and tomato,
cover and cook for 10 minutes.
3 Add the tomato passata, fish stock, tomato
paste, sugar and saffron (with the liquid) to the
pan. Stir well and bring to the boil, then reduce
the heat to low and simmer, uncovered, for
15 minutes.
4 Add the fish to the soup, cover and cook for
8 minutes, or until tender. Add salt and pepper,
to taste, and half the parsley. Discard the bay leaf.
Sprinkle the soup with the remaining parsley just
before serving. Delicious served with slices of
crusty bread.

*ABOVE: Mediterranean
fish soup*

CREAMY FISH SOUP

Preparation time: 10 minutes
Total cooking time: 35 minutes
Serves 4-6

¹/₄ teaspoon saffron threads
1 litre (32 fl oz) fish stock
¹/₂ cup (125 ml/4 fl oz) dry white wine
1 onion, finely chopped
1 small carrot, finely chopped
1 stick celery, chopped
1 bay leaf
45 g (1¹/₂ oz) butter
2 tablespoons plain flour
300 g (10 oz) skinless fish fillets (eg. snapper,
    orange roughy, bream), in bite-sized pieces
1 cup (250 ml/8 fl oz) cream
2 teaspoons chopped fresh chives, to garnish

1 In a small bowl, soak the saffron threads in 2 tablespoons boiling water.

2 Put the fish stock, wine, onion, carrot, celery and bay leaf in a large saucepan and slowly bring to the boil. Cover and simmer for 20 minutes. Strain and discard the vegetables. Stir the saffron (with the liquid) into the hot stock.

3 In a clean saucepan, melt the butter and stir in the flour for 2 minutes, or until pale and foaming. Remove from the heat and gradually stir in the fish stock. Return to the heat and stir until the mixture boils and thickens.

4 Add the fish and simmer for 2 minutes, or until the fish is cooked. Stir in the cream and heat through without boiling. Season with salt and ground white pepper, to taste. Serve garnished with chives.

NOTE: Saffron threads are quite costly, but they add a subtle flavour and vivid yellow touch to food. The bright orange threads are sold in small glass jars or tiny plastic packets. Some people squeeze the threads after soaking, to release more colour into the water.

BELOW: Creamy fish soup

SMOKED HADDOCK CHOWDER

Preparation time: 20 minutes
Total cooking time: 35 minutes
Serves 4-6

500 g (1 lb) smoked haddock or cod
1 potato, diced
1 stick celery, chopped
1 onion, finely chopped
50 g (1 3/4 oz) butter
1 rasher bacon, finely chopped
2 tablespoons plain flour
1/2 teaspoon dried mustard
1/2 teaspoon Worcestershire sauce
1 cup (250 ml/8 fl oz) milk
3 tablespoons chopped fresh parsley
1/4 cup (60 ml/2 fl oz) cream, optional

1 To make the fish stock, put the fish in a deep frying pan, add 1.25 litres (40 fl oz) water and bring to the boil. Reduce the heat and simmer for 8 minutes, or until the fish flakes easily. Drain; reserve the stock. Discard the skin and bones and flake the fish. Set aside.
2 Put the potato, celery and onion in a pan with 3 cups (750 ml/24 fl oz) reserved stock. Bring to the boil, reduce the heat and simmer for 8 minutes, or until the vegetables are tender. Set aside.
3 Melt the butter in a large pan over low heat, add the bacon and stir for 3 minutes. Stir in the flour, mustard and Worcestershire sauce and cook for 1 minute, or until pale and foaming. Remove from the heat and gradually stir in the milk. Return to the heat and stir until the chowder boils and thickens. Reduce the heat and simmer for 2 minutes. Stir in the vegetables and stock mixture, then add the parsley and fish. Simmer over low heat for 5 minutes, or until heated through. Season and serve with cream.

CREAMY MUSSEL SOUP

Preparation time: 30 minutes
Total cooking time: 40 minutes
Serves 4

750 g (1 1/2 lb) black mussels
1 stick celery, chopped
1 carrot, chopped
1 onion, chopped
10 black peppercorns
4 fresh parsley stalks
100 g (3 1/2 oz) butter, softened
3 spring onions, chopped
2 cloves garlic, crushed
1 large potato, cut into small dice
3/4 cup (185 ml/6 fl oz) white wine
1/3 cup (40 g/1 1/4 oz) plain flour
1 cup (250 ml/8 fl oz) cream
2 tablespoons chopped fresh parsley

1 Scrub the mussels and pull out the hairy beards. Place in a large saucepan with the celery, carrot, onion, peppercorns, parsley and 1.5 litres (48 fl oz) water. Bring to the boil, reduce the heat and simmer, covered, for 4–5 minutes.
2 Strain the stock through a fine sieve and discard any unopened mussels. Remove the meat from the remaining mussels and set aside. Discard the shells and vegetables. Return the

BELOW: Smoked haddock chowder

stock to the pan and simmer for 15 minutes. Remove from the heat.

3 Melt half the butter in a large saucepan, add the spring onion, garlic and potato and stir over medium heat for 3 minutes, or until the onion is soft. Add the wine, bring to the boil, then reduce the heat and simmer for 1 minute.

4 Blend the flour and remaining butter in a bowl to form a paste. Pour 3½ cups (875 ml/28 fl oz) of the stock into the saucepan with the garlic and potato. Gradually add the butter mixture, whisking until the mixture boils and thickens. Reduce the heat and simmer for 15 minutes, or until the potato is cooked. Stir in the mussel meat and cream until heated through. Stir in the parsley.

NEW ENGLAND CLAM CHOWDER

Preparation time: 35 minutes + soaking
Total cooking time: 45 minutes
Serves 4

1.5 kg (3 lb) clams (vongole) or pipis, in shell
2 teaspoons oil
3 rashers bacon, chopped
1 onion, chopped
1 clove garlic, crushed
750 g (1½ lb) potatoes, cut into small dice
1¼ cups (315 ml/10 fl oz) fish stock
2 cups (500 ml/16 fl oz) milk
½ cup (125 ml/4 fl oz) cream
3 tablespoons chopped fresh parsley

1 Discard any clams that are broken, already open or do not close when tapped on the bench. If necessary, soak in cold water for 1–2 hours to remove sand. Drain and put in a large heavy-based pan with 1 cup (250 ml/8 fl oz) water. Cover and simmer over low heat for 5 minutes, or until open. Discard any that do not open. Strain and reserve the liquid. Remove the clam meat from the shells.

2 Heat the oil in the cleaned pan. Add the bacon, onion and garlic and cook, stirring, over medium heat until the onion is soft and the bacon golden. Add the potato and stir well.

3 Measure the reserved liquid and add water to make 1¼ cups (315 ml/10 fl oz). Add to the pan with the stock and milk. Bring to the boil, reduce the heat, cover and simmer 20 minutes, or until the potato is tender. Uncover and simmer for 10 minutes, or until slightly thickened.

4 Add the cream, clam meat and parsley and season, to taste, with salt and pepper. Heat through gently before serving, but do not allow to boil or the liquid may curdle.

ABOVE: New England clam chowder

39

BISQUES
The basic ingredients in these rich, thick soups are chopped or puréed shellfish, stock and cream. Originally, bisques were made of boiled game or fowl but, after the seventeenth century, shellfish became the main ingredient. The most popular bisques are made from lobster, prawn, crab and clam. Sometimes, white meat stock is used instead of fish stock.

LOBSTER BISQUE

Preparation time: 20 minutes
Total cooking time: 1 hour
Serves 4-6

1 raw lobster tail, about 400 g (13 oz)
90 g (3 oz) butter
1 large onion, chopped
1 large carrot, chopped
1 stick celery, chopped
1/4 cup (60 ml/2 fl oz) brandy
1 cup (250 ml/8 fl oz) white wine
6 sprigs fresh parsley
1 sprig fresh thyme
2 bay leaves
1 tablespoon tomato paste (tomato purée)
1 litre (32 fl oz) fish stock
2 ripe tomatoes, chopped
2 tablespoons rice flour or cornflour
1/2 cup (125 ml/4 fl oz) cream

1 Remove the meat from the lobster tail. Wash the shell and crush into large pieces with a mallet or rolling pin, then set aside. Chop the meat into small pieces, cover and chill.
2 Melt the butter in a large pan, add the onion, carrot and celery and cook over low heat for 20 minutes, stirring occasionally, until the vegetables are softened but not brown.
3 In a small pan, heat the brandy, set alight with a long match and carefully pour over the vegetables. Shake the pan until the flame dies down. Add the white wine and the lightly crushed lobster shell. Increase the heat and boil until the liquid is reduced by half. Add the parsley, thyme, bay leaves, tomato paste, fish stock and chopped tomato. Simmer, uncovered, for 25 minutes, stirring occasionally.
4 Strain the mixture through a fine sieve or dampened muslin, pressing gently to extract all the liquid. Discard the vegetables and shell.
5 Return the liquid to the cleaned pan. Blend the rice flour or cornflour with the cream in a small bowl. Add to the liquid and stir over medium heat until the mixture boils and thickens. Add the lobster meat and season, to taste. Cook, without boiling, for 10 minutes, or until the lobster is just cooked. Serve hot.
NOTE: If you don't dampen the muslin when straining the mixture, it will soak up too much of the liquid.

PRAWN BISQUE

Preparation time: 25 minutes
Total cooking time: 15–20 minutes
Serves 4-6

500 g (1 lb) raw medium prawns
60 g (2 oz) butter
2 tablespoons plain flour
2 litres (64 fl oz) fish stock
1/2 teaspoon paprika
1 cup (250 ml/8 fl oz) cream
1/3 cup (80 ml/2 3/4 fl oz) dry sherry
1–2 tablespoons cream, extra, for serving
paprika, extra, to garnish

1 Peel the prawns and gently pull out the dark vein from each prawn back, starting at the head end. Reserve the heads and shells. Heat the butter in a pan, add the prawn heads and shells and cook, stirring, over medium heat for 5 minutes, lightly crushing the heads with a wooden spoon.
2 Add the flour to the pan and stir until combined. Add the fish stock and paprika and stir over the heat until the mixture boils. Reduce the heat and simmer, covered, over low heat for 10 minutes. Strain the mixture through a fine sieve set over a bowl, then return the liquid to the pan. Add the prawns and cook over low heat for 2–3 minutes. Allow to cool slightly, then process in batches in a blender or food processor until smooth. Return the mixture to the pan.
3 Add the cream and sherry to the pan and stir to heat through. Season, to taste, with salt and freshly ground black pepper. Serve topped with a swirl of cream and sprinkled with paprika.
NOTE: The prawn heads and shells give the bisque its rich flavour. A few of the small cooked prawns can be reserved for garnishing.

OPPOSITE PAGE:
Lobster bisque (top);
Prawn bisque

ABOVE: Seafood laksa

LAKSA

Of the many versions of this spicy soup from Malaysia and Indonesia, the most popular is known as Singapore Laksa or Laksa Lemak. It is enriched with coconut cream and includes seafood and rice noodles. If you are pushed for time, buy a laksa paste instead of all the spices. Use 2 tablespoons for the recipe on this page. A combination of different seafood can be used instead of the fish balls or tofu puffs.

SEAFOOD LAKSA

Preparation time: 45 minutes
Total cooking time: 45 minutes
Serves 4-6

1 kg (2 lb) raw medium prawns
1/3 cup (80 ml/2 3/4 fl oz) oil
2–6 fresh red chillies, seeded, finely chopped
1 onion, roughly chopped
3 cloves garlic, halved
2 cm (3/4 inch) piece ginger or galangal, chopped
1 teaspoon ground turmeric
1 tablespoon ground coriander
3 stems lemon grass, white part only, chopped
1–2 teaspoons shrimp paste
2 1/2 cups (600 ml/20 fl oz) coconut cream
2 teaspoons grated palm sugar or
  brown sugar
4 kaffir lime leaves, lightly crushed
1–2 tablespoons fish sauce

200 g (6 1/2 oz) packet fish balls
190 g (6 1/2 oz) packet tofu puffs
250 g (8 oz) dried rice vermicelli
250 g (8 oz) bean sprouts
4 tablespoons chopped fresh mint, for serving
2 teaspoons fresh coriander leaves, for serving

1 Peel the prawns and gently pull out the dark vein from each prawn back, starting at the head end. Set the shells, heads and tails aside. Cover the prawn meat and refrigerate.
2 To make the prawn stock, heat 2 tablespoons of the oil in a large, heavy-based pan or wok and add the prawn shells, heads and tails. Stir until the heads are bright orange, then add 1 litre (32 fl oz) water. Bring to the boil, reduce the heat and simmer for 15 minutes. Strain through a fine sieve, discarding the shells. Clean the pan.
3 Put the chilli, onion, garlic, ginger (or galangal), turmeric, coriander, lemon grass and 1/4 cup (60 ml/2 fl oz) of the prawn stock in a food processor and process until finely chopped.
4 Heat the remaining oil in the clean pan and add the chilli mixture and shrimp paste. Stir over

low heat for 3 minutes, or until fragrant. Pour in the remaining stock and simmer for 10 minutes. Add the coconut cream, sugar, lime leaves and fish sauce. Simmer for 5 minutes.

5 Add the prawns and simmer for 2 minutes, until just pink. Add the fish balls and tofu puffs and simmer gently until just heated through.

6 Soak the rice vermicelli in a bowl of boiling water for 2 minutes, drain and divide among serving bowls. Top with bean sprouts and ladle the soup over the top. Sprinkle with the mint and coriander.

NOTE: Fish balls and tofu puffs are available in the refrigerator section at Asian supermarkets.

CORN AND CRAB SOUP WITH CORIANDER

Preparation time: 15 minutes
Total cooking time: 10 minutes
Serves 4

1 1/2 tablespoons oil
6 cloves garlic, chopped
6 Asian shallots, chopped
2 stems lemon grass, white part only, chopped
1 tablespoon grated fresh ginger
1 litre (32 fl oz) chicken stock
1 cup (250 ml/8 fl oz) coconut milk
2 1/2 cups (375 g/12 oz) frozen corn kernels
2 x 170 g (5 1/2 oz) cans crab meat, drained
2 tablespoons fish sauce
2 tablespoons lime juice
1 teaspoon grated palm sugar or
    brown sugar
fresh coriander leaves, to garnish

1 Heat the oil in a large pan. Add the chopped garlic, Asian shallots, lemon grass and grated ginger to the pan and stir over medium heat for 2 minutes.

2 Add the stock and coconut milk to the pan and bring to the boil. Add the corn and cook for 5 minutes.

3 Add the crab meat, fish sauce, lime juice and sugar to the pan and stir. Season with salt and pepper and serve immediately, topped with coriander leaves, and sliced chillies if you like.

NOTES: For a variation, 2 eggs, beaten with 2 tablespoons of water, can be whisked into the soup before serving.

Red-skinned Asian shallots grow like garlic, in a clump. They are used extensively in Southeast Asian cookery.

BELOW: Corn and crab soup with coriander

TOM YUM GOONG

Preparation time: 25 minutes
Total cooking time: 45 minutes
Serves 4-6

✻ ✻

500 g (1 lb) raw medium prawns
1 tablespoon oil
2 tablespoons Thai red curry paste or
   tom yum paste
2 tablespoons tamarind purée
2 teaspoons ground turmeric
1 teaspoon chopped red chillies
4 kaffir lime leaves, shredded
2 tablespoons fish sauce
2 tablespoons lime juice
2 teaspoons grated palm sugar or brown sugar
2 tablespoons fresh coriander leaves, for
   serving

1 Peel the prawns, leaving the tails intact. Pull out the dark vein from each prawn back, starting at the head end. Reserve the shells and heads. Cover and refrigerate the prawn meat. Heat the oil in a large pan or wok and cook the shells and heads for 10 minutes over medium-high heat, stirring frequently, until the heads are deep orange.
2 Add 1 cup (250 ml/8 fl oz) water and the curry paste to the pan. Bring to the boil and cook for 5 minutes, or until reduced slightly. Add another 2 litres (64 fl oz) water and simmer for 20 minutes. Strain, discarding the shells and heads, and return the stock to the pan.
3 Add the tamarind, turmeric, chilli and lime leaves to the pan, bring to the boil and cook for 2 minutes. Add the prawns and cook for 5 minutes, or until pink. Stir in the fish sauce, lime juice and sugar. Serve sprinkled with coriander leaves.

WON TON SOUP

Preparation time: 40 minutes + 30 minutes
   soaking
Total cooking time: 5 minutes
Serves 4-6

✻ ✻

4 dried Chinese mushrooms
250 g (8 oz) raw prawns
250 g (8 oz) pork mince
1 tablespoon soy sauce

BELOW: Tom yum goong

1 teaspoon sesame oil

2 spring onions, finely chopped

1 teaspoon grated fresh ginger

2 tablespoons chopped canned water chestnuts

250 g (8 oz) packet won ton wrappers

1.5 litres (48 fl oz) chicken or beef stock

4 spring onions, very finely sliced, to garnish

1 Soak the mushrooms in a bowl of hot water for 30 minutes. Drain, then squeeze to remove any excess liquid. Discard the stems and chop the caps finely. Peel the prawns and pull out the dark vein from each prawn back, starting at the head end. Finely chop the prawn meat and mix with the mushrooms, pork, soy sauce, sesame oil, spring onion, ginger and water chestnuts in a bowl.

2 Cover the won ton wrappers with a damp tea towel to prevent them drying out. Working with one wrapper at a time, place a heaped teaspoon of mixture on the centre of each.

3 Moisten the pastry edges with water, fold in half diagonally and bring the two points together. Place on a tray dusted with cornflour.

4 Cook the won tons in rapidly boiling water for 4–5 minutes. Bring the stock to the boil in another pan. Remove the won tons with a slotted spoon and place in serving bowls. Top with spring onion. Ladle the stock over the won tons.

PUMPKIN, PRAWN AND COCONUT SOUP

Preparation time: 15 minutes
Total cooking time: 20 minutes
Serves 4-6

★ ★

500 g (1 lb) pumpkin, diced

4 tablespoons lime juice

1 kg (2 lb) raw large prawns

2 onions, chopped

1 small fresh red chilli, finely chopped

1 stem lemon grass, white part only, chopped

1 teaspoon shrimp paste

1 teaspoon sugar

1 1/2 cups (375 ml/12 fl oz) coconut milk

1 teaspoon tamarind purée

1/2 cup (125 ml/4 fl oz) coconut cream

1 tablespoon fish sauce

2 tablespoons fresh Thai basil leaves

1 Combine the pumpkin with half the lime juice in a bowl. Peel the prawns and pull out the dark vein from each back, starting at the head end.

2 Process the onion, chilli, lemon grass, shrimp paste, sugar and 3 tablespoons of the coconut milk in a food processor until a paste forms.

3 Combine the paste with the remaining coconut milk, tamarind purée and 1 cup (250 ml/8 fl oz) water in a large pan and stir until smooth. Add the pumpkin with the lime juice to the pan and bring to the boil. Reduce the heat and simmer, covered, for about 10 minutes or until the pumpkin is just tender.

4 Add the raw prawns and coconut cream, then simmer for 3 minutes, or until the prawns are just pink and cooked through. Stir in the fish sauce, the remaining lime juice and the Thai basil leaves. Pour the soup into warmed bowls and garnish with Thai basil leaves or sprigs.

ABOVE: Pumpkin, prawn and coconut soup

CLEAR SOUP WITH SALMON QUENELLES

Preparation time: 20 minutes
Total cooking time: 25 minutes
Serves 6

400 g (13 oz) salmon cutlets
1 litre (32 fl oz) fish stock
1/2 cup (125 ml/4 fl oz) dry white wine
2 teaspoons lemon juice
1 small carrot, finely chopped
2 spring onions, sliced
2 sprigs fresh dill
2 sprigs fresh parsley
3 black peppercorns
1 egg white, well chilled
1/2 cup (125 ml/4 fl oz) cream, well chilled
2 tablespoons fresh chervil leaves

1 Remove the skin and bones from the salmon and set aside. For the quenelles, weigh 150 g (5 oz) of the fish, chop roughly, cover and chill well. For the soup, in a large pan, combine the skin and bones with the remaining salmon, fish stock, wine, lemon juice, carrot, spring onion, dill, parsley and peppercorns. Slowly bring to the boil, then reduce the heat, cover and simmer for 15 minutes. Strain and discard the vegetables. (You won't be using the cooked salmon for this recipe, but you can use it as a sandwich filling. When cool, flake the salmon and mix with a little mayonnaise.)
2 Pour the soup into a clean pan, bring to the boil, then reduce the heat to just simmering. Season, to taste.
3 To make the quenelles, process the reserved salmon in a food processor until finely chopped. Gradually add the egg white and process until very smooth. Transfer to a chilled bowl and season well with salt and ground white pepper. Whip the cream and quickly fold into the salmon. Shape quenelles using 2 teaspoons dipped in cold water. Add to the soup in two batches and poach for 2 minutes, or until cooked. Transfer the quenelles to warm soup bowls.
4 Heat the soup to almost boiling and carefully ladle over the quenelles. Sprinkle with chervil leaves and serve.
NOTES: Ocean trout can also be used.
To make light fluffy quenelles, the ingredients used should be almost ice cold. The mixture will make about 24 quenelles.

MARMITE DIEPPOISE

Preparation time: 45 minutes
Total cooking time: 30 minutes
Serves 4

500 g (1 lb) raw medium prawns
600 g (1 1/4 lb) black mussels
350 g (11 oz) scallops
300 g (10 oz) assorted skinless fish fillets
  (eg. monkfish, snapper, orange roughy, salmon)
1/2 medium leek, white part only, sliced
1/2 small fennel bulb, sliced
1 1/2 cups (375 ml/12 fl oz) dry white wine
2 sprigs fresh thyme
1 bay leaf
150 g (5 oz) button mushrooms, sliced
1 cup (250 ml/8 fl oz) cream
1 tablespoon chopped fresh flat-leaf parsley

1 Peel the prawns and gently pull out the dark vein from each prawn back, starting at the head end.
2 Scrub the mussels with a stiff brush and pull out the hairy beards. Discard any broken mussels, or open ones that don't close when tapped on the bench. Rinse well.
3 Slice or pull off any vein, membrane or hard white muscle from the scallops, leaving any roe attached. Cut the fish into bite-sized cubes.
4 In a large heavy-based pan, combine the leek, fennel, wine, thyme, bay leaf and mussels. Bring to the boil, cover and simmer for 4–5 minutes, stirring occasionally, until the mussels are cooked. Remove the mussels from the pan with tongs, discarding any unopened ones. Remove the mussels from their shells and discard the shells.
5 Bring the cooking liquid to simmering point. Add the prawns and scallops, cover and simmer for 2 minutes, or until cooked. Remove the prawns and scallops and set aside.
6 Return the cooking liquid to simmering point and add the fish. Poach for 3 minutes, or until cooked, then remove and set aside. Line a sieve with a double layer of dampened muslin and strain the liquid into a clean pan. Bring to the boil, add the mushrooms and cook, uncovered, over high heat for 3 minutes. Stir in the cream, bring to the boil and simmer for about 5 minutes, stirring occasionally, until thick enough to coat the back of a spoon. Add the mussels, prawns, scallops and fish and simmer until heated through. Season, stir in the parsley and serve.

SALMON
When choosing salmon cutlets, there are indications of freshness you can look for. The central bone should be tightly adhered to the flesh—with ageing, the connective tissues break down and separate from the bone. There should be no signs of discolouration or blotches on the flesh, and no signs of dryness. Salmon flesh should look translucent, with a pleasant sheen or gloss. And, like all fresh seafood, it should have a pleasant sea smell. Avoid cutlets sitting in, or oozing, liquid.

OPPOSITE PAGE:
Clear soup with salmon quenelles (top);
Marmite dieppoise

BOUILLABAISSE

BOUILLABAISSE

Fishermen in Marseilles in southern France made this delicious soup to use up fish they had trouble selling. The fish were simmered in a pan of water with other ingredients, hence the name Bouillabaisse, from 'bouillir' (to boil) and 'abaisser' (to reduce). Any seafood combination can be used to make the soup.

ABOVE: Bouillabaisse

Preparation time: 40 minutes
Total cooking time: 30 minutes
Serves 4

300 g (10 oz) raw medium prawns
16–18 black mussels
200 g (6½ oz) scallops
1.5 kg (3 lb) assorted white fish fillets
    (eg. red rock cod, snapper, red mullet,
    orange roughy, monkfish)
2 tablespoons oil
1 fennel bulb, thinly sliced
1 onion, chopped
5 ripe tomatoes, peeled, seeded and chopped
1.25 litres (40 fl oz) fish stock
pinch of saffron threads
1 bay leaf
1 bouquet garni
5 cm (2 inch) strip of orange rind
1 tablespoon chopped fresh parsley, to garnish

Rouille

1 small red pepper (capsicum)
1 red chilli
1 slice white bread, crusts removed
2 cloves garlic
1 egg yolk
⅓ cup (80 ml/2¾ fl oz) olive oil

1 Peel the prawns and gently pull out the dark vein from each prawn back, starting at the head end. Scrub the mussels with a stiff brush and pull out the hairy beards. Discard any broken mussels, or open ones that don't close when tapped on the bench. Slice or pull off any vein, membrane or hard white muscle from the scallops, leaving any roe attached. Cut the fish into large bite-sized pieces. Refrigerate the seafood, covered.

2 Heat the oil in a large saucepan over medium heat and cook the fennel and onion for 5 minutes, or until golden. Add the tomato and cook for 3 minutes. Stir in the stock, saffron, bay leaf, bouquet garni and orange rind. Bring to the boil and boil for 10 minutes. Reduce the heat to simmer and add the scallops, prawns, mussels and fish. Simmer for 4–5 minutes, or until the mussels open. Discard any unopened mussels. Remove the bouquet garni and orange rind.

3 For the rouille, cut the red pepper and chilli into large flattish pieces. Remove the seeds and membrane and cook, skin-side-up, under a hot grill until the skin blackens and blisters. Place in a plastic bag and leave to cool, then peel.

4 Soak the bread in 3 tablespoons water, then squeeze out any excess. Process the pepper, chilli, bread, garlic and egg yolk in a food processor. With the motor running, add the oil in a thin stream, until the mixture is thick and smooth.

5 Ladle the bouillabaisse into bowls, sprinkle with parsley and serve with the rouille.

MANHATTAN-STYLE SEAFOOD CHOWDER

Preparation time: 30 minutes
Total cooking time: 30 minutes
Serves 4-6

60 g (2 oz) butter
3 rashers bacon, chopped
2 onions, chopped
2 cloves garlic, finely chopped
2 sticks celery, sliced
3 potatoes, diced
1.25 litres (40 fl oz) fish or chicken stock
3 teaspoons chopped fresh thyme
12 raw large prawns
1 tablespoon tomato paste (tomato purée)
425 g (14 oz) can chopped tomatoes
375 g (12 oz) skinless white fish fillets (eg. ling, cod, flake, hake), cut into bite-sized pieces
310 g (10 oz) can baby clams, undrained
2 tablespoons chopped fresh parsley
grated orange rind, to garnish

1 Melt the butter in a large pan and cook the bacon, onion, garlic and celery over low heat, stirring occasionally, for 5 minutes, or until soft but not brown.

2 Add the potato, stock and thyme to the pan and bring to the boil. Reduce the heat and simmer, covered, for 15 minutes.

3 Meanwhile, peel the prawns and pull out the dark vein from each prawn back, starting at the head end. Add the tomato paste and tomato to the pan, stir through and bring back to the boil. Add the fish pieces, prawns and clams with juice and simmer over low heat for 3 minutes. Season, to taste, and stir in the parsley. Serve garnished with the grated orange rind.

BELOW: Manhattan-style seafood chowder

FISH AND NOODLE SOUP

Preparation time: 15 minutes
Total cooking time: 20 minutes
Serves 4

200 g (6¹/₂ oz) dried rice vermicelli
1 tablespoon oil
2.5 cm (1 inch) piece of fresh ginger, grated
3 small red chillies, finely chopped
4 spring onions, chopped
800 ml (26 fl oz) coconut milk
2 tablespoons fish sauce
2 tablespoons tomato passata
500 g (1 lb) skinless fish fillets (eg. ocean perch,
    red mullet, cod, snapper), in bite-sized pieces
2 ham steaks, chopped into small cubes
150 g (5 oz) snake beans, cut into
    3 cm (1¹/₄ inch) lengths
2 cups (180 g/6 oz) bean sprouts
1 tablespoon fresh mint leaves
¹/₂ cup (80 g/2³/₄ oz) unsalted roasted peanuts

1 Soak the rice vermicelli in a bowl of boiling water for 5 minutes, then drain.
2 Heat the oil in a large, heavy-based pan, add the ginger, chilli and spring onion and cook over medium heat for 3 minutes.
3 Stir in the coconut milk, fish sauce and tomato passata, then cover and gently simmer for 10 minutes.
4 Add the fish, ham and snake beans to the pan and simmer for 10 minutes, or until the fish is tender. Divide the rice vermicelli among deep soup bowls and top with the bean sprouts and mint leaves. Carefully spoon the soup into the bowls and sprinkle with roasted peanuts.

CREAM OF OYSTER SOUP

Preparation time: 15 minutes
Total cooking time: 20 minutes
Serves 4

18 fresh oysters
15 g (¹/₂ oz) butter
1 small onion, finely chopped
¹/₂ cup (125 ml/4 fl oz) white wine
1¹/₂ cups (375 ml/12 fl oz) fish stock
1 cup (250 ml/8 fl oz) cream
6 whole black peppercorns
6 fresh basil leaves, torn
1 teaspoon lime juice
spring onions, shredded, to garnish
fresh basil leaves, shredded, to garnish

1 Drain the oysters in a small strainer and reserve the juice and oysters separately. Melt the butter in a small saucepan and add the onion. Cover and cook over low heat until soft but not brown, stirring occasionally. Add the wine and simmer for 5 minutes, or until reduced by half.
2 Add the stock to the pan, simmer for 2 minutes, then add the cream, peppercorns and basil and 6 roughly chopped oysters and simmer for 5 minutes. Strain, then push the mixture against the sides of the strainer, to extract as much flavour as possible. Discard the solids in the strainer.
3 Return the liquid to the pan and bring to the boil. Add the lime juice and reserved oyster juice. Season, to taste. Spoon into small cups and add 3 oysters to each. Top with cracked black pepper. Garnish with spring onion and basil.
NOTE: This soup is very rich, so serve only small portions for each person.

BELOW: Fish and noodle soup

PRAWN AND UDON NOODLE SOUP

Preparation time: 20 minutes
Total cooking time: 30 minutes
Serves 6

500 g (1 lb) raw medium prawns
1 1/2 tablespoons oil
1 stem lemon grass, white part only, chopped
2 cloves garlic, chopped
2 small fresh red chillies, cut in half
2 fresh kaffir lime leaves
1 lime, quartered
4 spring onions, sliced on the diagonal
500 g (1 lb) dried udon noodles
2 tablespoons soy sauce
100 g (3 1/2 oz) shiitake mushrooms, halved
1 tablespoon fresh coriander leaves
500 g (1 lb) baby bok choy, trimmed,
 leaves separated

1 Peel the prawns, reserving the heads and shells. Gently pull out the dark vein from each prawn back, starting at the head end.
2 Heat the oil in a large pan, add the prawn heads and shells and cook over high heat until pink. Add the lemon grass, garlic, red chillies, kaffir lime leaves, lime quarters, half the spring onion and 2 litres (64 fl oz) water. Bring to the boil, reduce the heat and simmer for 20 minutes. Pour through a fine strainer into a bowl and discard the solids. Rinse the pan and return the stock to the pan.
3 Add the noodles to a large pan of boiling salted water and cook for 5 minutes, or until tender. Drain well.
4 Bring the stock to the boil. Add the soy sauce and prawns to the pan and cook for 5 minutes, or until the prawns turn pink and are cooked through. Add the remaining ingredients and season with salt and pepper, to taste.
5 Divide the cooked noodles among the soup bowls, then ladle the soup over them. The soup can be served garnished with extra lime wedges if you wish.

UDON NOODLES
These are long, thick, white noodles made with wheat flour. The thickness varies and they can be round, square or flat. Udon noodles come dried, fresh or precooked and are mostly used in Japanese soups and simmered dishes.

ABOVE: Prawn and udon noodle soup

51

SOUPE DE POISSON

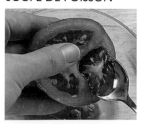

Scoop the seeds out of the tomatoes with a teaspoon.

Skim off any scum that forms on the surface.

Strain the soup through dampened muslin, into a clean pan.

SOUPE DE POISSON

Preparation time: 30 minutes
Total cooking time: 45 minutes
Serves 6

✭✭

1 large ripe tomato
1 1/2 kg (3 lb) chopped fish bones from
    white-fleshed fish
1 leek, white part only, chopped
1 carrot, chopped
1 stick celery, chopped
1 large clove garlic, chopped
1 bay leaf
3 fresh parsley stalks
6 black peppercorns
1 cup (250 ml/8 fl oz) dry white wine
1 tablespoon lemon juice
250 g (8 oz) skinless fish fillets (eg. snapper,
    perch, cod, red mullet), cut into
    bite-sized pieces
2 tablespoons chervil leaves
1/4 lemon, cut into very fine slices

1 Score a cross in the base of the tomato. Place in a heatproof bowl and cover with boiling water. Leave for 30 seconds, transfer to cold water, drain and peel away from the cross. Cut the tomato in half, scoop out the seeds with a teaspoon and finely chop the flesh.
2 Rinse the bones well in cold water and combine in a large pan with the leek, carrot, celery, garlic, bay leaf, parsley, peppercorns, wine, lemon juice and 2 litres (64 fl oz) water. Slowly bring to the boil, skimming off any scum that forms on the surface. Reduce the heat and simmer for 20 minutes.
3 Strain and discard the fish and vegetables. Strain the soup again, through a sieve lined with dampened muslin, into a clean pan. Simmer, uncovered, for 10 minutes.
4 Add the fish pieces and simmer for 2 minutes, or until tender. Season, to taste, with salt and ground white pepper.
5 Divide the chopped tomato and chervil among six warm bowls and ladle the hot soup over them. Float some lemon slices on top and serve immediately.
NOTE: The straining muslin is dampened so it won't absorb too much of the cooking liquid.

ZUPPA DI COZZE

Preparation time: 25 minutes
Total cooking time: 35 minutes
Serves 6

✭✭

200 g (6 1/2 oz) ripe tomatoes
1 kg (2 lb) black mussels
2 tablespoons olive oil
40 g (1 1/4 oz) butter
1 leek, white part only, finely chopped
3 cloves garlic, crushed
pinch of saffron threads or powder
1 tablespoon finely chopped fresh coriander
    or parsley
1 small fresh red chilli, finely chopped
2/3 cup (170 ml/5 1/2 fl oz) dry white wine

1 Score a cross in the base of each tomato. Place in a heatproof bowl and cover with boiling water. Leave for 30 seconds, transfer to cold water, drain and peel away from the cross. Cut the tomatoes in half, scoop out the seeds with a teaspoon and finely chop the flesh.
2 Scrub the mussels with a stiff brush and pull out the hairy beards. Discard any broken mussels, or open ones that don't close when tapped on the bench. Rinse well.
3 Heat the oil and butter in a large saucepan and cook the leek and garlic over low heat until the leek is soft but not brown. Add the saffron, coriander or parsley and chilli and cook, stirring, for 1–2 minutes. Increase the heat and add the wine. Bring to the boil and cook for 1–2 minutes, then add the chopped tomato and 1 cup (250 ml/8 fl oz) water. Cover and simmer for 20 minutes.
4 Add the mussels to the pan and cook, covered, until they are opened. After 4–5 minutes, discard any unopened mussels. So the soup is not too crowded with shells, remove one third of the remaining mussels, remove the mussel meat and add to the soup. Discard the empty shells. Season, to taste, with salt and pepper. Serve immediately with crusty bread.

OPPOSITE PAGE:
Zuppa di cozze (top);
Soupe de poisson

SCALLOP AND EGG FLOWER SOUP

Preparation time: 30 minutes
  + 10 minutes chilling
Total cooking time: 45 minutes
Serves 4

★ ★

300 g (10 oz) scallops
1 tablespoon dry sherry
1/4 teaspoon ground white pepper
1 teaspoon grated fresh ginger
7 spring onions
2 tablespoons oil
1 tablespoon cornflour
3 cups (750 ml/24 fl oz) chicken stock
2 tablespoons soy sauce
1/3 cup (75 g/2 1/2 oz) canned straw mushrooms,
    cut in halves
1/3 cup (50 g/1 3/4 oz) frozen peas
1 egg, lightly beaten
dry sherry, extra, to taste
2 teaspoons soy sauce, extra

ABOVE: Scallop and egg flower soup

1 Slice or pull off any vein, membrane or hard white muscle from the scallops, leaving any roe attached. Combine with the sherry, pepper and ginger in a bowl and refrigerate for 10 minutes.
2 Finely chop the spring onions, keeping the green and white parts separate.
3 Heat the oil in a wok or heavy-based frying pan, swirling gently to coat the base and side. Add the white part of the spring onion and cook for 30 seconds. Add the scallops and their liquid and cook, turning, over high heat until the scallops turn milky white. Transfer to a bowl.
4 Blend the cornflour in a little of the stock until smooth, add to the wok with the remaining stock and soy sauce and bring to the boil, stirring until the mixture boils and thickens. Add the straw mushrooms and peas and cook for 2 minutes. Return the scallops to the wok, stirring the soup constantly.
5 Pour in the egg and cook, stirring until it turns opaque. Stir the spring onion greens through and add a little more sherry and soy sauce, to taste. Can be garnished with extra spring onion strips.
NOTE: Drain and rinse straw mushrooms before using. Leftover canned mushrooms can be chilled, covered with water, for up to 3 days. They can be used in dishes such as stir-fries.

ASIAN-STYLE SEAFOOD SOUP

Preparation time: 30 minutes
Total cooking time: 40 minutes
Serves 6

4 ripe tomatoes
1 tablespoon oil
5 cm (2 inch) piece fresh ginger, grated
3 stems lemon grass, white part only,
　finely chopped
3 small fresh red chillies, finely chopped
2 onions, chopped
3 cups (750 ml/24 fl oz) fish stock
4 kaffir lime leaves, finely shredded
160 g (5 1/2 oz) fresh pineapple,
　chopped into small pieces
1 tablespoon tamarind concentrate
1 tablespoon grated palm sugar or
　brown sugar
2 tablespoons lime juice
1 tablespoon fish sauce
500 g (1 lb) raw medium prawns

500 g (1 lb) skinless white fish fillets
　(eg. snapper, ocean perch, red rock cod,
　red mullet), cut into bite-sized pieces
2 tablespoons chopped fresh coriander

1 Score a cross in the base of each tomato. Place in a heatproof bowl and cover with boiling water. Leave for 30 seconds, transfer to cold water, drain and peel away from the cross. Cut the tomatoes in half, scoop out the seeds with a teaspoon and finely chop the flesh.
2 Heat the oil in a large pan, add the ginger, lemon grass, chilli and onion and stir over medium heat for 5 minutes, or until the onion is golden brown.
3 Add the tomato to the pan and cook for 3 minutes. Stir in the fish stock, kaffir lime leaves, pineapple, tamarind, sugar, lime juice, fish sauce and 3 cups (750 ml/24 fl oz) water. Cover and bring to the boil. Reduce the heat and simmer for 15 minutes.
4 Meanwhile, peel the prawns and gently pull out the dark vein from each prawn back, starting at the head end. Add the prawns, fish and coriander to the pan and simmer for 10 minutes, or until the seafood is tender. Season, to taste.

*BELOW: Asian-style
seafood soup*

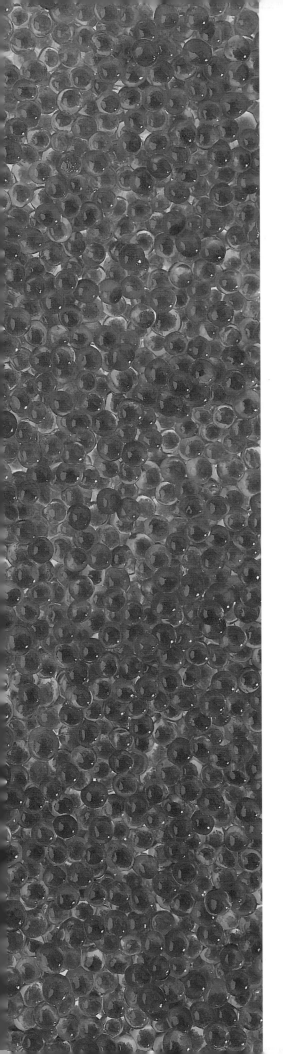

DIPS, PATES & LIGHT BITES

Perfect for a picnic, light supper, lunchtime get-together with a few friends or even a full-blown party, light bites come in all shapes and sizes. From a steaming bowl of moules marinière to be mopped up with crusty bread, or smoked fish pâté to spread on hot buttered toast, seafood can be ideal comfort food. But in this chapter you'll also find prawn and pea noodle baskets elegant enough to hold their own at any posh dinner, and detailed instructions on how to make those darlings of the modern party, sushi and sashimi.

3 Alternatively, this dip can be mixed in a food processor or blender. Serve with sliced bread.
NOTE: Taramasalata can be stored, covered, in an airtight container in the refrigerator for up to 3 days.

MOULDED EGG AND CAVIAR DIP

Preparation time: 1 hour + 2 hours chilling
Total cooking time: 6 minutes
Serves 10–12

✬ ✬

7 eggs
3 tablespoons finely chopped fresh parsley
3 tablespoons whole egg mayonnaise
80 g (2³/₄ oz) chives, finely chopped
500 g (1 lb) cream cheese, softened to
  room temperature
90 g (3 oz) lumpfish roe or caviar
300 g (10 oz) sour cream
chives and lumpfish roe or caviar, for serving

1 Fill a pan with cold water and gently add the eggs. Bring to the boil, then reduce the heat and simmer for 6 minutes. Drain, then plunge the eggs in cold water to stop the cooking process. Cool thoroughly and drain. Peel the eggs and mash well, then stir in the parsley and mayonnaise. Season, to taste, with salt and pepper.
2 Line a deep 18 cm (7 inch) loose-based fluted flan tin with plastic wrap, leaving a wide overhang to help you remove the moulded dip from the tin later.
3 Spoon half the egg mixture into the lined tin. Firmly press down and smooth the surface with a spatula or the back of a spoon, pressing well into the side of the tin. Sprinkle with half the chives, pressing them down into the dip. Using a clean, warm spatula, spread half the cream cheese over the top. Spoon half the roe over the top and gently press down.
4 Repeat the layering with the remaining egg mixture, chives, cream cheese and roe. Cover the moulded dip with plastic wrap, pressing down firmly so the layers stick together, and refrigerate for 2 hours.
5 Remove the top cover of plastic wrap and place a plate over the mould. Flip over onto the plate while holding the tin, and then gently ease the tin off. Remove the plastic wrap, trying not to damage the fluted edges.

TARAMASALATA

The authentic version of this traditional Greek dip is made from tarama, the orange-coloured, salted and dried roe of the grey mullet. This is sometimes obtainable from stores that specialise in Greek or Turkish food products. The smoked roe from cod is often used instead. As well as a dip, taramasalata can be served with bread as part of a meze plate.

ABOVE: Taramasalata

TARAMASALATA

Preparation time: 10 minutes
Total cooking time: Nil
Makes 1 cup (250 ml/8 fl oz)

✬

4 slices white bread, crusts removed
1 small onion, finely grated
100 g (3¹/₂ oz) tarama or smoked cod's roe
2 tablespoons lemon juice
¹/₄ cup (60 ml/2 fl oz) olive oil

1 Place the bread in a bowl and cover with cold water. Drain and squeeze out as much water as possible, then return the bread to the dried bowl.
2 Add the onion, tarama, lemon juice and oil to the bread and mix together with a fork. Season, to taste, with salt and pepper.

6 Spoon dollops of the sour cream over the top of the mould and spread out a little. Decorate with the extra chives and roe. Serve with water crackers.

CHILLI CRAB AND TOMATO DIP

Preparation time: 25 minutes
Total cooking time: Nil
Serves 6

1 small ripe tomato
2 x 170 g (5½ oz) cans crab meat, drained
200 g (6½ oz) neufchatel cheese (see Note)
2 tablespoons chilli sauce
2 teaspoons tomato paste (tomato purée)
1 teaspoon grated lemon rind
2 teaspoons lemon juice
1 small onion, finely grated
2 spring onions, finely sliced

1 Score a cross in the base of the tomato. Place in a heatproof bowl and cover with boiling water. Leave for 30 seconds, transfer to cold water, drain and peel away from the cross. Cut the tomato in half, scoop out the seeds with a teaspoon and finely chop the flesh.
2 Squeeze any liquid from the crab meat with your hands. Beat the neufchatel in a bowl with a wooden spoon until smooth, then stir in the crab meat, chilli sauce, tomato paste, lemon rind, lemon juice and grated onion. Season well with salt and pepper. Mix together and spoon into a serving bowl.
3 Scatter the sliced spring onion and chopped tomato over the top. Refrigerate, covered, before serving. Can be served with thinly sliced or lightly toasted bread. A small serving spoon makes it easier for guests.
NOTE: Neufchatel is a smooth, mild, good-quality cream cheese available from delicatessens. If it is not available, another cream cheese can be used instead.

BELOW: Chilli crab and tomato dip

1 Peel the prawns and gently pull out the dark vein from each prawn back, starting at the head end. Pat them dry with paper towels and place in a bowl. Add the lime juice to the prawns, cover and refrigerate for 10 minutes.

2 Cook the corn in boiling water for 2–3 minutes, or until tender. Drain and plunge the kernels into iced water to prevent further cooking, then drain and pat dry with paper towel.

3 Process the prawns and lime juice in a food processor in short bursts for 2–3 seconds, until the prawns are finely chopped but not minced. Transfer to a bowl and stir in the corn, lime rind, cream cheese and chives. Add the chilli sauce and mix well. Cover with plastic wrap and refrigerate for at least 2 hours.

4 Just before serving, peel the large prawns, leaving the tails intact. Gently pull out the dark vein from each prawn back, starting at the head end. Transfer the dip to a serving bowl and garnish with the peeled prawns. Serve with some extra cooked and peeled prawns, or Melba toast or pitta bread, for dipping.

SMOKED FISH PATE

Preparation time: 10 minutes + several
  hours chilling
Total cooking time: Nil
Serves 4-6

4 smoked mackerel or smoked trout fillets
2–3 tablespoons lemon or lime juice
125 g (4 oz) cream cheese, softened
200 g (6¹/₂ oz) butter, melted
sprigs of fresh herbs (dill, fennel,
  flat-leaf parsley)
lemon slices, to garnish

1 Remove the skin and bones from the fish and roughly flake the flesh. Place the flesh in a blender or food processor with the juice, cream cheese and butter. Blend or process until smooth. Season, to taste, with pepper.

2 Spread into a 2-cup (500 ml/16 fl oz) capacity serving dish and chill for several hours. Garnish with sprigs of fresh herbs and lemon slices. Serve with Melba toast or crackers.

PRAWN, CORN AND SWEET CHILLI DIP

Preparation time: 1 hour + 2 hours chilling
Total cooking time: 3 minutes
Serves 8

1 kg (2 lb) cooked medium prawns
¹/₄ cup (60 ml/2 fl oz) lime juice
³/₄ cup (110 g/3¹/₂ oz) frozen corn kernels
3 teaspoons finely grated lime rind
250 g (8 oz) cream cheese, softened
3 tablespoons finely chopped chives
1 tablespoon sweet chilli sauce
4 cooked large prawns, to garnish

ABOVE: Prawn, corn and sweet chilli dip

SALMON AND CHIVE LOG

Preparation time: 10 minutes + several
  hours chilling
Total cooking time: Nil
Serves 4-6

250 g (8 oz) cream cheese, softened

2 tablespoons sour cream

1 tablespoon lemon juice

3 spring onions, chopped

420 g (14 oz) can red salmon, drained, skin
  and bones removed, flaked

1 teaspoon freshly ground black pepper

1/3 cup (40 g/1 1/4 oz) finely chopped pecan nuts

80 g (2 3/4 oz) fresh chives, finely chopped

1 Beat the cream cheese, sour cream and lemon juice in a bowl until smooth. Stir in the spring onion, salmon, pepper, pecan nuts and a quarter of the chives until combined. Refrigerate for several hours to firm.
2 Place the mixture on a sheet of plastic wrap and roll into a log shape. Roll the log in the remaining chives and refrigerate until needed. Serve with crackers or bread.

*ABOVE: Smoked fish
pâté (top); Salmon and
chive log*

GRAVLAX

Remove any bones from the salmon with tweezers.

Rub the remaining sugar mixture into the second salmon fillet.

Whisk all the ingredients of the mustard sauce together.

For serving, the salmon can be sliced thinly on an angle towards the tail.

OPPOSITE PAGE: Potted prawns (top); Gravlax

POTTED PRAWNS

Preparation time: 12 minutes + overnight chilling
Total cooking time: 3 minutes
Makes 1¹/3 cups (350 g/11 oz)

250 g (8 oz) small cooked prawns
100 g (3¹/2 oz) butter
¹/4 teaspoon ground nutmeg
¹/4 teaspoon ground ginger
pinch of cayenne pepper

1 Peel the prawns and gently pull out the dark vein from each prawn back, starting at the head end. Chop the prawns very finely. Melt 60 g (2 oz) of the butter over low heat in a small saucepan. Add the prawns, nutmeg, ginger, cayenne pepper and salt and pepper, to taste.
2 Stir over low heat for 2 minutes, or until all the butter has been absorbed into the mixture. Spoon into a 1¹/3 cup (350 ml/11 fl oz) capacity ramekin, press down, then smooth the surface.
3 Melt the remaining butter in a small pan and pour over the surface (leaving the white sediment behind in the pan) to cover completely. Refrigerate overnight to allow the flavours to develop. Bring back to room temperature and serve with toast.

GRAVLAX

Preparation time: 10 minutes + 24 hours chilling
Total cooking time: 5 minutes
Serves 12

¹/4 cup (60 g/2 oz) sugar
2 tablespoons sea salt
1 teaspoon crushed black peppercorns
2.5 kg (5 lb) salmon, filleted, skin on
1 tablespoon vodka or brandy
4 tablespoons very finely chopped fresh dill

Mustard sauce

1¹/2 tablespoons cider vinegar
1 teaspoon caster sugar
¹/2 cup (125 ml/4 fl oz) olive oil
2 teaspoons chopped fresh dill
2 tablespoons Dijon mustard

1 Combine the sugar, salt and peppercorns in a small dish. Remove any bones from the salmon with tweezers. Pat dry with paper towels and lay a fillet skin-side-down in a shallow tray or baking dish. Sprinkle the fillet with half the vodka, rub half the sugar mixture into the flesh, then sprinkle with half the dill. Sprinkle the remaining vodka over the second salmon fillet and rub the remaining sugar mixture into the flesh. Lay it flesh-side-down on top of the other fillet. Cover with plastic wrap, place a heavy board on top and then weigh the board down with 3 heavy cans or a foil-covered brick. Refrigerate for 24 hours, turning it over after 12 hours.
2 For the mustard sauce, whisk all the ingredients together, then cover until needed.
3 Uncover the salmon and lay both fillets on a wooden board. Brush off all the dill and seasoning with a stiff pastry brush. Sprinkle with the remaining fresh dill and press it onto the salmon flesh, shaking off any excess. Serve whole on the serving board, or thinly sliced on an angle towards the tail, with the sauce.
NOTE: Gravlax can be refrigerated, covered, for up to a week.

SCOTCH WOODCOCK

Preparation time: 10 minutes
Total cooking time: 5 minutes
Serves 4

2 eggs
4 egg yolks
150 ml (5 fl oz) cream
2 tablespoons finely chopped fresh parsley
pinch of cayenne pepper
45 g (1¹/2 oz) can anchovy fillets, drained
20 g (³/4 oz) softened butter
4 thick slices bread, toasted

1 Whisk together the whole eggs, egg yolks, cream, half the parsley and the cayenne in a bowl until smooth. Add a little salt and pepper. Pour the mixture into a small heavy-based pan and cook over low heat, stirring frequently, until the egg has set and forms soft curds. Do not overheat or overmix.
2 Mash the anchovies and butter with a fork to form a smooth paste. Spread over the toast.
3 Spoon the egg over the anchovy toasts, sprinkle with the remaining parsley and serve. The toasts can be cut into small triangles.

ABOVE: Tuna patties

TUNA PATTIES

Preparation time: 30 minutes + 30 minutes chilling
Total cooking time: 40 minutes
Makes 8

3 floury potatoes, quartered
30 g (1 oz) butter
1 onion, finely chopped
1 clove garlic, crushed
1 red pepper (capsicum), finely chopped
415 g (13 oz) can tuna
1 egg, lightly beaten
2 tablespoons lemon juice
3 tablespoons chopped fresh parsley
1/4 cup (30 g/1 oz) plain flour
1 cup (100 g/3 1/2 oz) dry breadcrumbs
1 egg, lightly beaten, extra
2 tablespoons milk
oil, for shallow-frying

1 Steam or boil the potatoes for 8–10 minutes, or until tender (pierce with the point of a small sharp knife—if the potato comes away easily, it is ready). Drain and return to the pan. Stir over medium heat, then mash. Set aside to cool.
2 Melt the butter in a frying pan, add the onion and garlic and stir over medium heat for 5 minutes, or until soft. Add the red pepper and cook, stirring, for 5 minutes, or until soft.
3 Drain the tuna, transfer to a bowl and flake with a fork. Mix in the potato, beaten egg, onion mixture, lemon juice and parsley.
4 Place the flour on a shallow plate and the breadcrumbs on another plate. Combine the beaten egg and milk in a shallow dish or bowl. Form the mixture into 8 patties, coat lightly in flour, then in the egg and milk. Finally, coat with the breadcrumbs. Place on a plate or baking tray. Reshape if necessary, then cover and chill for 30 minutes.
5 Heat about 3 tablespoons of oil in a heavy-based frying pan over medium heat and cook the patties in batches for 2–3 minutes on each side, or until golden brown. Drain and serve hot.
NOTE: Drained, canned salmon can be used instead of tuna.

BAGNA CAUDA

Preparation time: 5 minutes
Total cooking time: 8 minutes
Makes about 1 cup (250 ml/8 fl oz)

1 1/4 cups (315 ml/10 fl oz) cream
45 g (1 1/2 oz) can anchovy fillets, drained
10 g (1/4 oz) butter
2 cloves garlic, crushed

1 Bring the cream slowly to the boil in a small heavy-based saucepan. Boil for 8 minutes, stirring frequently. Take care that the cream does not boil over. This cooking time reduces and thickens the cream.
2 Meanwhile, chop the anchovies finely. Melt the butter in a small saucepan, add the anchovies and garlic and cook, stirring, for 1 minute over low heat without allowing to brown.
3 Pour in the cream and mix thoroughly, then add salt and pepper, to taste, if necessary. Pour into a serving bowl. Serve at room temperature as a dipping sauce, with vegetable crudités. The mixture will thicken on standing.

PRAWN AND PEA NOODLE BASKETS

Preparation time: 40 minutes
Total cooking time: 20–25 minutes
Serves 4

★ ★ ★

700 g (1 lb 7 oz) raw medium prawns
oil, for deep-frying
200 g (6¹/2 oz) fresh egg noodles
2 spring onions, chopped
1 clove garlic, crushed
¹/2 teaspoon finely grated fresh ginger
¹/2 teaspoon sesame oil
¹/2 teaspoon fish sauce
100 g (3¹/2 oz) green peas, cooked
3 canned water chestnuts, sliced
1 tablespoon chopped fresh mint
2 teaspoons chopped fresh chives
80 g (2³/4 oz) snow pea (mangetout) sprouts
chive stalks or spring onion greens, to garnish

1 Peel the prawns and pull out the dark vein from each prawn back, starting at the head end.
2 Fill a deep-fryer or large heavy-based pan one third full of oil and heat to 180°C (350°F), or until a noodle dropped into the oil browns in 8–10 seconds. Before the oil is too hot, dip 2 wire baskets (see Note), one slightly smaller than the other, in the oil, then shake dry. The oil will prevent the noodles sticking.
3 Separate the noodles; divide into 4 portions. Arrange the first portion inside the large basket and press the smaller basket inside to mould the noodles. Holding the handles firmly together, ease the baskets into the oil, keeping the noodles under. Gently twist the top basket to prevent sticking, tipping from side to side, and cook the noodles to an even golden brown. Remove from the baskets, taking care, as the metal will be hot. Drain on crumpled paper towels and keep warm. Repeat with the other noodles.
4 Heat 2 tablespoons of oil in a wok. Stir-fry the prawns, spring onion, garlic and ginger over high heat for 2 minutes, or until the prawns turn pink. Stir in the sesame oil, fish sauce, peas and water chestnuts. Remove from the heat and season, to taste, with salt and pepper. Stir in the mint, chives and snow pea sprouts.
5 Pile the prawn and pea mixture into the noodle baskets, garnish and serve.
NOTE: Wire baskets, available at kitchenware shops, come clipped together. Otherwise, use a large and a small metal Asian straining spoon.

PRAWN AND PEA NOODLE BASKETS

Separate the egg noodles and divide them into four bundles.

Arrange one of the bundles inside the larger basket.

Fit the baskets together, hold firmly, then gently lower them into the oil.

Stir-fry the prawns, spring onion, garlic and ginger over high heat until the prawns turn pink.

LEFT: Prawn and pea noodle baskets

PRAWN, NOODLE
AND NORI PARCELS

Carefully peel all the prawns, leaving the tails intact.

Use a sharp knife to cut the noodles the same length as the prawn bodies to the base of the tails.

Neatly roll each batter-dipped prawn in noodles, then wrap with a nori strip.

Lower the prawn and noodle parcels into the hot oil and deep-fry for about 1 minute, until golden.

RIGHT: Prawn, noodle and nori parcels

PRAWN, NOODLE AND NORI PARCELS

Preparation time: 45 minutes
Total cooking time: 10 minutes
Makes 24

★ ★ ★

1 kg (2 lb) raw medium prawns
250 g (8 oz) dried somen noodles
2 sheets nori (dried seaweed)
1/2 cup (60 g/2 oz) plain flour
2 egg yolks
oil, for deep-frying

Dipping sauce

1/3 cup (80 ml/2^{3}/4 fl oz) Tonkatsu sauce
  or barbecue sauce
2 tablespoons lemon juice
1 tablespoon sake or mirin
1–2 teaspoons grated fresh ginger

1 Peel the prawns, leaving the tails intact. Gently pull out the dark vein from each prawn back, starting at the head end. Set aside.

2 Using a sharp knife, cut the noodles to the same length as the prawn bodies to the base of the tail. Keep the noodles in neat bundles and set aside. Cut the nori into 2.5 cm (1 inch) wide strips.

3 Sift the flour into a large bowl and make a well in the centre. Mix the egg yolks with 3 tablespoons of water. Gradually add to the flour, whisking to make a smooth lump-free batter. Add another tablespoon of water if the mixture is too thick. Set aside.

4 Mix the dipping sauce ingredients in a small bowl, adding the ginger according to taste.

5 Dip a prawn in the batter, letting the excess run off. Roll the prawn lengthways in noodles to coat it with a single layer. Secure the noodles by rolling a seaweed strip around the centre of the prawn, securing the seaweed with a little batter. Repeat with the rest of the prawns.

6 Fill a deep, heavy-based pan one third full of oil and heat to 180°C (350°F), or until a cube of bread browns in 15 seconds. Deep-fry 2–3 coated prawns at a time, for about 1–2 minutes, or until the prawns are cooked. Drain on crumpled paper towels and keep warm while cooking the remainder. Serve warm with the dipping sauce.

NOTE: Nori, Tonkatsu sauce and sake are available at Asian speciality stores.

PRAWN TOASTS

Preparation time: 20 minutes
Total cooking time: 10–15 minutes
Makes 48

★★

350 g (11 oz) raw medium prawns

1 clove garlic

75 g (2¹/₂ oz) canned water chestnuts
   or bamboo shoots, drained

1 tablespoon chopped fresh coriander

2 cm (³/₄ inch) piece fresh ginger

2 eggs, separated

¹/₄ teaspoon white pepper

¹/₄ teaspoon salt

12 slices white bread

1 cup (155 g/5 oz) sesame seeds

oil, for deep-frying

chilli sauce, for serving

1 Peel the prawns and gently pull out the dark vein from each prawn back, starting at the head end.

2 Process the prawns, together with the garlic, chestnuts or bamboo shoots, coriander, ginger, egg whites, pepper and salt, in a food processor for 20–30 seconds, or until smooth. Cut rounds from the bread with a 5 cm (2 inch) cutter.

3 Brush the top of each bread round with lightly beaten egg yolk, then spread evenly with the prawn mixture. Sprinkle generously with sesame seeds.

4 Fill a deep, heavy-based pan one third full of oil and heat to 180°C (350°F), or until a cube of bread dropped into the oil browns in 15 seconds. Deep-fry the toasts in small batches, with the prawn mixture face down, for 10–15 seconds each batch, or until golden, crisp and cooked on both sides. Remove from the oil with tongs or a slotted spoon. Drain on sheets of crumpled paper towel. Serve hot with chilli sauce.

WATER CHESTNUTS

The Chinese water chestnut is grown in China, Japan and in the East Indies. It is the white-fleshed root of a type of water grass. Water chestnuts have a crisp texture and sweetish taste and are used in both savoury and sweet dishes. Usually sold canned, they are readily available. After opening, they can be stored, covered in water in an airtight container, for up to three days.

ABOVE: Prawn toasts

THAI MUSSELS

After scrubbing all the mussels, pull out the hairy beards.

Remove the mussels from the water as soon as the shells open.

Loosen the mussel meat from the shells with a sharp knife.

OPPOSITE PAGE: Thai mussels (top left); Fresh oysters with tarragon; Smoked salmon in dill dressing

THAI MUSSELS

Preparation time: 15 minutes + 10 minutes
 standing
Total cooking time: 15 minutes
Serves 4

1 kg (2 lb) black mussels
1/3 cup (80 ml/2³/₄ fl oz) lime juice
1 tablespoon sweet chilli sauce
1 tablespoon grated palm sugar or
 brown sugar
1 tablespoon fish sauce
1 tablespoon finely chopped lemon grass,
 white part only
2 tablespoons chopped fresh coriander
1 red chilli, finely chopped

1 Scrub the mussels with a stiff brush and pull out the hairy beards. Discard any broken mussels, or open ones that don't close when tapped on the bench. Rinse well.
2 Mix together the remaining ingredients in a small bowl. Leave for 10 minutes.
3 Place the mussels, in batches, in a pan of simmering water. Remove as soon as the shells open and discard any that do not open after 4–5 minutes. Loosen the mussels from the shells with a sharp knife and serve immediately, in half shells, topped with the sauce.

SMOKED SALMON
IN DILL DRESSING

Preparation time: 15 minutes
Total cooking time: Nil
Serves 4

400 g (13 oz) smoked salmon
2 tablespoons light olive oil
2 tablespoons oil
2 tablespoons lemon juice
3 teaspoons soft brown sugar
3 tablespoons chopped fresh dill

1 Arrange the smoked salmon slices in a single layer, on individual plates or a large platter.
2 Combine the oils, juice and sugar in a bowl and stir until the sugar dissolves. Season, to taste, then mix in 2 tablespoons of the dill.

3 Drizzle the dressing over the salmon. Using the back of a spoon, cover the salmon with the dressing. Sprinkle with the remaining dill and some cracked black pepper and serve with extra lemon wedges and slices of rye bread.

FRESH OYSTERS
WITH TARRAGON

Preparation time: 15 minutes + 30 minutes
 marinating
Total cooking time: Nil
Serves 4

1 tablespoon chopped fresh tarragon
2 teaspoons very finely chopped spring onion
2 teaspoons white wine vinegar
1 tablespoon lemon juice
2 tablespoons extra virgin olive oil
24 fresh oysters

1 Whisk together the tarragon, spring onion, vinegar, lemon juice and olive oil in a bowl.
2 Remove the oysters from their shells, keeping the shells. Mix the oysters with the vinaigrette, cover and chill for 30 minutes. Rinse and refrigerate the oyster shells as well.
3 To serve, spoon the oysters back into their shells. Drizzle with any remaining vinaigrette.

CRAB AND PRAWN
NORI ROLLS

Drain a 170 g (5½ oz) can crabmeat and process with 350 g (11 oz) peeled and deveined raw medium prawns, 1 egg white and 2 teaspoons finely grated fresh ginger until smooth. Add 2 tablespoons chopped fresh coriander and 1 finely chopped spring onion and process until just combined. Add salt and pepper, to taste. Divide the mixture between 2 nori sheets and spread evenly over the sheets. Roll up to enclose the filling. Using a sharp knife, cut each roll into 8 rounds, wiping the knife clean between slices. Place 2 cm (³/₄ inch) apart on a lightly oiled bamboo or metal steamer. Steam over a large pan of simmering water for about 5 minutes, until just cooked. Serve warm, topping each with a fresh coriander leaf. Makes 16.

THAI FISH CAKES

Preparation time: 30 minutes
Total cooking time: 10 minutes
Serves 4-6

450 g (14 oz) skinless firm white fish fillets
  (eg. cod, hake, ling, redfish), chopped
1/4 cup (45 g/1 1/2 oz) rice flour or cornflour
1 tablespoon fish sauce
1 egg, lightly beaten
3 tablespoons fresh coriander leaves
3 teaspoons red curry paste
1–2 teaspoons chopped fresh red chillies,
  optional
100 g (3 1/2 oz) green beans, very
  finely sliced
2 spring onions, finely chopped
1/2 cup (125 ml/4 fl oz) oil, for frying
sweet chilli sauce, or other dipping sauce,
  for serving

1 Process the fish in a food processor for 20 seconds, or until smooth. Add the rice flour, fish sauce, egg, coriander leaves, curry paste and chillies, if using. Process for 10 seconds, or until well combined, then transfer to a large bowl. Mix in the green beans and spring onion.
2 With wet hands, form 2 tablespoons of mixture at a time into flattish patties.
3 Heat the oil in a heavy-based frying pan over medium heat. Cook 4 fish cakes at a time until golden brown on both sides. Drain on crumpled paper towels, then serve with sweet chilli sauce. The sauce can be garnished with a sprinkle of chopped peanuts and finely diced cucumber.
NOTES: Red curry paste is available from most supermarkets, or from Asian speciality stores.

The fish cakes can be prepared up to the end of Step 2 and stored, covered, in the refrigerator for up to 4 hours. Cook just before serving.

BELOW: Thai fish cakes

JAPANESE PRAWN AND CUCUMBER SALAD

Preparation time: 20 minutes + 1 hour
   marinating
Total cooking time: Nil
Serves 4

1 medium telegraph cucumber
375 g (12 oz) cooked medium prawns
1/4 cup (60 ml/2 fl oz) rice vinegar
1 tablespoon caster sugar
1 tablespoon soy sauce
1 teaspoon finely grated fresh ginger
1 tablespoon sesame seeds, toasted

1 Halve the cucumber lengthways and remove the seeds with a teaspoon. Slice thinly, sprinkle with 1/2 teaspoon of salt and leave on a plate covered with paper towels for 5 minutes. Gently squeeze the moisture from the cucumber and set aside on more paper towels.
2 Peel the prawns, leaving the tails intact. Gently pull out the dark vein from each prawn back, starting at the head end.
3 Combine the vinegar, sugar, soy sauce and ginger in a large bowl, then stir until the sugar dissolves. Add the prawns and cucumber and refrigerate, covered, for 1 hour. Stir occasionally.
4 Drain the prawn and cucumber mixture in a colander. Divide the salad among the serving plates and sprinkle with the toasted sesame seeds.

PRAWNS STEAMED IN BANANA LEAVES

Preparation time: 30 minutes + 2 hours
   marinating
Total cooking time: 15 minutes
Serves 4

1 kg (2 lb) raw medium prawns
2.5 cm (1 inch) piece fresh ginger, grated
2 small fresh red chillies, finely chopped
4 spring onions, finely chopped
2 stems lemon grass, white part only,
   finely chopped
2 teaspoons soft brown sugar
2 tablespoons lime juice
1 tablespoon fish sauce

1 tablespoon sesame seeds, toasted
2 tablespoons chopped fresh coriander
6–8 small banana leaves

1 Peel the prawns and gently pull out the dark vein from each prawn back, starting at the head end. Process the ginger, chilli, spring onion and lemon grass in a food processor, in short bursts, until a paste forms. Transfer to a bowl and mix in the brown sugar, lime juice, fish sauce, sesame seeds and coriander. Add the prawns and toss to coat. Cover and refrigerate for 2 hours.
2 Cut the banana leaves into eight 18 cm (7 inch) squares. Soak the leaves in boiling water for 3 minutes, to soften. Drain, then pat dry.
3 Divide the prawn mixture into eight portions and place a portion on the centre of each banana leaf square. Fold up, then secure the parcels closed with bamboo skewers.
4 Place the parcels in a bamboo steamer over a large pan of simmering water and steam for 8–10 minutes, or until the filling is cooked.
NOTE: Banana leaves are available from Asian food stores and some supermarkets. Alternatively, use foil or baking paper.

ABOVE: Prawns steamed in banana leaves

SUSHI & SASHIMI
Only the freshest ingredients are used by the Japanese to prepare these traditional dishes. They are beautifully presented to appeal to the eye as well as the taste buds.

WHAT'S THE DIFFERENCE?
Japanese *sashimi* is very thin slices of raw fish or other seafood, prepared in various delicate ways and usually served as an appetizer with dipping sauces.

Sushi consists of cold vinegar-flavoured rice topped with sashimi and a limitless variety of ingredients, including omelette or vegetables. Alternatively, for sushi the rice can be rolled, with fillings in the centre, in precooked nori (seaweed). Sushi is served as a main meal with pickled ginger, soy and wasabi.

For making sushi, you will need a bamboo mat. They are not expensive and are available at Asian grocery stores. There isn't really a successful substitute.

TUNA/SALMON NORI ROLLS
You will need a bamboo mat, 5 sheets of nori, each cut in half lengthways, 4 cups (800 g/1 lb 10 oz) cooked sushi rice (see page 74), wasabi and 200 g (6½ oz)

sashimi tuna or salmon, cut into thin strips. Place a piece of nori on the mat, shiny-side-down, and spread 4 tablespoons rice over it, leaving a 2 cm (¾ inch) border along one end. Make a slight indentation along the centre to hold the fish in place, then dab a small amount of wasabi along the ridge. Top with the fish. Roll the mat over to enclose the filling, pressing gently to form a firm roll. Slice the roll in half and then each half into three. Makes 60.

HAND ROLLS

You will need 10 sheets of nori, each cut in half diagonally, 2 cups (400 g/13 oz) cooked sushi rice (see page 74), wasabi, 20 peeled, deveined raw small prawns, 1 thinly sliced avocado and 1 cup (125 g/4 oz) tempura flour. Prepare the tempura batter, following the instructions on the flour packet. Dip the prawns in the batter and deep-fry in hot oil, in batches, until crisp and golden. Drain on crumpled paper towel. Hold a sheet of nori shiny-side-down, flat in your hand, place 2 tablespoons rice on the left-hand side and spread over half of the nori sheet. Dab with wasabi. Place a prawn on the rice with a slice of avocado, then roll the nori to form a cone, enclosing the smaller end. Repeat to use all the remaining ingredients. Makes 20.

PRAWN AND TUNA NIGIRI

You will need 10 peeled, butterflied cooked prawns, 250 g (8 oz) sashimi tuna, wasabi and 2 cups (400 g/13 oz) cooked sushi rice (see page 74). Trim the tuna into a rectangle, removing any connective tissue or blood. Cut thin slices, wiping the knife after each slice. Form a tablespoon of sushi rice into an oval the same length and width as the fish. Place one of the tuna slices flat on your hand, then spread a small dab of wasabi over the centre. Place the rice on the fish and cup your palm. Press the rice onto the fish, firmly pushing with a slight upward motion to make a neat shape. Turn over and repeat the shaping process, finishing with the fish on top. Repeat until you have used the remaining cooked sushi rice and prawns. Makes 16–20.

SASHIMI SALMON, CUCUMBER AND CHIVE ROLLS

Cut a 200 g (6½ oz) fillet of salmon into paper-thin slices, on an angle. Cut 1 small Lebanese cucumber in half and discard the seeds. Cut the flesh into long thin strips. Place a salmon slice on a board, top with strips of cucumber, roll up and tie with trimmed chives. Serve with ginger, shoyu and wasabi. Makes 25.

NOTE: Shoyu is Japanese-style soy sauce, a much lighter and sweeter sauce than the Chinese one. It should be refrigerated after opening.

FROM LEFT: Tuna and salmon nori rolls; Hand rolls; Prawn and tuna nigiri; Sashimi salmon, cucumber and chive rolls

SUSHI & SASHIMI

MAKING SUSHI RICE

Rinse 2½ cups (550 g/1 lb 2 oz) white short-grain rice under cold running water until the water runs clear; drain in the strainer for 1 hour. Transfer to a large saucepan with 3 cups (750 ml/24 fl oz) water, bring to the boil and cook for 5–10 minutes, without stirring, or until tunnels form on the surface. Reduce the heat to low, cover and cook for 12–15 minutes, or until tender. Remove from the heat, place a tea towel over the rice; leave for 15 minutes. Combine 5 tablespoons rice vinegar, 1 tablespoon mirin, 2 teaspoons salt and 2 tablespoons sugar in a bowl and stir until the sugar dissolves. Spread the rice over a flat non-metallic tray, top with the dressing and

stir to mix through. Spread out and cool to body temperature. If the rice gets too cold, it will turn hard and be difficult to work with. Spread a damp tea towel over the rice and keep it covered as you work. To prevent rice sticking to your hands, dip your fingers in a bowl of warm water with a few drops of rice vinegar added. Makes 6 cups (1.2 kg/2 lb 6½ oz).

SASHIMI

Preparing sashimi is relatively simple. You will need a good, very sharp knife. There are four ways of cutting fish for sashimi, all used for different types of fish. The simplest is the straight down cut, about 2 cm (¾ inch) wide. For a cubed cut, the straight pieces are cut into cubes.

There is also an angled cut and a paper-thin slice used for white fish.

CALIFORNIA ROLLS

To make these, you will need 4 sheets of nori, 3 cups (600 g/1¼ lb) cooked sushi rice, 10 g (¼ oz) flying fish roe, 1 sliced avocado, 10 cooked peeled, deveined prawns, each halved lengthways, or 2 crab sticks, and 2 tablespoons Japanese mayonnaise (kyuupi). Place 1 sheet of nori on a bamboo mat, shiny-side-down. Spread 2–3 tablespoons of rice in the middle of the nori, leaving a 2 cm (¾ inch) border along the end nearest you. Make a slight indentation along the centre of the rice to hold the filling in, then spread a small line of mayonnaise

along the ridge. Spread about 1 tablespoon of flying fish roe over the centre of the rice and top with some prawn and avocado. Roll the mat over to enclose the filling, then roll the mat, pressing gently to form a firm roll. Slice the roll in half and then each half into three. Makes 24.

INSIDE-OUT ROLLS

These have the rice on the outside. Use 8 sheets of nori and 6 cups (1.2 kg/2 lb 6½ oz) cooked sushi rice. Place a sheet of nori on a bamboo mat and spread 1 cm (½ inch) rice over the top, leaving a 1 cm (½ inch) border. Cover with a sheet of plastic wrap, slightly larger than the nori. In one quick motion, turn the whole thing over, then place it back on the mat, so the plastic is under the rice and the nori on top. Spread a little wasabi on the nori, along the short end, 4 cm (1½ inches)

from the edge. Lay strips of cucumber, avocado and fresh crab on top of the wasabi, then roll from this end, using the plastic as a guide. Rewrap in plastic, then roll up in the mat. Remove the plastic and roll in flying fish roe or sesame seeds. Cut in half, trim the ends, and cut each half into three. Serve with shoyu. Makes 48.

CHIRASHI-ZUSHI

A Japanese sushi meal in a bowl, chirashi means scattered, and that is how it is prepared. A bed of cooked sushi rice is placed in the bottom of a lacquered bowl, then vegetables and seafood are scattered over the top. The seafood can be raw or cooked, but usually the fish will be sashimi. Chirashi-zushi is accompanied by pickled ginger, wasabi, and soy sauce. To make chirashi-zushi, you will need 4 cups (800 g/1 lb 10 oz) cooked sushi rice, 3 tablespoons each

of toasted white sesame seeds, shredded pickled daikon and shredded nori. Soak 6 dried shiitake mushrooms in boiling water for 10 minutes, then drain. Cut the mushrooms into thin strips and combine in a saucepan with 3 tablespoons soy sauce, 1 cup (250 ml/8 fl oz) dashi stock and 1 tablespoon mirin, and simmer for 10 minutes, then drain. Spread the sushi rice into a large bowl or four individual bowls. Top with the sesame seeds, pickled daikon, nori and mushrooms. Over the top, decoratively arrange 1 thinly sliced cucumber, 16 blanched snow peas (mangetout), 100 g (3½ oz) each of sashimi tuna and salmon and 16 cooked, peeled, deveined and butterflied prawns. Serves 4–6.

FROM LEFT: Sashimi tuna (top) and salmon; California rolls; Inside-out rolls; Chirashi-zushi

75

PRAWN CROUSTADE

Preparation time: 45 minutes
Total cooking time: 25 minutes
Serves 6

★ ★

1/2 loaf unsliced white bread
1/2 cup (125 ml/4 fl oz) olive oil
I clove garlic, crushed

Filling

500 g (I lb) raw medium prawns
1 1/2 cups (375 ml/12 fl oz) fish stock
2 slices lemon
50 g (1 3/4 oz) butter
6 spring onions, chopped
1/4 cup (30 g/1 oz) plain flour
I tablespoon lemon juice
1/2–I teaspoon chopped fresh dill
1/4 cup (60 ml/2 fl oz) cream

BELOW: Prawn croustade

I Preheat the oven to hot 210°C (415°F/Gas 6–7). Remove the crust from the bread and cut the bread into slices about 5 cm (2 inches) thick. Cut each slice diagonally to form triangles. Cut triangles 1 cm (1/2 inch) inside the others, leaving a base on each, then scoop out the centres to create cavities for the filling. Heat the oil and garlic in a small pan, brush all over the bread cases, then place on a baking tray and bake for 10 minutes, or until golden brown.
2 For the filling, peel the prawns and gently pull out the dark vein from each prawn back, starting at the head end. Roughly chop the prawns, place in a small pan and cover with stock. Add the lemon slices, simmer for 15 minutes, strain and reserve the liquid and prawns separately.
3 Melt the butter in a small pan, add the spring onion and stir over medium heat until soft. Stir in the flour and some pepper and cook for 2 minutes. Remove from the heat and gradually stir in the reserved prawn liquid. Return to the heat and stir constantly over medium heat for 5 minutes, or until the sauce boils and thickens. Add the lemon juice, dill, cream and reserved prawns, and stir until heated through.
4 To serve, spoon the filling into the warm bread cases.

SEAFOOD VOL-AU-VENTS

Preparation time: 30 minutes
Total cooking time: 20 minutes
Serves 4

★

250 g (8 oz) raw medium prawns
250 g (8 oz) black mussels
125 g (4 oz) scallops
4 large cooked vol-au-vent cases
I cup (250 ml/8 fl oz) fish stock
60 g (2 oz) butter
1 1/2 tablespoons plain flour
I tablespoon white wine
I tablespoon cream
60 g (2 oz) button mushrooms, diced
I tablespoon fresh lemon juice
I–2 tablespoons chopped fresh parsley

I Peel the prawns and gently pull out the dark vein from each prawn back, starting at the head end. Scrub the mussels with a stiff brush and pull out the hairy beards. Discard any broken mussels, or open ones that don't close when tapped on the bench. Rinse well. Slice or pull off any vein, membrane or hard white muscle from the scallops, leaving any roe attached.

2 Preheat the oven to 160°C (315°F/Gas 2–3). Place the vol-au-vent cases on a baking tray and heat in the oven while preparing the filling.

3 Heat the fish stock in a small pan, add the prawns and mussels and simmer for 4–5 minutes. Add the scallops and cook for 1 minute, or until tender. Drain and cool, reserving the stock. Remove the meat from the mussels, discarding any unopened mussels.

4 Melt half the butter in a small pan over low heat. Stir in the flour and cook for 2 minutes, or until pale and foaming. Remove from the heat and gradually stir in the reserved stock and wine. Return to the heat and stir constantly until the sauce boils and thickens. Simmer for 5 minutes. Remove from the heat and stir in the cream.

5 Melt the remaining butter in a pan and cook the mushrooms for 2–3 minutes, or until soft. Add the seafood, sauce, lemon juice, parsley, and salt and pepper, to taste. Stir until heated through.

6 Spoon the seafood mixture into the warm vol-au-vent cases and serve immediately.

PRAWN FRITTERS

Preparation time: 25 minutes
Total cooking time: 15 minutes
Serves 4-6

50 g (1³⁄₄ oz) dried rice vermicelli
300 g (10 oz) raw medium prawns
1 egg
1 tablespoon fish sauce
1 cup (125 g/4 oz) plain flour
¹⁄₄ teaspoon shrimp paste
3 spring onions, sliced
1 small fresh red chilli, finely chopped
oil, for deep-frying
dipping sauce (see page 128) or bottled sweet
   chilli sauce, for serving

1 Soak the rice vermicelli in a bowl of boiling water for 5 minutes, then drain, pat dry and cut into short lengths.

2 Peel the prawns and gently pull out the dark vein from each prawn back, starting at the head end. Process half the prawns in a food processor until smooth, then transfer to a bowl. Chop the remaining prawns and add to the bowl.

3 Beat the egg, fish sauce and ³⁄₄ cup (185 ml/ 6 fl oz) water in a small jug. Sift the flour into a bowl, make a well in the centre and gradually add the egg mixture, whisking to make a smooth lump-free batter.

4 Add the prawns, shrimp paste, spring onion, red chilli and rice vermicelli to the bowl, then mix until well combined.

5 Fill a deep, heavy-based pan one third full of oil and heat to 180°C (350°F), or until a cube of bread browns in 15 seconds. Drop tablespoons of mixture into the oil and deep-fry in batches for 3 minutes, or until crisp and golden. Drain on crumpled paper towels. Repeat until all the mixture is used. Serve hot, with your choice of dipping sauce.

ABOVE: Prawn fritters

PRAWN COCKTAIL

Preparation time: 20 minutes
Total cooking time: Nil
Serves 4-6

1 kg (2 lb) cooked medium prawns
1 cup (250 ml/8 fl oz) cocktail sauce
  (see page 128)
lettuce, for serving
lemon wedges, for serving
sliced bread, for serving

1 Peel the prawns and pull out the dark vein
from each prawn back, starting at the head end.
2 Reserve some prawns to use as a garnish.
Remove the tails from the remaining prawns and
add to the cocktail sauce. Mix gently to coat the
prawns in the sauce.
3 Arrange the lettuce in serving dishes or bowls.
Spoon some prawns into each dish. Garnish with
the reserved prawns. Serve with lemon wedges
and bread.
NOTE: You can make the cocktail sauce several
hours ahead and refrigerate. Stir in 2 tablespoons
of thick cream for a creamier sauce.

PRAWN CUTLETS

Preparation time: 30 minutes + 15 minutes
  chilling
Total cooking time: 10 minutes
Serves 4-6

1 kg (2 lb) raw large prawns
4 eggs
2 tablespoons soy sauce
cornflour, for coating
2 cups (200 g/6 1/2 oz) dry breadcrumbs
oil, for deep-frying
tartare sauce (see page 128), for serving
lemon wedges, for serving

1 Peel the prawns, leaving the tails intact. Slit
them all open down the backs, remove the veins
and then gently flatten open with your fingers.
2 Beat the eggs and soy sauce in a small bowl.
Coat the prawns in cornflour, shake off the
excess, then dip in the egg mixture and finally
press in the breadcrumbs. Chill for 15 minutes.

3 Fill a deep, heavy-based pan one third full of
oil and heat to 180°C (350°F), or until a cube of
bread browns in 15 seconds. Deep-fry the
prawns in batches until lightly golden. Drain on
crumpled paper towels, then serve with tartare
sauce and lemon wedges.

PANCAKES WITH CAVIAR

Preparation time: 15 minutes + 1 hour standing
Total cooking time: 20 minutes
Serves 4-6

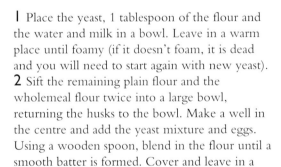

10 g (1/4 oz) fresh yeast
  or 1/2 teaspoon dry yeast
3/4 cup (90 g/3 oz) plain flour
2/3 cup (170 ml/5 1/2 fl oz) warm water
2/3 cup (170 ml/5 1/2 fl oz) milk, warmed
3/4 cup (110 g/3 1/2 oz) wholemeal flour
2 eggs, lightly beaten
2/3 cup (170 ml/5 1/2 fl oz) sour cream or
  crème fraîche
200 g (6 1/2 oz) lumpfish roe or caviar

1 Place the yeast, 1 tablespoon of the flour and
the water and milk in a bowl. Leave in a warm
place until foamy (if it doesn't foam, it is dead
and you will need to start again with new yeast).
2 Sift the remaining plain flour and the
wholemeal flour twice into a large bowl,
returning the husks to the bowl. Make a well in
the centre and add the yeast mixture and eggs.
Using a wooden spoon, blend in the flour until a
smooth batter is formed. Cover and leave in a
warm place for 1 hour.
3 Lightly grease a heavy-based frying pan with
melted butter. Stir the batter for 10 seconds.
Drop 2 tablespoons of batter into the pan for
each pancake, cooking a few at a time. Cook
until bubbles appear on the surface, turn and
cook the other side. Keep warm. Serve topped
with sour cream or crème fraîche and lumpfish
roe or caviar.
NOTE: True caviar, the ripe eggs from various
species of the sturgeon family, is very expensive.
Cheaper imitations, the fish eggs from other
types of fish, are often marketed as caviar. One
of these, lumpfish roe, can be used as a substitute
in many recipes.

OPPOSITE PAGE:
Prawn cocktail (top);
Prawn cutlets

2 Place the mussels, 1 onion, the celery and wine in a large pan and bring rapidly to the boil. Cover and cook, shaking the pan frequently, for 3 minutes. After 3 minutes, start removing the mussels as they open. Discard any mussels that have not opened after 4–5 minutes.

3 Pull off and discard the empty side of each shell. Set aside the mussels in the shells, cover and keep warm.

4 Strain and reserve the cooking liquid, discarding the vegetables.

5 In a pan, heat the fish stock, parsley, thyme and bay leaf. Bring to the boil, then reduce the heat, cover and simmer for 10 minutes. Remove the herbs.

6 Melt the butter in a large pan, add the garlic and remaining onion and stir over low heat for 5–10 minutes, or until the onion is soft but not brown. Stir in the flour and cook for 1 minute, or until pale and foaming. Remove from the heat and gradually stir in the reserved mussel liquid and fish stock. Return to the heat and stir until the mixture boils and thickens. Reduce the heat and simmer, uncovered, for 10 minutes.

7 Divide the reserved mussels among 4 soup bowls. Ladle liquid over the mussels and garnish with dill sprigs. Serve immediately with slices of fresh crusty bread.

MOULES MARINIERE

Preparation time: 15 minutes + 2 hours soaking
Total cooking time: 30–35 minutes
Serves 4

26 black mussels
3 onions, chopped
1 stick celery, chopped
1 cup (250 ml/8 fl oz) white wine
1 1/2 cups (375 ml/12 fl oz) fish stock
4 sprigs of fresh parsley
1 sprig of fresh thyme
1 bay leaf
60 g (2 oz) butter
2 cloves garlic, crushed
1 teaspoon plain flour
fresh dill sprigs, for serving

1 Scrub the mussels with a stiff brush and pull out the hairy beards. Discard any broken mussels, or open ones that don't close when tapped on the bench. Rinse well.

ABOVE: Moules marinière

COQUILLES SAINT JACQUES

Preparation time: 20 minutes
Total cooking time: 10 minutes
Serves 4

24 scallops on shells
1 cup (250 ml/8 fl oz) fish stock
1 cup (250 ml/8 fl oz) white wine
60 g (2 oz) butter
4 spring onions, chopped
1 rasher bacon, finely chopped
100 g (3 1/2 oz) button mushrooms, thinly sliced
1/4 cup (30 g/1 oz) plain flour
3/4 cup (185 ml/6 fl oz) cream
1 teaspoon lemon juice
1 cup (80 g/2 3/4 oz) fresh breadcrumbs
30 g (1 oz) butter, melted, extra

1 Slice or pull off any vein, membrane or hard white muscle from the scallops, leaving any roe attached. Remove the scallops from the shells and cut the scallops in half.

2 Heat the fish stock and white wine in a pan and add the scallops. Cover and simmer over medium heat for 2–3 minutes, or until the scallops are opaque and tender. Remove the scallops with a slotted spoon, cover and set aside. Bring the liquid in the pan to the boil and reduce until 1 1/2 cups (375 ml/12 fl oz) remain.

3 Melt the butter in a pan and add the spring onion, bacon and mushrooms. Cook over medium heat for 3 minutes, stirring occasionally, until the onion is soft but not brown.

4 Stir in the flour and cook for 2 minutes. Remove from the heat and gradually stir in the reduced stock. Return to the heat and stir until the mixture boils and thickens. Reduce the heat and simmer for 2 minutes. Stir in the cream, lemon juice and salt and freshly ground black pepper, to taste. Cover, set aside and keep warm.

5 Combine the breadcrumbs and extra butter in a small bowl. Preheat the grill to high.

6 Divide the scallops among the shells. Spoon the warm sauce over the scallops and sprinkle with the breadcrumb mixture. Place under the grill until the breadcrumbs are golden brown. Serve immediately.

MARINATED OCTOPUS WITH SWEET CHILLI DRESSING

Preparation time: 30 minutes + 4 hours marinating
Total cooking time: 4 minutes
Serves 4-6

1 kg (2 lb) baby octopus
1/2 cup (125 ml/4 fl oz) olive oil
2 cloves garlic, crushed
2 tablespoons finely chopped fresh coriander
I red chilli, finely chopped
2 tablespoons lemon juice

Sweet chilli dressing

I red chilli, finely chopped
1/4 cup (60 ml/2 fl oz) lemon juice
2 tablespoons soft brown sugar
I tablespoon fish sauce
2 tablespoons finely chopped fresh coriander
I tablespoon sweet chilli sauce

I To clean the octopus, use a small sharp knife to cut off the head. Discard the head and gut. Pick up the octopus body and push up the beak with your index finger. Remove and discard the beak. Clean the octopus under running water and drain on crumpled paper towels.

2 In a glass or ceramic bowl, combine the oil, garlic, coriander, chilli and lemon juice. Add the octopus, mix well, then cover and refrigerate overnight, or for at least 4 hours.

3 Drain the octopus on crumpled paper towels. Heat the barbecue or grill plate to very hot. Coat the plate with oil. Cook the drained octopus, turning frequently, for 3–4 minutes, or until tender, basting with marinade often to keep the octopus moist. Do not overcook, or the octopus will toughen. Serve either warm with dressing, or cold as part of a salad.

4 For the dressing, combine all the ingredients in a small screw top jar and shake well.

NOTE: Traditionally, octopus are hit hard against rocks to tenderise them before cooking. These days, octopus are successfully tenderised by being tossed in a clean cement mixer, or a device specially designed for this purpose.

BELOW: Marinated octopus with sweet chilli dressing

FRESH SALMON TARTARE

Preparation time: 20 minutes
Total cooking time: Nil
Serves 4

400 g (13 oz) salmon fillet
2 spring onions, finely chopped
1 tablespoon tiny capers or finely chopped
　regular capers
1 tablespoon finely chopped gherkin
chopped fresh dill, to garnish
1 lemon, cut into wedges

1 Remove the skin and any connective tissue or bones from the salmon. This should leave you with about 70 g (2¼ oz) of fish per person. Using a large, sharp knife, finely chop the salmon until it has the texture of mince. Mix in a bowl with the spring onion, capers, gherkin and some salt and freshly ground black pepper. Refrigerate, covered, until just before serving.
2 When ready to serve, roughly pile onto individual plates and sprinkle with dill. Grind some more black pepper over the fish and serve

with lemon wedges. Can be served with slices of buttered rye bread.
NOTE: You can also use fresh tuna fillet.

HERRINGS IN SOUR CREAM

Preparation time: 20 minutes
Total cooking time: Nil
Serves 4-6

2 x 150 g (5 oz) jars pickled herrings
1 cup (250 ml/8 fl oz) sour cream
2 tablespoons white wine vinegar
½ teaspoon sugar
1 red onion, sliced into rings
1 tablespoon chopped fresh chives

1 Drain the herrings and remove any visible bones with tweezers. Cut the herrings into strips about 2.5 cm (1 inch) wide and arrange on serving plates.
2 Mix the sour cream, vinegar and sugar in a bowl to dissolve the sugar. Spoon over the fillets. Garnish with the onion and chives.

*RIGHT: Fresh
salmon tartare*

OMELETTE ARNOLD BENNETT

Preparation time: 10 minutes
Total cooking time: 10 minutes
Serves 2

100 g (3¹/2 oz) smoked haddock or cod fillets
60 g (2 oz) butter
2 tablespoons cream
4 eggs, separated
¹/4 cup (60 ml/2 fl oz) cream, extra
60 g (2 oz) Parmesan or Gruyère cheese, grated

1 Place the haddock in a small frying pan and cover with water. Bring slowly to boil, then turn off the heat. Cover and leave for 10 minutes, then drain. Remove any skin and bones, then flake the flesh and set aside.
2 Wipe out the pan, return to the heat and melt half the butter. Add the cream and the flaked fish. Stir over medium heat for 2–3 minutes. Remove from the heat and allow to cool.

3 Beat the egg yolks and 1 tablespoon of the extra cream in a small bowl. Whisk the egg whites in a clean dry bowl until soft peaks form. Fold in the yolks, haddock mixture and half the grated cheese.
4 Melt the remaining butter in a non-stick frying pan. When hot, add the egg mixture. Cook until golden and set on the bottom. Do not fold.
5 Sprinkle with the remaining cheese and pour the remaining cream over the omelette. Sprinkle with salt and freshly ground black pepper, to taste. Brown quickly under a preheated grill. Slide onto a serving plate, then cut into wedges. Serve with lime wedges and mixed salad.
NOTE: Arnold Bennett was an English novelist who died in 1931. This dish was created for him at the Savoy Hotel. Traditionally, grated Parmesan cheese was used.

SMOKED HADDOCK
Smoked haddock and smoked cod are interchangeable in most recipes, although smoked haddock has a finer flavour. Smoked haddock can be a little salty, depending on the cure. To lessen the salty taste, soak the fillets in water for a couple of hours. Smoked haddock can be gently poached in water or milk, or fried, grilled, or baked. After cooking, you can flake the flesh and use it in many ways. It is often used in combination with cheese as a pancake or omelette filling, baked in a quiche filling, or in soups and bakes.

ABOVE: Omelette Arnold Bennett

STUFFED MUSSELS

Insert a strong knife or oyster shucker in the side of the mussel, near the hinge, then twist to open.

Spread spinach mixture over each mussel and smooth with a wet knife.

STUFFED MUSSELS

Preparation time: 40 minutes + 10 minutes soaking
Total cooking time: 20 minutes
Serves 4

1 kg (2 lb) black mussels
500 g (1 lb) English spinach
4 anchovy fillets
2 tablespoons milk
1 egg, hard-boiled
1 clove garlic, crushed
2–3 tablespoons lemon juice
100 g (3 1/2 oz) butter, melted
pinch of grated nutmeg
1 cup (80 g/2 3/4 oz) fresh white breadcrumbs
60 g (2 oz) Parmesan, grated

1 Preheat the oven to moderately hot 200°C (400°F/Gas 6). Scrub the mussels with a stiff brush and pull out the hairy beards. Discard any broken mussels, or open ones that don't close when tapped on the bench. Rinse well.
2 Wash the spinach thoroughly, then drain. Discard the stalks and finely shred the leaves. Put the spinach in a pan, cover and cook over low heat, stirring occasionally, for 3–5 minutes, or until wilted. Drain well and, when cool, squeeze out as much liquid as possible with your hands.
3 Cover the anchovy fillets with milk in a small bowl, cover and leave for 10 minutes, then drain. Process the spinach, anchovies, egg and garlic in a food processor until finely chopped. Transfer to a large bowl, add the lemon juice, butter and nutmeg. Season with salt and pepper, to taste. Add enough of the breadcrumbs to form a spreadable mixture.
4 Wrap one hand in a tea towel and, with the other, open the mussels by inserting a short strong knife, or oyster shucker, near the hinge, then twisting the knife quickly to open the shell. Break off and discard the top shell.
5 Spread about 1 tablespoon of spinach mixture over each mussel and smooth with a knife dipped in water. Place the mussels on baking trays, sprinkle with the Parmesan and bake for 10–12 minutes, or until the mussels are cooked.

INSALATA DI MARE

Preparation time: 40 minutes + 1 hour 15 minutes standing
Total cooking time: 15 minutes
Serves 6

4 cloves garlic, cut into thick slices
1/2 cup (125 ml/4 fl oz) lemon juice
8 baby squid hoods, cut into thick rings, then halved
800 g (1 lb 10 oz) raw medium prawns
1 kg (2 lb) black mussels
1 kg (2 lb) fresh baby clams (vongole) or pipis
1/3 cup (80 ml/2 3/4 fl oz) extra virgin olive oil
3 tablespoons chopped fresh flat-leaf parsley
baby spinach leaves, for serving, optional

1 Place the garlic and lemon juice in a small bowl and set aside for 1 hour. Remove the garlic and discard. (This infuses the lemon juice with the garlic flavour.)
2 Cook the squid in a pan of boiling salted water for 5 minutes, or until tender. Remove the squid.
3 Cook the prawns in the same water for 2 minutes, or until pink and cooked through. Drain and cool slightly, then peel and pull out the dark vein from each prawn back, starting at the head end.
4 Scrub the mussels with a stiff brush and pull out the hairy beards. Discard any broken mussels, or open ones that don't close when tapped on the bench. Rinse well. Scrub the clams. Cook the mussels and clams in separate pans with 1 cup (250 ml/8 fl oz) water in each pan. Cover and steam for about 4–5 minutes, until the shells open. Discard any shells that do not open. Allow to cool slightly. Remove the mussels and clams from their shells.
5 Combine the seafood with the garlic-infused lemon juice, olive oil and parsley, then season with salt and cracked black pepper. Allow to stand for 15 minutes at room temperature, before serving. Can be served on a bed of baby spinach leaves.

OPPOSITE PAGE:
Stuffed mussels (top):
Insalata di mare

EGGS

The colour of the eggshell has nothing to do with the quality of the egg, rather the breed of hen which laid the egg. Eggs are best refrigerated away from strong smelling foods, the flavours of which can be absorbed through the porous shells. Refrigerate whole unbroken egg yolks in a container, covered with water, for 2–3 days. Whites keep for 4–5 days, covered with plastic in the fridge, or can be frozen for up to 6 months. Freeze individually in an ice cube tray to make it easy to thaw out just the quantity required. Thaw at room temperature.

ABOVE: Fish croquettes

FISH CROQUETTES

Preparation time: 30 minutes + 1½ hours chilling
Total cooking time: 30 minutes
Makes 16

★ ★

1½ cups (375 ml/12 fl oz) milk
500 g (1 lb) skinless white fish fillets
   (eg. ling, flake, hake, coley, flathead)
90 g (3 oz) butter
4 spring onions, finely chopped
¾ cup (90 g/3 oz) plain flour
½ teaspoon ground nutmeg
2 teaspoons grated lemon rind
1 tablespoon lemon juice
4 tablespoons chopped fresh parsley
½ cup (60 g/2 oz) plain flour, for dusting
2 eggs, lightly beaten
1½ cups (150 g/5 oz) dry breadcrumbs
oil, for deep-frying

1 Heat the milk in a large frying pan and add the fish fillets in a single layer. Cook over low heat for 3–4 minutes, or until the fish flakes easily when tested with a fork. Transfer to a plate with a slotted spoon. Reserve the milk. Flake the fish well with a fork and set aside.
2 Melt the butter in a large heavy-based pan, add the spring onion and cook for 2 minutes, or until soft. Add the flour and nutmeg and stir for 1 minute, or until pale and foaming. Remove from the heat and add 1 cup (250 ml/8 fl oz) of the reserved milk all at once. Whisk until smooth, then return to the heat. Stir over medium heat until the mixture thickens. Continue to stir for 2 minutes over medium heat. The mixture will be very thick.
3 Add the flaked fish, lemon rind, juice and parsley. Season, to taste. Transfer to a bowl, cover and refrigerate for at least 1 hour.
4 Form into 16 croquette shapes 8 x 3 cm (3 x 1¼ inches). Dust each with plain flour, then dip in the egg and coat with breadcrumbs. Refrigerate again for at least 20 minutes.
5 Fill a deep, heavy-based pan one third full of oil and heat to 180°C (350°F), or until a cube of bread dropped into the oil browns in 15 seconds. Cook a few croquettes at a time for 2–3 minutes, or until golden brown. Drain on crumpled paper towels. Serve hot.
NOTE: You can freeze uncooked croquettes for up to 1 month.

CRAB CAKES WITH AVOCADO SALSA

Preparation time: 15 minutes + 30 minutes
  chilling
Total cooking time: 6 minutes
Serves 4

2 eggs, lightly beaten
340 g (11 oz) can crab meat, drained
1 spring onion, finely chopped
1 tablespoon mayonnaise
2 teaspoons sweet chilli sauce
1¼ cups (100 g/3½ oz) fresh white
  breadcrumbs
oil, for shallow-frying
lime wedges, for serving

Avocado salsa

2 ripe Roma (egg) tomatoes, chopped
1 small red onion, finely chopped
1 large ripe avocado, diced
¼ cup (60 ml/2 fl oz) lime juice
2 tablespoons fresh chervil leaves
1 teaspoon caster sugar

1 Combine the eggs, crab meat, spring onion, mayonnaise, sweet chilli sauce and breadcrumbs in a bowl and stir well. Season, to taste, with salt and freshly ground black pepper. Using wet hands, form the crab mixture into 8 small flat patties. Cover and refrigerate for 30 minutes.
2 For the avocado salsa, put the tomato, onion, avocado, lime juice, chervil leaves and sugar in a bowl. Season, to taste, with salt and pepper, and toss gently to combine.
3 Heat the oil in a large heavy-based pan to 180°C (350°F), or until a cube of bread dropped into the oil browns in 15 seconds. Cook the crab cakes over medium heat for 6 minutes, or until golden brown on both sides. Drain well on crumpled paper towels. Serve the crab cakes with the bowl of avocado salsa and some lime wedges.

BELOW: Crab cakes with avocado salsa

OYSTERS
Fresh oysters served in the shell are one of nature's works of art. It is impossible to improve on perfection... but these recipes certainly come close.

OYSTERS ROCKEFELLER
Arrange 24 oysters in their shells on a bed of rock salt on a baking tray. Cover and refrigerate. Melt 60 g (2 oz) butter in a pan. Add 2 finely chopped bacon rashers and cook until browned. Add 8 finely chopped English spinach leaves, 2 finely chopped spring onions, 2 tablespoons finely chopped fresh parsley, 4 tablespoons dry breadcrumbs and a drop of Tabasco. Cook over medium heat until the spinach has wilted. Spoon onto the oysters and grill for 2–3 minutes, or until golden. Makes 24.

OYSTERS MORNAY
Melt 30 g (1 oz) butter in a small pan. Stir in 1 tablespoon plain flour and cook for 2 minutes. Remove from heat. Gradually add ²⁄₃ cup (170 ml/5¹⁄₂ fl oz) hot milk. Return to medium heat and stir until the mixture boils and thickens. Add salt and pepper, to taste, and a pinch of cayenne pepper. Simmer for 2 minutes, stirring occasionally. Remove. Drain the juice from 24 oysters. Arrange the oysters in the shells on a bed of rock salt on a baking tray. Top each with a teaspoon of the sauce and sprinkle with grated Cheddar. Grill for 2–3 minutes, or until golden. Makes 24.

GINGER AND SOY OYSTERS

Arrange 24 oysters in their shells on a bed of rock salt on a baking tray. Combine in a bowl 2 tablespoons each of soy sauce and sweet sherry, 3 teaspoons sesame oil, 1 tablespoon finely shredded fresh ginger, 1 spring onion cut into long shreds, and ground pepper. Divide evenly among the oysters. Bake in a preheated moderate 180°C (350°F/Gas 4) oven for 5–10 minutes, or until the oysters are just cooked. Makes 24.

OYSTERS KILPATRICK

Arrange 24 oysters in their shells on a bed of rock salt on a baking tray. Sprinkle lightly with Worcestershire. Sprinkle with 3 finely chopped bacon rashers and ground black pepper. Grill for 3–4 minutes. Makes 24.

MEDITERRANEAN OYSTERS

Arrange 24 oysters in their shells on a bed of rock salt on a baking tray. Sprinkle the oysters lightly with balsamic vinegar. Chop 6 slices of prosciutto and divide among the oysters. Sprinkle with cracked black pepper. Grill for 1 minute, or until the prosciutto is crisp. Makes 24.

OYSTERS WITH SALMON ROE AND CREME FRAICHE

Spread rock salt over a large serving platter. Arrange 24 shucked oysters on the rock salt (the salt helps to steady the oysters). Spoon 1 teaspoon crème fraîche onto each oyster and top with 1/2 teaspoon salmon roe (you will need about 120 g/4 oz altogether). Season with freshly ground black pepper. Serve with lime wedges. Makes 24.

OYSTERS WITH SESAME SEED MAYONNAISE

Remove 24 oysters from their shells and pat dry. Wash the shells, replace the oysters and cover with a damp cloth. Refrigerate. Stir 1 tablespoon sesame oil, 1 clove crushed garlic and 2 tablespoons toasted sesame seeds into 1/3 cup (80 g/2 3/4 oz) whole-egg mayonnaise. Season and spoon a teaspoonful onto each oyster. Garnish each with a sprig of fresh dill. Makes 24.

CLOCKWISE, FROM LEFT: Oysters Rockefeller; Ginger and soy oysters; Oysters Kilpatrick; Oysters with salmon roe and crème fraîche; Oysters with sesame seed mayonnaise; Mediterranean oysters; Oysters mornay

89

MUSSELS SAGANAKI

Preparation time: 45 minutes
Total cooking time: 25 minutes
Serves 6

★ ★

750 g (1 1/2 lb) black mussels

1/2 cup (125 ml/4 fl oz) dry white wine

3 sprigs fresh thyme

1 bay leaf

1 tablespoon olive oil

1 large onion, finely chopped

1 clove garlic, finely chopped

420 g (14 oz) ripe tomatoes, halved, grated and skin discarded

2 tablespoons tomato paste (tomato purée)

1/2 teaspoon sugar

1 tablespoon red wine vinegar

70 g (2 1/4 oz) feta, crumbled

1 teaspoon fresh thyme leaves

1 Scrub the mussels with a stiff brush and pull out the hairy beards. Discard any broken mussels, or open ones that don't close when tapped on the bench. Rinse well.

2 Bring the wine, thyme and bay leaf to the boil in a large pan, add the mussels and cook for 4–5 minutes. Pour the mussel liquid through a strainer into a heatproof jug and reserve. Discard any unopened mussels. Remove one half shell from each mussel and discard.

3 Heat the oil in a saucepan, add the onion and stir over medium heat for 3 minutes. Add the garlic and cook for 1 minute, or until fragrant. Pour in the reserved mussel liquid, increase the heat and bring to the boil, then boil for 2 minutes, or until almost dry. Add the tomato, tomato paste and sugar, then reduce the heat and simmer for 5 minutes. Add the vinegar and simmer for another 5 minutes.

4 Add the mussels to the saucepan and cook over medium heat for 1 minute, or until heated through. Spoon into a warm serving dish. Top with the crumbled feta and fresh thyme leaves. Serve hot.

RIGHT: Mussels saganaki

STUFFED SARDINES

Preparation time: 20 minutes
Total cooking time: 30 minutes
Serves 4-6

1 kg (2 lb) fresh sardines

1/4 cup (60 ml/2 fl oz) olive oil

1/2 cup (40 g/1 1/4 oz) soft white breadcrumbs

1/4 cup (30 g/1 oz) sultanas

1/4 cup (40 g/1 1/4 oz) pine nuts, toasted

20 g (3/4 oz) can anchovies, drained and mashed

1/2 teaspoon sugar

1 tablespoon finely chopped fresh parsley

2 spring onions, finely chopped

1 Preheat the oven to moderate 180°C (350°F/ Gas 4). Cut the heads from the sardines, split open the bellies with a sharp knife and remove the insides. Open out each sardine and place skin-side-up on a chopping board. Press each sardine lightly, yet firmly, to open out. Turn each over and pull out the backbone. Cut off at the tail end of the bones. Wash in salted water and dry on paper towels.

2 Heat half the oil in a frying pan, add the breadcrumbs and cook quickly, stirring until lightly golden. Drain on paper towels.

3 Put half the fried breadcrumbs in a bowl and stir in the sultanas, toasted pine nuts, mashed anchovies, sugar, parsley and spring onion. Season with salt and pepper, to taste. Spoon about 2 teaspoons of the mixture into each prepared sardine, then carefully fold up to enclose the stuffing.

4 Place the stuffed sardines in a single layer in a well-greased baking dish. Sprinkle any remaining stuffing over the top of the sardines, with the cooked breadcrumbs. Drizzle the remaining olive oil over the top. Bake for 30 minutes. The sardines can be served with lemon wedges.

NOTE: You can also use butterflied sardines for this recipe.

ABOVE: Stuffed sardines

91

VIETNAMESE FRESH PRAWN ROLLS

Roughly cut the drained noodles into shorter lengths with scissors.

Brush both sides of each rice paper wrapper with water.

Fold in the sides of the wrapper, adding a garlic chive and letting it point out of the roll.

OPPOSITE PAGE:
Vietnamese fresh prawn rolls (top); Scallops and vegetables with balsamic dressing

VIETNAMESE FRESH PRAWN ROLLS

Preparation time: 50 minutes + 5 minutes soaking
Total cooking time: 25 minutes
Makes about 20

100 g (3½ oz) dried mung bean vermicelli (cellophane noodles)
1 kg (2 lb) cooked large prawns
20–25 rice paper wrappers, about 16 cm (6½ inches) diameter
40 fresh mint leaves
10 garlic chives, halved

Dipping sauce

2 tablespoons satay sauce
3 tablespoons hoisin sauce
1 fresh red chilli, finely chopped
1 tablespoon chopped roasted unsalted peanuts
1 tablespoon lemon juice

1 Soak the cellophane noodles for 5 minutes in a small bowl with enough hot water to cover. Drain well and use scissors to roughly chop the noodles into shorter lengths. Peel the prawns and gently pull out the dark vein from each back, starting at the head end. Cut the prawns in half horizontally.

2 Using a pastry brush, brush both sides of each rice paper wrapper with water. Leave for about 2 minutes, or until the wrappers become soft and pliable. Stack the wrappers on top of each other and sprinkle lightly with water to prevent them sticking together and drying out. Be careful as the wrappers can tear easily when softened (we've allowed a few extra just in case).

3 Place 1 softened wrapper on a work surface and spoon about 1 tablespoon of the noodles along the bottom third of the wrapper, leaving enough space at the sides to fold the wrapper over. Top with 2 mint leaves and 2 prawn halves. Fold in the sides towards each other and firmly roll up the wrapper, adding a garlic chive and allowing it to point out of one end. Repeat with the remaining wrappers and ingredients and place the spring rolls, seam-side-down, on a serving plate. Cover with a damp tea towel to prevent them drying out.

4 For the dipping sauce, mix the satay sauce, hoisin sauce, red chilli, peanuts and lemon juice in a small bowl. Serve with the spring rolls.

SCALLOPS AND VEGETABLES WITH BALSAMIC DRESSING

Preparation time: 30 minutes
Total cooking time: 8 minutes
Serves 4

16 large scallops, in shells
olive oil, for brushing
1 tablespoon olive oil
2 spring onions, finely chopped
2 bacon rashers, finely chopped
½ small red pepper (capsicum), seeded and finely diced
½ stick celery, finely diced
1 tablespoon finely chopped fresh parsley
100 g (3½ oz) mixed salad leaves
60 g (2 oz) snow pea (mangetout) sprouts, trimmed
1 spring onion, cut into thin shreds, to garnish

Balsamic dressing

⅓ cup (80 ml/2¾ fl oz) olive oil
1 tablespoon balsamic vinegar
½ teaspoon Dijon mustard
½ teaspoon honey

1 Slice or pull off any vein, membrane or hard white muscle from the scallops, leaving any roe attached. Gently pat dry with paper towels. Very lightly brush with olive oil and place on a large baking tray in their shells. Preheat the grill to hot.

2 Heat the oil in a heavy-based frying pan. Add the spring onion and bacon, cook for 2 minutes, then add the red pepper and celery. Cook and stir frequently for 3 minutes, or until the vegetables are softened. Add the parsley and season well with salt and black pepper.

3 Combine the balsamic dressing ingredients in a glass jar and shake well.

4 Grill the scallops for 1–2 minutes. Take care not to overcook. Arrange 4 shells around the outside of four large serving plates. Spoon some warm vegetable mixture over each scallop. Divide the mixed salad leaves and snow pea sprouts into 4 portions and place some in the centre of each plate. Garnish the salad with the spring onion shreds. Drizzle a little dressing over the scallops and the salad. Serve at once.

SALMON RILLETTES

Preparation time: 10 minutes + overnight chilling
Total cooking time: 10 minutes
Serves 4-6

200 g (6¹/2 oz) salmon fillet
125 g (4 oz) unsalted butter, softened
100 g (3¹/2 oz) smoked salmon, finely chopped
1 egg yolk, lightly beaten
1 tablespoon olive oil
1 teaspoon lemon juice
1 tablespoon chopped fresh dill

1 Remove the skin and any bones from the salmon fillet. Melt 50 g (1³/4 oz) of the butter in a frying pan over low heat and cook the salmon for 5 minutes, then turn and cook for another 5 minutes. Remove from the pan and cool slightly before flaking into small pieces and combining with the remaining softened butter and smoked salmon, egg yolk, oil, lemon juice and dill. Season with salt and pepper, to taste.
2 Transfer to a serving dish and refrigerate overnight. Serve with Melba toasts.

ABOVE: Salmon rillettes

SALMON MOUSSE

Preparation time: 15 minutes + overnight chilling
Total cooking time: 2 minutes
Serves 8-10

645 g (1 lb 5 oz) canned red salmon, drained
¹/2 cup (125 ml/4 fl oz) chicken stock
1 tablespoon powdered gelatine
1¹/2 tablespoons lemon juice
1¹/2 cups (375 ml/12 fl oz) cream
few drops of red food colouring, optional

1 Lightly oil a 4¹/2 cup (1.125 litre) capacity savarin or fish mould. Remove and discard the salmon bones and dark skin. You will need about 500 g (1 lb) salmon flesh.
2 Heat the stock in a small saucepan, remove from the heat and sprinkle the gelatine over the stock. Stir until dissolved, then cool. Blend or process the salmon and stock mixture until smooth. Transfer to a large bowl and stir in the lemon juice and salt and pepper, to taste.
3 Beat the cream in a small bowl with electric beaters until soft peaks form. Gently fold into the

salmon and lightly tint with food colouring, if desired. Spoon into the mould, cover and refrigerate overnight.

4 To unmould, loosen the edges, quickly dip the mould in warm water and turn onto a plate. Holding the mould and plate together firmly, give a quick sharp shake to release the mould. Serve with toast, crackers or vegetables sticks.

DRESSED CRAB

Preparation time: 40 minutes + freezing
Total cooking time: 10–15 minutes
Serves 1–2

★★★

1 kg (2 lb) mud crab
2–3 teaspoons lemon juice
1½ tablespoons good-quality whole-egg
    mayonnaise
1 cup (80 g/2¾ oz) fresh breadcrumbs
1 teaspoon Worcestershire sauce
2 hard-boiled eggs
2 tablespoons chopped fresh parsley
1 tablespoon chopped fresh chives

1 Freeze the crab for about 1 hour to immobilize it, then drop it into a large pan of boiling water. Reduce the heat and simmer for 10–15 minutes, or until bright orange all over—it should be cooked through by this stage. Drain and cool.

2 Twist the claws off the crab. Pull back the small flap on the underside of the crab and prise off the top shell. Scrape out any creamy brown meat and set aside. Wash and dry the top shell and set aside. Remove the intestines and grey feathery gills from the main body and discard. Scrape out any remaining creamy brown meat and add to the rest. Cut the crab in half and remove the white meat. Crack the claws and remove any meat. Keep white meat separate.

3 Finely chop the brown crab meat and combine with the lemon juice, mayonnaise and enough of the breadcrumbs to combine. Add the sauce and salt and pepper, to taste. Press the egg yolks and whites separately through a sieve. Place the white crab meat on both the outside edges of the dry shell. Spoon the brown meat mixture into the centre of the shell and arrange the combined parsley and chives, sieved yolks and whites in rows over the crab meat. Serve with bread, lemon wedges and extra mayonnaise.
NOTE: Heavy crabs have the most meat.

ABOVE: Dressed crab

THAI PRAWN OMELETTE

Preparation time: 15 minutes
Total cooking time: 15 minutes
Serves 2–4

★ ★ ★

500 g (1 lb) raw small prawns
2 tablespoons oil
3 cloves garlic, chopped
2 stems lemon grass, white part only, finely
  chopped
2 coriander roots, finely chopped
1–2 teaspoons chopped fresh red chillies
3 spring onions, chopped
1 tablespoon fish sauce
2 teaspoons grated palm sugar or brown sugar
4 eggs
2 teaspoons fish sauce, extra
2 spring onions, finely shredded, for garnish
fresh coriander sprigs, for garnish

BELOW: Thai
prawn omelette

1 Peel the prawns and gently pull out the dark vein from each back, starting at the head end.

2 Heat half the oil in a large wok or heavy-based pan. Add the garlic, lemon grass, coriander root and chilli to the wok and stir over medium heat for 20 seconds. Add the prawns to the wok and stir-fry until the prawns change colour. Add the chopped spring onion, ½ teaspoon black pepper, fish sauce and palm sugar to the wok and toss well. Remove from the wok.

3 Beat the eggs, fish sauce and 2 tablespoons water in a bowl until foamy. Add the remaining oil to the wok and swirl around to coat the sides. Heat the wok and, when very hot, pour in the egg and swirl around the wok. Allow to set on the underneath edges, frequently lifting the edges once set, and slightly tilting the wok to let the unset mixture run underneath. Repeat until the omelette is nearly all set.

4 Place three-quarters of the prawn mixture in the centre of the omelette and fold in the sides to form a square, overlapping the sides a little, or simply fold the omelette in half. Slide onto a serving plate and place the remaining prawn mixture on the top. Sprinkle with the shredded spring onion. Garnish with coriander and serve with chilli sauce and steamed rice.

NOTE: You can also use a mixture of seafood such as prawns and scallops.

STUFFED PRAWNS IN CRISPY WON TON

Preparation time: 40 minutes
Total cooking time: 10 minutes
Makes 12

15 won ton wrappers
12 raw large prawns
400 g (13 oz) raw medium prawns, peeled and finely chopped
4 spring onions, very finely chopped
1 egg white
1/2 cup (60 g/2 oz) cornflour
1 egg, lightly beaten
oil, for deep-frying

1 Using a very sharp knife, thinly shred the won ton wrappers. Peel the large prawns and gently pull out the dark vein from each prawn back, starting at the head end. Cut an incision along the inside of each prawn, to form a pocket.
2 Combine the chopped prawns and spring onion in a bowl and mix well. Add the egg white, 3 teaspoons of the cornflour, and salt and pepper, to taste, and mix together well with your fingertips.
3 Using a flat-bladed knife, spread about 1 tablespoon of the prawn mixture along each large prawn, pressing as much mixture as possible into the pocket. With wet hands, press any remaining mixture around the prawn. Toss each prawn in the remaining cornflour and shake off the excess. Dip in the egg, then loosely sprinkle with won ton shreds, pressing very firmly so they stick.
4 Fill a deep, heavy-based pan or wok one third full of oil and heat to 180°C (350°F), or until a cube of bread dropped into the oil browns in 15 seconds. Cook the prawns in batches for 4 minutes, or until golden brown all over. You may need to turn them with tongs or a long-handled slotted metal spoon. Drain on crumpled paper towels and serve immediately.
NOTE: The prawns can be stuffed up to a day in advance and refrigerated. Coat with shredded won ton just before frying.

WON TON WRAPPERS
These are wafer-thin wrappers made from flour and egg. Usually they are wrapped around savoury fillings before steaming or deep-frying to serve as a snack. Sometimes, the filled won tons are boiled and served in soups. In the recipe on this page, we have used them shredded to add a crisp decorative coating to deep-fried prawns. You will find won ton wrappers in the refrigerated section in Asian food stores. Leftovers can be frozen.

ABOVE: Stuffed prawns in crispy won ton

97

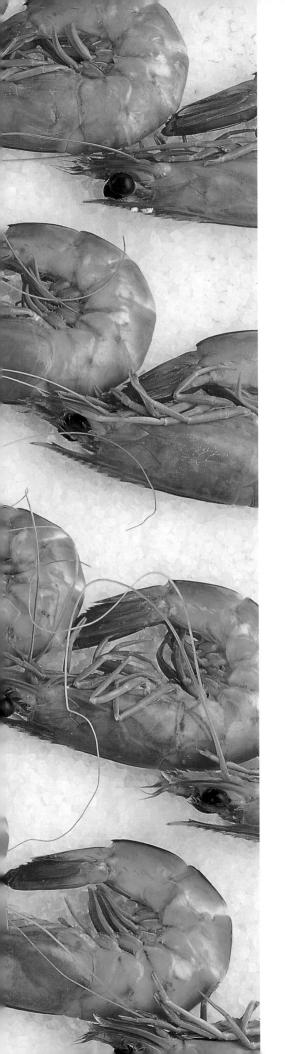

SALADS

The seafood salad really is the epitome of freshness. Every single ingredient has to be in tip-top, just-picked (or 'just-caught') condition because there won't be a great deal of cooking to hide behind. However, once you've chosen these perfect ingredients, you've done all the hard work. It is difficult to go wrong with flakes of fish or plump prawns mixed with crisp greens and herbs. A tangy vinaigrette is tossed through to soften the leaves, blend the flavours and bind the whole together. The result is a seafood salad light enough to serve for a summer's lunch, colourful enough for guests, thoughtful enough to serve to friends.

SALAD NICOISE

Preparation time: 30 minutes
Total cooking time: 25 minutes
Serves 4-6

★

4 eggs
500 g (1 lb) baby new potatoes
250 g (8 oz) green beans, topped and tailed
6 artichoke hearts in oil, drained
350 g (11 oz) mixed salad leaves
4 tomatoes, cut into wedges
425 g (14 oz) can tuna, drained and
   separated into chunks
1 red pepper (capsicum), cut into strips
1 tablespoon drained bottled capers
10 niçoise olives
1 tablespoon chopped fresh tarragon, to garnish

Dressing

1 clove garlic, crushed
3 teaspoons Dijon mustard
2 anchovy fillets in oil, drained and finely chopped
1/4 cup (60 ml/2 fl oz) white wine vinegar
1/2 cup (125 ml/4 fl oz) extra virgin olive oil

1 Fill a pan with cold water and gently add the eggs. Bring to the boil, then reduce the heat and simmer for 6 minutes. Drain and plunge the eggs in cold water to stop the cooking process. Peel and cut into wedges.
2 Steam or boil the potatoes for 10 minutes, until just tender (pierce with the point of a small sharp knife—if the potato comes away easily, it is ready). Drain, cool and cut into thick slices.
3 Place the beans into a pan of boiling water, return to the boil for 2 minutes, then drain and rinse under cold water. Chill in a bowl of iced water. Halve or quarter the artichokes.
4 Arrange the salad leaves on a serving platter or individual plates. Top with the potato, beans, tomato, artichoke, tuna, egg and red pepper. Sprinkle with the capers and olives.
5 For the dressing, use a food processor or whisk to mix the garlic, mustard, anchovies and vinegar until smooth. Gradually add the oil and blend until smooth. Season with salt and pepper and drizzle over the salad. Sprinkle with tarragon.

ABOVE: Salad niçoise

PRAWN AND PAPAYA SALAD WITH LIME DRESSING

Preparation time: 25 minutes
Total cooking time: 5 minutes
Serves 4

750 g (1 1/2 lb) cooked medium prawns
1 large papaya, chopped
1 small red onion, finely sliced
2 sticks celery, finely sliced
2 tablespoons shredded fresh mint

Lime dressing

1/2 cup (125 ml/4 fl oz) oil
1/4 cup (60 ml/2 fl oz) lime juice
2 teaspoons finely grated fresh ginger
1 teaspoon caster sugar

1 Peel the prawns, leaving the tails intact. Gently pull out the dark vein from each prawn back, starting at the head end. Put the prawns in a bowl.
2 For the lime dressing, put the oil, lime juice, ginger and sugar in a small bowl and whisk to combine. Season, to taste, with salt and freshly ground black pepper.

3 Add the lime dressing to the prawns and toss gently to coat the prawns. Add the papaya, onion, celery and fresh mint and gently toss to combine. Serve the salad at room temperature, or cover and refrigerate for up to 3 hours before serving. Can be served garnished with extra sprigs of fresh mint.

PUMPKIN AND PRAWN SALAD WITH ROCKET

Cut 800 g (1 lb 10 oz) firm pumpkin into 3 cm (1 1/4 inch) cubes and 2 small red onions into thick wedges. Toss with 1 tablespoon oil and 2 cloves crushed garlic and place in a single layer on a baking tray. Bake in a moderately hot 200°C (400°F/ Gas 6) oven for 35 minutes, or until tender. Toss in a bowl with 300 g (10 oz) small cooked, peeled and deveined prawns. Add 200 g (6 1/2 oz) torn rocket leaves. Whisk together in a bowl 1–2 tablespoons balsamic vinegar, 1 tablespoon olive oil and salt and freshly ground black pepper, to taste. Drizzle over the salad. Serves 4–6.

BELOW: Prawn and papaya salad with lime dressing

little lime friands

PREPARATION TIME 20 MINUTES   COOKING TIME 15 MINUTES (plus cooling time)

6 egg whites
185g butter, melted
1 cup (125g) almond meal
1½ cups (240g) icing sugar mixture
½ cup (75g) plain flour
1 tablespoon finely grated lime rind
1 tablespoon lime juice
30 whole blanched almonds (60g)

1 Preheat oven to moderately hot. Grease 30 1½-tablespoon (30ml) mini muffin pan holes.

2 Place egg whites in medium bowl; whisk lightly until combined. Add butter, almond meal, sifted icing sugar and flour, then rind and juice. Whisk until just combined. Divide mixture among prepared pans; top mixture in each hole with an almond.

3 Bake in moderately hot oven about 15 minutes. Turn onto wire racks to cool, right way up. Serve warm or at room temperature.

makes 30
per friand 8.5g fat; 517kJ (124 cal)
tips This recipe can be made 2 days ahead.
Recipe suitable to freeze; butter suitable to microwave.

MUSSEL SALAD WITH SAFFRON DRESSING

Preparation time: 40 minutes
Total cooking time: 30 minutes
Serves 4-6

500 g (1 lb) new potatoes, unpeeled
1 kg (2 lb) black mussels
2/3 cup (170 ml/5 1/2 fl oz) dry white wine
1 small onion, sliced
2 sprigs fresh thyme
2 bay leaves
large pinch of powdered saffron or threads
4 tablespoons sour cream
2 teaspoons chopped fresh parsley

1 Place the potatoes in a pan of cold, lightly salted water. Bring to the boil, then reduce the heat and simmer for 20 minutes, or until tender. (When pierced with the point of a small knife, the potato will come away easily.) Drain and leave to cool.
2 Scrub the mussels with a stiff brush and pull out the hairy beards. Discard any broken mussels, or open ones that don't close when tapped on the bench. Rinse well. Place the wine, onion, thyme sprigs, bay leaves and half the mussels in a saucepan with a tight-fitting lid. Cover and cook over high heat, stirring once, for about 4–5 minutes, or until the mussels start to open. Remove the mussels as they open, using tongs. Discard any unopened mussels. Cook the remaining mussels the same way, and leave to cool.
3 Strain the mussel cooking liquid and reserve 1/2 cup (125 ml/4 fl oz) of the liquid. While it is still warm, stir in the saffron. Whisk in the sour cream and season well with salt and cracked pepper.
4 Cut the potatoes into quarters if large, or halves if small. Remove the mussels and discard the shells. Combine the potatoes and mussels in a bowl and add the saffron dressing. Sprinkle with chopped parsley and serve immediately.

ESCABECHE

Preparation time: 20 minutes + overnight chilling
Total cooking time: 15 minutes
Serves 4

plain flour, for dusting
500 g (1 lb) skinless fish fillets (eg. red mullet, whiting, redfish, garfish)
5 tablespoons extra virgin olive oil
1 red onion, thinly sliced
2 cloves garlic, thinly sliced
2 sprigs fresh thyme
1 teaspoon ground cumin
2 spring onions, chopped
1/2 teaspoon finely grated orange rind
1/4 cup (60 ml/2 fl oz) orange juice
3/4 cup (185 ml/6 fl oz) white wine
3/4 cup (185 ml/6 fl oz) white wine vinegar
60 g (2 oz) pitted green olives, roughly chopped
1/2 teaspoon caster sugar

1 Mix a little salt and pepper into the flour and dust the fish lightly with the flour. Heat 2 tablespoons of the oil in a frying pan over medium heat and add the fish in batches. Cook on both sides until lightly browned and cooked through (the fish should flake easily when tested with a fork). Remove from the pan and place in a single layer in a large shallow, non-metallic dish.
2 Heat the remaining oil in the same pan, add the onion and garlic and cook, stirring over medium heat for about 5 minutes, or until soft.
3 Add the thyme, cumin and spring onion and stir until fragrant. Add the orange rind, juice, wine, vinegar, olives and sugar and salt and pepper, to taste. Bring to the boil and pour over the fish. Allow to cool in the liquid, or refrigerate overnight. Serve at room temperature. Can be served on a bed of watercress sprigs and finely sliced spring onion.
NOTE: Escabeche is a Spanish dish, served cold, traditionally made using whole fish. We have used fish fillets which also work well.

RED MULLET
Red mullet is also known as goatfish, barbounia and rouget. A small red fish with two long barbels attached to the lower jaw, it is available all year round and always sold as a whole fish. The flesh can be quite soft, sometimes a little dry, and has a medium to large flake. Red mullet has a delicate flavour. To cook, you can bake, barbecue, grill, pan-fry or poach it.

OPPOSITE PAGE: Mussel salad with saffron dressing (top); Escabeche

MIXED SEAFOOD SALAD

Preparation time: 1 hour + 1 hour chilling
Total cooking time: 20 minutes
Serves 8

1.25 kg (2¹/₂ lb) large cooked prawns
12 cooked yabbies or crayfish
500 g (1 lb) scallops
¹/₂ cup (125 ml/4 fl oz) white wine
pinch of dried thyme
pinch of dried tarragon or a bay leaf
400 g (13 oz) salmon, trout or firm white
   fish fillets (eg. flake, hake, ling)

Vinaigrette

¹/₂ cup (125 ml/4 fl oz) extra virgin olive oil
2 tablespoons white wine vinegar
1 teaspoon sugar
2 teaspoons Dijon mustard
1 tablespoon chopped fresh dill

6 hard-boiled eggs
150 g (5 oz) mixed lettuce leaves
2 tablespoons chopped fresh flat-leaf parsley
2 ripe avocados, sliced
2 tablespoons lemon juice

Green goddess dressing

1¹/₄ cups (310 g/10 oz) whole-egg mayonnaise
4 canned anchovy fillets, drained, finely chopped
1 clove garlic, crushed
¹/₄ cup (60 g/2 oz) sour cream
3 tablespoons chopped fresh herbs
   (chives, parsley, dill)

1 Peel the prawns and pull out the dark vein from each prawn back, starting at the head end.
2 Cut down each side of the shell on the underside of each yabby with kitchen scissors, starting at the head and working towards the tail. Pull back the flap and remove the meat from each shell. Gently pull out the vein from each back and discard each shell.
3 Slice or pull off any vein, membrane or hard white muscle from the scallops.
4 Put 1 cup (250 ml/8 fl oz) water with the wine, herbs, and a pinch each of salt and pepper, in a pan. Bring to the boil, then reduce the heat and simmer for 5 minutes. Add the scallops and poach for a few minutes, or until they have just turned white, then remove with a slotted spoon and drain on a wire rack. Add the fish fillets to the gently simmering liquid. Poach until cooked and just tender, remove with a slotted spoon and drain on a wire rack. Break into large pieces.
5 Combine the prawns, yabbies, scallops and fish in a bowl. Whisk together the oil, vinegar, sugar, mustard and dill, and season, to taste. Pour over the seafood, cover and refrigerate for 1 hour.
6 Peel and slice the eggs, reserving 2 yolks. Put half the lettuce leaves in a deep serving bowl. Arrange half the seafood over the lettuce, reserving the vinaigrette. Sprinkle with half the parsley, top with half the avocado, drizzle with half the lemon juice, then finish with half the sliced eggs, including the extra whites. Season with salt and pepper. Repeat the layers and season, to taste. Drizzle with the reserved vinaigrette. Crumble the reserved egg yolks over the top. Serve with the green goddess dressing.
7 For the green goddess dressing, mix all the ingredients in a bowl and season, to taste.

SCALLOP CEVICHE

Preparation time: 20 minutes + 2 hours
   marinating
Total cooking time: Nil
Serves 2–4

16 scallops, in shells
1 teaspoon finely grated lime rind
2 cloves garlic, chopped
2 fresh red chillies, seeded and chopped
¹/₄ cup (60 ml/2 fl oz) lime juice
1 tablespoon chopped fresh parsley
1 tablespoon olive oil

1 Take the scallops off their shells. Reserve the shells. If they need to be cut off, use a small, sharp knife to slice the scallop free, being careful to leave as little meat on the shell as possible. Slice or pull off any vein, membrane or hard white muscle, leaving any roe attached.
2 In a non-metallic bowl, mix together the lime rind, garlic, chilli, lime juice, parsley and olive oil, and season with salt and freshly ground black pepper. Place the scallops in the dressing and stir to coat. Cover with plastic wrap and refrigerate for 2 hours to 'cook' the scallop meat.
3 To serve, slide each scallop back onto a half shell and spoon the dressing over. Serve cold.
NOTE: These will keep for 2 days in the dressing.

YABBIES
Yabbies are also known as lobby, crawbob and freshwater crayfish. They have a delicious, sweet moist flesh and are available alive and cooked. Ensure live yabbies are active and have all their claws intact. If sluggish, it means the yabbies are either immobilized by the cold, or dying and not as fresh as they could be. They should have a pleasant sea smell. Cooked yabbies should have a firm shell, all the claws intact and no discolouration on the underside.

OPPOSITE PAGE: Mixed seafood salad

SMOKED TROUT WITH WARM CHILLI AND RASPBERRY DRESSING

Preparation time: 25 minutes
Total cooking time: 10 minutes
Serves 4-6

250 g (8 oz) sorrel
310 g (10 oz) fresh asparagus
1 smoked trout (about 400 g/13 oz)
1 red onion, thinly sliced
250 g (8 oz) teardrop tomatoes, cut in halves
200 g (6½ oz) fresh raspberries

BELOW: Smoked trout with warm chilli and raspberry dressing

Warm chilli and raspberry dressing
125 g (4 oz) fresh raspberries
1 teaspoon chilli paste
2 cloves garlic, crushed
½ cup (125 ml/4 fl oz) olive oil
2 tablespoons raspberry vinegar or white wine vinegar

1 Trim the stalks from the sorrel, rinse well, then dry and refrigerate to crisp.
2 For the dressing, gently stir all the ingredients in a small pan over low heat until the raspberries begin to break up and colour the liquid. Transfer to a bowl, whisk together well and season with salt and freshly ground black pepper.
3 Boil, steam or microwave the asparagus until just tender. Drain and refresh under cold water. Peel away and discard the skin and bones from the trout. Break the flesh into pieces.
4 Divide the sorrel among individual plates. Arrange the asparagus, trout, onion, tomatoes and raspberries on top. Drizzle with the dressing.

HAWAIIAN POKE SALAD

Preparation time: 15 minutes + 15 minutes soaking + 4 hours marinating
Total cooking time: 5 minutes
Serves 4-6

5 g dried wakame (dried curly-leaved seaweed), optional
500 g (1 lb) fish steaks (eg. tuna, swordfish, striped marlin)
1 large onion, finely chopped
6 spring onions, sliced
2 small red chillies, cut into fine strips
⅓ cup (80 ml/2¾ fl oz) low-salt soy sauce
1 tablespoon sesame oil
lettuce leaves, for serving
1 tablespoon sesame seeds, toasted
lime wedges, for serving

1 Soak the wakame in a bowl of cold water for 15 minutes. Drain.
2 Cut the fish into small cubes. Put the wakame, fish, onion, spring onion, chilli, soy and sesame oil in a bowl, cover and refrigerate for 4 hours.
3 Line a serving platter with lettuce leaves. Top with the marinated fish and sprinkle with the toasted sesame seeds. Serve with lime wedges.

WARM PRAWN, ROCKET AND FETA SALAD

Preparation time: 30 minutes
Total cooking time: 10 minutes
Serves 4-6

1 kg (2 lb) raw medium prawns
4 spring onions, chopped
4 Roma (egg) tomatoes, chopped
1 red pepper (capsicum), chopped
425 g (14 oz) can chickpeas, drained
1 tablespoon chopped fresh dill
3 tablespoons finely shredded fresh basil
1/4 cup (60 ml/2 fl oz) extra virgin olive oil
60 g (2 oz) butter
2 small fresh red chillies, finely chopped
4 cloves garlic, crushed
2 tablespoons lemon juice
300 g (10 oz) rocket leaves
150 g (5 oz) feta cheese

1 Peel the prawns, leaving the tails intact. Gently pull out the dark vein from each prawn back, starting at the head end.
2 Combine the spring onion, tomato, pepper, chickpeas and herbs in a bowl.
3 Heat the oil and butter in a large frying pan or wok, add the prawns and cook, stirring over high heat for 3 minutes. Add the chilli and garlic, and continue cooking until the prawns turn pink. Remove from the heat and stir in the lemon juice.
4 Arrange the rocket leaves on a large platter, top with the tomato mixture, then the prawn mixture. Crumble the feta cheese over the top.

CAESAR SALAD

Preparation time: 15 minutes
Total cooking time: 20 minutes
Serves 4

4 slices white bread, crusts removed, cut into cubes
3 rashers bacon, chopped
1 cos lettuce, leaves torn into pieces
50 g (1 3/4 oz) Parmesan shavings
Parmesan shavings, extra, to garnish

Dressing
2–4 anchovies in oil, drained
1 egg
2 tablespoons lemon juice
1 clove garlic, crushed
1/2 cup (125 ml/4 fl oz) olive oil

1 Preheat the oven to moderately hot 190°C (375°F/Gas 5). Spread the bread on a baking tray and bake for 15 minutes, or until golden.
2 Cook the bacon over medium heat until it is crisp. Drain on paper towels.
3 Put the lettuce leaves in a serving bowl with the bread cubes, bacon and Parmesan.
4 For the dressing, process the anchovies, egg, lemon juice and garlic in a food processor for 20 seconds, or until smooth. With the motor running, add the oil in a thin stream until the dressing is thick and creamy. Season with salt and pepper. Drizzle over the salad, sprinkle with the extra Parmesan and serve immediately.

ABOVE: Warm prawn, rocket and feta salad

PICKLED SEAFOOD
Ensure glass storage jars are clean by rinsing them with boiling water and drying in a warm oven. Don't use a tea towel to dry them.

PICKLED MUSSELS/SARDINES

Scrub 1 kg (2 lb) black mussels. Remove the hairy beards. Discard any broken mussels or open ones that don't close when tapped on the bench. Place in a large saucepan, cover with water, cover and cook for 4–5 minutes, or until all the mussels have opened. Discard any that do not open. Cool slightly before removing the mussel meat from the shells. Toss the meat in flour, then shallow-fry batches in hot oil, until brown and crisp. Remove

and arrange in a single layer in a large non-metallic dish. Combine 2 cups (500 ml/16 fl oz) white wine vinegar, 6 sliced spring onions, 1 finely chopped fresh chilli, 2 bay leaves and 2 teaspoons sugar in a saucepan. Stir over low heat until the sugar dissolves, then boil for 1 minute. Stir in 1 tablespoon chopped fresh mint. Pour over the mussels and refrigerate at least overnight, and up to 5 days, turning once. Serve at room temperature. Serves 4–6. To prepare

12 fresh sardines, gut them, rinse in water, toss in flour and follow the same method.

PICKLED PRAWNS

Peel and devein 40 cooked large prawns, leaving the tails intact. Thinly slice 1 fennel bulb. Put the prawns, fennel, 2 thinly sliced small red onions, and the rind of 2 oranges and 2 limes, cut into thin strips, in a non-metallic container and mix. Mix 2/3 cup (170 ml/5 1/2 fl oz) lime juice, 1/3 cup (80 ml/2 3/4 fl oz)

orange juice, 1 cup (250 ml/8 fl oz) olive oil, ½ cup (125 ml/4 fl oz) tarragon vinegar, 2 finely sliced bird's eye red chillies and 1 teaspoon each of salt and sugar. Pour over the prawn mixture. Cover and refrigerate for at least 2 days, and up to 5 days. Serves 4–6.

PICKLED OCTOPUS

Clean 1 kg (2 lb) octopus (see page 31) and combine in a pan with 2 bay leaves and 12 black peppercorns. Cover and cook over medium–low heat, in its own liquid, for 1 hour, or until tender. Drain and cool. Put the peppercorns, bay leaves and cooled octopus in a 4 cup (1 litre) clean jar. Add 1 tablespoon fresh oregano leaves, 2 teaspoons fresh thyme and 1 thinly sliced garlic clove. Pour in 1 cup (250 ml/8 fl oz) red wine vinegar and enough olive oil to completely cover the

octopus. Seal, then gently turn the jar upside down a couple of times. Refrigerate for at least 2 days, and up to 5 days. Return to room temperature to serve. Serves 4–6.

ROLLMOPS

Wash 8 herrings. Place your knife behind the gill and fin and cut off the head. Cut along the belly, remove the gut and open the fish out flat. Pinch the bone at the tail end and carefully lift out, pulling the bone towards the head. Remove any small bones with tweezers. Place the butterflied fillets in a large non-metallic dish. Combine 4 cups (1 litre) water with 200 g (6½ oz) salt and stir over medium heat until the salt dissolves. Allow to cool before pouring over the fish. Cover and refrigerate overnight. Meanwhile, prepare the pickling vinegar then allow it to cool.

Combine 4 cups (1 litre) white wine vinegar, 2 bay leaves, 1 tablespoon pickling spice (available from most supermarkets) and 5 black peppercorns. Rinse and dry the brined herring fillet and place skin-side-down on a wooden board. Place a thin slice of onion on the centre of each fillet and top with a slice of gherkin. Roll each fillet up from the head end and secure with a toothpick. Pack the rollmops into a 4 cup (1 litre) clean jar, pour the spiced vinegar over and seal. Refrigerate for at least 2 days, and up to 5 days, before serving. Serve with sour cream, onion and pumpernickel. Serves 4–6.

FROM LEFT: Pickled mussels; Pickled sardines; Pickled prawns; Pickled octopus; Rollmops

SQUID

Found in temperate waters throughout the world, squid are commonly used in cookery in most of Asia and the Mediterranean. The torpedo-shaped body varies in length from small, 5 cm (2 inches), to very long. As well as eight arms, squid have two long tentacles at the back of the body. Squid are not difficult to prepare and, when cooked, the flesh is tender and sweet. In Italy, squid are called calamari.

ABOVE: Salmon and fennel salad

SALMON AND FENNEL SALAD

Preparation time: 15 minutes
Total cooking time: Nil
Serves 4

2 teaspoons Dijon mustard
1 teaspoon caster sugar
1/2 cup (125 ml/4 fl oz) olive oil
2 tablespoons lemon juice
2 fennel bulbs, thinly sliced
200 g (6 1/2 oz) smoked salmon, cut into strips
2 tablespoons chopped fresh chives
1 tablespoon chopped fresh fennel fronds from the top of the fennel, or chopped fresh dill
fresh rocket leaves, for serving
lemon wedges, for serving

1 For the dressing, whisk together the mustard, sugar, olive oil and lemon juice in a large bowl.
2 Add the sliced fennel, salmon, chives and fennel fronds to the bowl. Season with salt and pepper and toss gently. Serve with the rocket leaves, lemon wedges and maybe some toast.

SQUID AND SCALLOPS WITH CHERMOULA DRESSING

Preparation time: 30 minutes + 30 minutes chilling
Total cooking time: 5 minutes
Serves 4

2 oranges
8 baby squid
200 g (6 1/2 oz) scallops
2 tablespoons oil
150 g (5 oz) rocket leaves
3 ripe Roma (egg) tomatoes, chopped

Chermoula dressing

1 cup (50 g/1 3/4 oz) finely chopped fresh coriander
1 cup (30 g/1 oz) finely chopped fresh flat-leaf parsley
2 teaspoons ground cumin
1 teaspoon ground paprika
1/4 cup (60 ml/2 fl oz) lime juice
1/4 cup (60 ml/2 fl oz) olive oil

1 Remove the skin and white pith from the oranges. Use a small sharp knife to cut between the membranes to release the segments. Set aside.

2 To clean the squid, gently pull the tentacles away from the hoods (the intestines should come away at the same time). Remove the intestines from the tentacles by cutting under the eyes, then remove the beak if it remains in the centre of the tentacles by using your finger to push up the centre. Pull away the soft bones (quill) from the hoods. Rub the hoods under cold running water and the skin should come away easily. Wash the hoods and tentacles and drain well. Place in a bowl of water with ¼ teaspoon salt and mix well. Cover and refrigerate for about 30 minutes. Drain well, then cut the tubes into long thin strips and the tentacles into pieces.

3 Slice or pull off any vein, membrane or hard white muscle from the scallops. Rinse the scallops and pat dry with paper towels.

4 Heat the oil in a large deep frying pan and cook the squid in batches for 1–2 minutes, over high heat, until it turns white. Do not overcook, or it will become chewy. Drain on crumpled paper towels. Add the scallops to the pan and cook until golden and tender. Do not overcook.

5 Arrange the rocket on a large platter, top with seafood, tomatoes and orange segments.

6 Whisk the dressing ingredients together in a non-metallic bowl. Pour over the seafood.

MARINATED FISH SALAD WITH CHILLI AND BASIL

Preparation time: 30 minutes + several hours marinating
Total cooking time: Nil
Serves 4

500 g (1 lb) skinless firm white fish fillets
   (eg. mahi mahi, coral trout, snapper,
   red emperor)
¼ cup (60 ml/2 fl oz) lime juice
¼ cup (60 ml/2 fl oz) coconut milk
3 tomatoes, diced
3 Lebanese cucumbers, diced
5 spring onions, finely sliced
2 fresh red chillies, seeded and sliced
2 cloves garlic, crushed
1 teaspoon grated fresh ginger
½ cup (15 g/½ oz) fresh basil leaves, torn
mixed salad leaves, for serving

1 Slice the fish into thin strips and place in a glass or ceramic bowl.

2 For the marinade, combine the lime juice, coconut milk, 1 teaspoon salt and ¼ teaspoon cracked black pepper in a jug. Mix well, then pour over the fish. Cover and refrigerate for several hours or overnight, turning once or twice.

3 Add the tomato, cucumber, spring onion, chilli, garlic, ginger and basil to the fish. Mix well and serve spooned over salad leaves.

NOTES: The action of acid in the lime juice 'cooks' the fish, firming the flesh and turning it opaque.

When mangoes are in season, dice roughly and toss through the finished salad for extra flavour and sweetness.

BELOW: Marinated fish salad with chilli and basil

SWEET AND SOUR SARDINES

Preparation time: 20 minutes + marinating
Total cooking time: 15–20 minutes
Serves 4

12 fresh butterflied sardines
plain flour, for dusting
olive oil, for frying
1/2 red onion, thinly sliced
1 clove garlic, crushed
2 bay leaves
1 tablespoon raisins
1 tablespoon pine nuts
1/2–1 teaspoon dried chilli flakes
1 teaspoon soft brown sugar
1/3 cup (80 ml/2³/4 fl oz) balsamic vinegar
1/3 cup (80 ml/2³/4 fl oz) red wine

SARDINES

These small fish have an oily soft flesh with a fine texture. Although they have quite a lot of bones, the backbone is easily removed and the remaining bones are edible. Sardines are sold whole or filleted and deboned (butterflied). Often confused with pilchards, sardines are simply juvenile pilchards. They have a strong, distinct flavour and are suitable for baking, grilling, barbecuing and pan-frying.

1 Dust the sardines with the flour and season well with salt and pepper.
2 Add enough olive oil to a large heavy-based frying pan to come about 1 cm (1/2 inch) up the side. Heat the oil over medium heat and fry the sardines in batches for about 5–10 minutes, until crisp and golden. Drain well on crumpled paper towels, then lay them in a non-metallic dish.
3 Fry the onion in a little olive oil over medium heat for about 5 minutes, until tender but not brown. Add the garlic, bay leaves, raisins, pine nuts and chilli flakes. Stir well, then add the sugar, vinegar and red wine, and bring everything to a simmer. Pour this mixture over the sardines, cover and marinate in the refrigerator until cool. Serve at room temperature, perhaps on a bed of snow pea (mangetout) sprouts or mixed lettuce leaves.
NOTE: If butterflied sardines are unavailable, buy whole sardines and to prepare, slit open the belly, remove the gut and cut off the head. Place the sardine skin-side-up on a chopping board. Press each sardine lightly, yet firmly, to open out. Turn each over and pull out the backbone. Cut off at the tail end of the bones. Wash in lightly salted water and dry on paper towels.

TUNA SALAD WITH GARLIC MAYONNAISE

Preparation time: 25 minutes
Total cooking time: 10 minutes
Serves 6

6 medium potatoes such as pontiac, sebago, coliban
150 g (5 oz) snow peas (mangetout)
200 g (6¹/2 oz) asparagus
250 g (8 oz) cherry tomatoes
2 x 425 g (14 oz) cans tuna, drained

Garlic mayonnaise

3 egg yolks
1 clove garlic, crushed
1/2 teaspoon French mustard
2 tablespoons lemon juice
1 cup (250 ml/8 fl oz) olive oil

1 Cut the peeled potatoes into 2 cm (3/4 inch) cubes and steam or boil for 8–10 minutes, or until just tender (pierce with the point of a small knife—if the potato comes away easily, it is ready). Drain and set aside.
2 Cook the snow peas in a pan of boiling water for 1 minute, remove from the water with a slotted spoon and plunge into iced water. Drain and set aside.
3 Trim the woody ends from the asparagus and blanch as for snow peas.
4 To make garlic mayonnaise, place the yolks, garlic, mustard and juice in a bowl and beat with electric beaters for 1 minute. Add the oil in a thin steady stream, about 1 teaspoon at a time, beating constantly until thick and creamy. Start to add the oil more quickly as the mayonnaise thickens. Continue beating until all the oil is incorporated. Season, to taste, with salt and cracked black pepper.
5 Arrange the potato, snow peas, asparagus, tomatoes and chunks of tuna on individual plates. Place a spoonful of mayonnaise on each plate or serve separately. Serve immediately.
NOTE: The mayonnaise can also be made in a blender or food processor, or by hand with a large balloon whisk.

OPPOSITE PAGE: Sweet and sour sardines (top); Tuna salad with garlic mayonnaise

SALMON AND GREEN BEAN SALAD

Preparation time: 20 minutes
Total cooking time: 30 minutes
Serves 4-6

350 g (11 oz) skinless salmon fillet

oil, for deep-frying

4 cloves garlic, thinly sliced

200 g (6½ oz) white sweet potato, thinly sliced

100 g (3½ oz) green beans, halved lengthways

1 red onion, thinly sliced

20 g (¾ oz) sesame seeds, toasted

1 mizuna lettuce, stems trimmed

Dressing

2 cloves garlic, crushed

2 tablespoons tahini

1 tablespoon rice vinegar

2 tablespoons lime juice

1 tablespoon soy sauce

¼ cup (60 ml/2 fl oz) olive oil

1 Chargrill or grill the fish fillet until medium-rare or cooked to your taste. Allow to cool slightly before cutting into large pieces.

2 Heat the oil in a deep heavy-based saucepan to 180°C (350°F), or until a cube of bread dropped into the oil browns in 15 seconds. Deep-fry the garlic and sweet potato separately until crisp and golden. Drain on crumpled paper towels.

3 Cook the beans in boiling water until tender. Rinse, plunge into iced water and drain. Combine with the onion, sesame seeds, sweet potato, garlic and mizuna. Divide among serving plates. Top with the fish.

4 For the dressing, whisk the ingredients together in a bowl. Drizzle over the salad and serve immediately.

NOTES: Ocean trout is also suitable for using in this recipe.

Tahini is made from crushed sesame seeds and is available in the health food section at supermarkets. If you find the flavour too strong, you can substitute with 1 teaspoon of sesame oil and 2 tablespoons orange juice.

BELOW: Salmon and green bean salad

THAI NOODLE SALAD

Preparation time: 25 minutes
Total cooking time: 5 minutes
Serves 4

Dressing

2 tablespoons grated fresh ginger
2 tablespoons soy sauce
2 tablespoons sesame oil
1/3 cup (80 ml/2 3/4 fl oz) red wine vinegar
1 tablespoon sweet chilli sauce
2 cloves garlic, crushed
1/3 cup (80 ml/2 3/4 fl oz) kecap manis

500 g (1 lb) cooked large prawns
250 g (8 oz) thin instant noodles
5 spring onions, sliced
2 tablespoons chopped fresh coriander
1 red pepper (capsicum), chopped
100 g (3 1/2 oz) snow peas (mangetout), sliced

1 For the dressing, put the ingredients in a large bowl and whisk together with a fork.
2 Peel the prawns and gently pull out the dark vein from each prawn back, starting at the head end. Cut the prawns in half lengthways.
3 Cook the noodles in a large pan of boiling water for 2 minutes, then drain well. Add to the dressing and mix well. Leave to cool.
4 Add the prawns and remaining ingredients to the noodles and toss through gently. Serve at room temperature.
NOTE: Kecap manis (sweet soy sauce) is available from supermarkets and Asian food stores.

TUNA AND WHITE BEAN SALAD

Preparation time: 15 minutes
Total cooking time: Nil
Serves 4-6

750 g (1 1/2 lb) canned tuna in oil
1 clove garlic, crushed
1–2 teaspoons fresh thyme leaves
1–2 teaspoons finely chopped fresh parsley
1/4 cup (60 ml/2 fl oz) white wine vinegar
1/3 cup (80 ml/2 3/4 fl oz) extra virgin olive oil

400 g (13 oz) can cannellini beans, drained and rinsed
1 large red onion, coarsely chopped
3 hard-boiled eggs, cut into wedges
3 tomatoes, cut into wedges

1 Drain the tuna and flake into chunks. Combine the garlic, thyme, parsley, vinegar and olive oil in a bowl, and whisk with a fork. Season, to taste, with salt and black pepper.
2 Combine the beans and onion in a large bowl, add the dressing and toss. Add the tuna, toss gently, then add half the egg wedges and half the tomato. Lightly combine. Pile on a platter and garnish with the remaining egg and tomato.

ABOVE: Thai noodle salad

CRAB AND MANGO SALAD

Using a sharp knife, peel the mango and cut the flesh into thin strips.

Shave the coconut into thin slices with a vegetable peeler.

Pour the dressing over the combined crab, prawns, mango and coconut.

ABOVE: Crab and mango salad

CRAB AND MANGO SALAD

Preparation time: 25 minutes
Total cooking time: 5 minutes
Serves 4

☆

Dressing

1/3 cup (80 ml/2³/4 fl oz) light olive oil
1/4 cup (60 ml/2 fl oz) lime juice
1 teaspoon fish sauce
1/2 small green chilli, finely chopped
1 tablespoon finely chopped fresh coriander
2 teaspoons grated fresh ginger

2 x 4 cm (1 1/2 inch) squares of fresh coconut
1 teaspoon olive oil
2 cups (60 g/2 oz) trimmed watercress
100 g (3 1/2 oz) snow pea (mangetout) sprouts
100 g (3 1/2 oz) small cooked prawns
400 g (13 oz) cooked fresh or canned crab meat, drained

1 firm ripe mango, cut into thin strips
fresh coriander leaves, to garnish
1 lime, cut into slices, to garnish

1 For the dressing, combine the ingredients and season with salt and freshly ground black pepper. Set aside to allow the flavours to develop.
2 Peel the coconut into wafer-thin slices with a vegetable peeler. Heat the olive oil in a pan and gently fry the coconut, stirring, until golden. Drain on crumpled paper towels.
3 Combine the watercress and snow pea sprouts and arrange on a platter.
4 Peel the prawns and gently pull out the dark vein from each prawn back, starting at the head end. Lightly toss the crab meat, prawns, mango and three-quarters of the toasted coconut and dressing together. Pile in the centre of the watercress and snow pea sprout mixture, scatter the remaining coconut over the top and garnish with the coriander leaves and lime slices.
NOTE: If you can't get fresh coconut, use 1/2 cup (30 g/1 oz) flaked coconut and toast it.

SPANISH-STYLE SEAFOOD SALAD

Preparation time: 40 minutes
  + 2 hours chilling
Total cooking time: 10 minutes
Serves 6

750 g (1 1/2 lb) raw medium prawns

200 g (6 1/2 oz) scallops

12–15 black mussels

2 slices lemon

2 bay leaves

pinch of dried thyme

250 g (8 oz) broccoli, cut into small florets

3 teaspoons capers

20 dry-cured black olives

3 spring onions, chopped

1/2 green pepper (capsicum), diced

1/4 cup (60 ml/2 fl oz) olive oil

2 tablespoons lemon juice

1 teaspoon Dijon mustard

1 clove garlic, crushed

1 Peel the prawns and pull out the dark vein from each prawn back, starting at the head end.

2 Slice or pull off any vein, membrane or hard white muscle from the scallops, leaving any roe attached.

3 Scrub the mussels with a stiff brush and pull out the hairy beards. Discard any broken mussels, or open ones that don't close when tapped on the bench. Rinse well.

4 Put the lemon, bay leaves, thyme and 3 cups (750 ml/24 fl oz) water in a large pan and bring to the boil. Add the scallops and cook for 30 seconds to 1 minute, or until opaque. Remove with a slotted spoon and drain on crumpled paper towels. Add the prawns to the pan and cook for 2–3 minutes, or until cooked. Remove with a slotted spoon and drain on paper towels. Add the mussels to the pan, cover and cook for 4–5 minutes, or until they have opened, shaking the pan occasionally. Drain the mussels on crumpled paper towels, discarding any that haven't opened. Discard one half shell from each mussel. Put all the seafood in a bowl.

5 Cook the broccoli in boiling water for 2 minutes. Refresh in cold water. Drain and add to the seafood with the capers, olives, spring onion and diced green pepper.

6 Whisk the oil, lemon juice, mustard, garlic and some salt and freshly ground black pepper in a bowl. Pour over the seafood and gently toss to coat the seafood. Cover and refrigerate for about 2 hours before serving.

PRAWNS

For the seafood lover, there are few things more delicious than fresh prawns. Fresh prawns should always have a pleasant sea smell and a nice sheen or gloss. The shells should be quite firm to the touch. Avoid any that smell of ammonia, or have dark discolouration around the head and legs, as these are early signs of deterioration.

LEFT: Spanish-style seafood salad

PAN-FRIES, DEEP-FRIES & STIR-FRIES

It is generally accepted that fresh fish, with bright eyes and sea salt still clinging to its skin, requires nothing but a little foaming butter and a hot pan (and perhaps a quick squeeze of lemon) to achieve true greatness. That is not to say that deep-fried seafood doesn't have its ardent supporters... for many, a newspaper-wrapped parcel of hot beer-battered fish and crunchy chips, stinging the fingertips with salt and vinegar, is the final word in culinary perfection. And stir-fried seafood? Just think of chilli crab and nothing more need be said.

PAN-FRIED FISH

Coat both sides of the fish cutlets with seasoned flour, shaking off any excess.

After 3 minutes cooking, turn the fish and brown the other side.

Reduce the heat and cook the fish until the flesh flakes easily with a fork.

PAN-FRIED FISH

Preparation time: 5 minutes
Total cooking time: 8 minutes
Serves 4

★

2–3 tablespoons plain flour
4 firm white fish cutlets (eg. blue-eye, jewfish, warehou, snapper)
olive oil, for shallow-frying

1 Sift the flour together with a little salt and pepper onto a dinner plate. Pat the fish dry with paper towels, then coat both sides of the cutlets with seasoned flour, shaking off any excess.
2 Heat about 3 mm (1/8 inch) oil in a large frying pan until very hot. Put the fish into the hot oil immediately and cook for 3 minutes on one side, then turn and cook the other side for 2 minutes, or until the coating is crisp and well browned. Reduce the heat to low and cook for another 2–3 minutes, until the flesh flakes easily when tested with a fork.
3 Remove the fish from the pan and drain briefly on crumpled paper towels. If cooking in batches, keep warm while cooking the remaining cutlets. Serve immediately.
NOTE: This method is good for any fish cutlet, fillet or steak. However, the cooking time will vary depending on the thickness of the fish.

FISH CRUSTED WITH PARMESAN AND HERBS

Lightly dust 4 x 200 g (6½ oz) skinless white fillets of ling, snapper or perch with seasoned flour. Dip into a beaten egg whisked with 1 tablespoon of milk, then coat with a mixture of ½ cup (50 g/1¾ oz) dry breadcrumbs, 2 tablespoons each of chopped fresh dill and parsley, 4 tablespoons grated Parmesan and 4 tablespoons lightly crushed flaked almonds. Press on firmly. Heat 1 tablespoon oil and 30 g (1 oz) butter in a frying pan, add the fish and cook over medium heat on both sides until golden and cooked. Top with guacamole, or serve with tartare sauce (see page 128). Serves 4.

RIGHT: Pan-fried fish

WARM PRAWN AND SCALLOP STIR-FRY

Preparation time: 30 minutes + 10 minutes marinating
Total cooking time: 15 minutes
Serves 4

★ ★

500 g (1 lb) raw small prawns

300 g (10 oz) scallops

2 teaspoons five-spice powder

1–2 small fresh red chillies, seeded and finely chopped

2–3 cloves garlic, crushed

2 tablespoons oil

2 teaspoons sesame oil

200 g (6¹/2 oz) fresh asparagus, cut into short lengths

150 g (5 oz) snow peas (mangetout), trimmed

125 g (4 oz) rocket leaves, torn into pieces

2 tablespoons light soy sauce

2 tablespoons lemon juice

1 tablespoon mirin

1 tablespoon oil, extra

1 tablespoon honey

6 spring onions, chopped

1 tablespoon chopped fresh coriander

1 tablespoon sesame seeds, lightly toasted

1 Peel the prawns, leaving the tails intact. Gently pull out the dark vein from each prawn back, starting at the head end. Slice or pull off any vein, membrane or hard white muscle from the scallops, leaving any roe attached.
2 Combine the five-spice powder, chilli, garlic and oils in a large glass or ceramic bowl. Add the prawns and scallops and toss to coat. Cover and refrigerate for at least 10 minutes.
3 Blanch the asparagus and snow peas briefly in a pan of boiling water. Drain and plunge into a bowl of iced water, then drain again. Arrange the asparagus, snow peas and rocket on 4 plates.
4 Put the soy sauce, lemon juice, mirin, extra oil and honey in a small bowl. Stir to combine.
5 Heat the wok, and stir-fry the prawns, scallops and spring onion over high heat, in batches, for 3–4 minutes, or until cooked through. Remove from the wok and set aside.
6 Add the sauce and coriander to the wok, and bring to the boil. Cook over high heat for 1–2 minutes. Return the seafood to the wok and toss. Divide among the serving plates and sprinkle with the sesame seeds.

ABOVE: Warm prawn and scallop stir-fry

FISH AND CHIPS

A cube of bread will brown in 30 seconds when the oil is ready.

Handle the fish with tongs, turning if necessary.

OPPOSITE PAGE: Fish and chips (top); Breaded scampi and Crumbed calamari with chilli plum sauce

FISH AND CHIPS

Preparation time: 25 minutes + soaking
Total cooking time: 25 minutes
Serves 4

★ ★

1¼ cups (155 g/5 oz) plain flour
1½ cups (375 ml/12 fl oz) beer
4 floury potatoes (desiree, spunta or russet)
oil, for deep-frying
4 firm white fish fillets (eg. bream, cod, coley,
    flake, flathead, pollack, snapper)
cornflour, for coating
lemon wedges, for serving

1 Sift the flour into a large bowl and make a well. Gradually add the beer, whisking to make a smooth lump-free batter. Cover and set aside.
2 Peel the potatoes and cut into chips 1 cm (¾ inch) thick. Soak for 10 minutes in cold water. Drain and pat dry. Fill a deep heavy-based pan one third full of oil and heat to 160°C (315°F), or until a cube of bread browns in 30 seconds. Cook batches of chips for 4–5 minutes, or until pale golden. Remove with tongs or a slotted spoon. Drain on crumpled paper towels.
3 Just before serving, reheat the oil to moderate 180°C (350°F), or until a cube of bread browns in 15 seconds. Cook the chips again, in batches, until crisp and golden. Drain on crumpled paper towels. Keep hot in the oven. Serve with the fish.
4 Pat the fish dry with paper towels. Dust with cornflour, dip into the batter and drain off excess. Deep-fry in batches for 5–7 minutes, or until cooked. Turn with tongs if necessary. Drain on crumpled paper towels. Serve with lemon wedges.

CRUMBED CALAMARI WITH CHILLI PLUM SAUCE

Preparation time: 25 minutes
Total cooking time: 12 minutes
Serves 4

★ ★

500 g (1 lb) squid hoods
¼ cup (30 g/1 oz) plain flour, seasoned
1–2 eggs, lightly beaten
3 cups (240 g/7½ oz) fresh white
    breadcrumbs
oil, for deep-frying

Chilli plum sauce
1 teaspoon oil
1 clove garlic, crushed
1 cup (315 g/10 oz) dark plum jam
⅓ cup (80 ml/2¾ fl oz) white vinegar
1–2 tablespoons sweet chilli sauce

1 Pat the squid with paper towels. Remove the quill and any skin. Cut into 1 cm (½ inch) rings.
2 Put the flour in a plastic bag, add the rings and toss. Dip each ring in beaten egg, drain off excess, then coat in breadcrumbs. Pat the crumbs lightly onto the rings and shake off any excess crumbs.
3 Fill a deep deavy-based pan one third full of oil and heat to 180°C (350°F), or until a cube of bread dropped into the oil turns golden brown in 15 seconds. Cook batches of rings for 3 minutes, or until golden. Drain on crumpled paper towels. Keep warm. Skim crumbs from the surface of the oil between batches. Serve hot, with the sauce.
4 For the sauce, heat the oil in a small pan over low heat and cook the garlic until softened. Stir in the jam, vinegar and chilli over medium heat until combined.

BREADED SCAMPI

Preparation time: 15 minutes
Total cooking time: 10 minutes
Serves 4 as a first course

★ ★

1 kg (2 lb) peeled raw scampi (scampi meat)
    or peeled raw large prawns
½ cup (60 g/2 oz) plain flour
4 eggs, lightly beaten
2 cups (200 g/6½ oz) dry breadcrumbs
1 tablespoon finely chopped fresh parsley
oil, for deep-frying
tartare sauce (see page 128), for serving
lemon wedges, for serving

1 Pat the scampi or prawns dry with paper towel, then toss in the flour and shake off any excess. Dip into the egg, then the combined crumbs and parsley.
2 Fill a deep heavy-based pan one third full of oil and heat to 180°C (350°F), or until a cube of bread dropped into the oil browns in 15 seconds. Deep-fry the scampi in batches for 2 minutes, or until golden and cooked through. Drain. Serve with tartare sauce and lemon wedges.

SHRIMP PASTE

Shrimp paste, also known as *blachan* or *balachan*, is a paste made from salted, sun-fermented shrimps or prawns, dried, ground and formed into blocks. It has a pungent odour. Although it doesn't need to be chilled, you can reduce the smell by wrapping in plastic and sealing in an airtight container before storing in the fridge or freezer. Always roast or fry before adding to a dish, and use sparingly. Shrimp paste is used as a flavouring in Thailand, Malaysia and Indonesia.

ABOVE: Thai-style fish with sweet chilli glaze

THAI-STYLE FISH WITH SWEET CHILLI GLAZE

Preparation time: 30 minutes + 2 hours marinating
Total cooking time: 35 minutes
Serves 4-6

★ ★ ★

2 whole fish (eg. snapper, bream, murray cod, ocean perch, flathead, about 1 kg/2 lb each)
1 stem lemon grass, white part only, bruised with the side of a knife, cut into quarters
6 kaffir lime leaves, cut in half
25 g (3/4 oz) fresh coriander leaves and stalks
1/2 cup (125 ml/4 fl oz) fish sauce
1/3 cup (80 ml/2 3/4 fl oz) lime juice
peanut oil, for deep-frying

Sweet chilli glaze

1 teaspoon oil
1 teaspoon shrimp paste
180 g (6 oz) grated palm sugar or brown sugar
1 stem lemon grass, white part only, bruised with the side of a knife, cut in half
5 cm (2 inch) piece fresh galangal, cut in half

4 small red chillies, finely sliced
2 teaspoons finely grated lime rind
1/3 cup (80 ml/2 3/4 fl oz) lime juice

1 Wash the fish and pat dry inside and out. Make deep cuts in the thickest part of the fish. Fill each cavity with half the lemon grass, lime leaves and coriander. Secure the openings with skewers. Place in a shallow, non-metallic dish.
2 Combine the fish sauce and lime juice, pour over the fish and marinate in the refrigerator for about 2 hours, turning the fish after an hour. Drain and pat dry with crumpled paper towels.
3 For the glaze, heat the oil in a small pan and fry the shrimp paste until fragrant. Add the sugar, lemon grass, galangal, red chilli, lime rind and juice, and 3/4 cup (185 ml/6 fl oz) water. Stir over medium heat until the sugar has dissolved, bring to the boil, then reduce the heat and simmer for 10 minutes, or until slightly thickened. Discard the galangal and lemon grass. Keep warm.
4 Fill a wok one third full of oil and heat to 180°C (350°F), or until a cube of bread dropped into the oil browns in 15 seconds. Cook each fish for 10 minutes, or until crisp and golden, spooning hot oil over the fish with a long-handled metal spoon. Drain on crumpled paper towels. Serve drizzled with the glaze.

SALMON WITH LEEK AND CAMEMBERT

Preparation time: 10 minutes
Total cooking time: 15 minutes
Serves 4

500 g (1 lb) skinless salmon fillet
1/4 cup (60 g/2 oz) wholegrain mustard
1 tablespoon lime juice
2 tablespoons oil
1 leek, white part only, julienned
2 tablespoons tamari
2 teaspoons fish sauce
1 tablespoon honey
75 g (2 1/2 oz) snow pea (mangetout) sprouts
2 tablespoons fresh coriander leaves
100 g (3 1/2 oz) Camembert, sliced
fresh coriander leaves, extra, to garnish
lime wedges, for serving

1 Cut the salmon into thick strips and place in a glass or ceramic bowl with the mustard and lime juice. Toss to coat the salmon.
2 Heat a wok until very hot, add the oil and swirl it around to coat the side. Add the salmon in batches and stir-fry over high heat until it turns soft pink and is slightly browned on the outside. Remove from the wok.
3 Add 1 tablespoon water to the wok, then add the leek and stir-fry until it is golden brown. Return the salmon to the wok, along with the tamari, fish sauce and honey. Cook until the salmon is heated through.
4 Remove the wok from the heat and toss the snow pea sprouts and coriander leaves through the salmon. Serve topped with the Camembert and extra coriander, and lime wedges on the side.
NOTES: Tamari is a thick Japanese-style soy sauce made from soy beans.

Ocean trout fillets can also be used to make this recipe.

BELOW: Salmon with leek and Camembert

SWORDFISH WITH BOK CHOY

Preparation time: 20 minutes
Total cooking time: 10 minutes
Serves 4

☆

500 g (1 lb) swordfish steak, cut into
   bite-sized pieces
1 tablespoon freshly cracked black pepper
3 tablespoons oil
3 cloves garlic, thinly sliced
1 onion, sliced
1 kg (2 lb) baby bok choy, leaves separated
100 g (3 1/2 oz) fresh shiitake mushrooms, sliced
2 tablespoons hoisin sauce
2 tablespoons rice wine
1 tablespoon oyster sauce
1 tablespoon soy sauce
1 tablespoon toasted sesame seeds
1 teaspoon sesame oil

1 Press the pieces of swordfish into the cracked black pepper until coated on all sides, then shake off any excess.

2 Heat a wok until very hot, add 2 tablespoons of the oil and swirl it around to coat the side. Stir-fry the swordfish in batches over high heat until tender. Do not overcook or the fish will break up. Remove from the wok and keep warm.

3 Reheat the wok, add 1 tablespoon of the oil and stir-fry the garlic until crisp and golden brown. Add the onion and stir-fry until golden brown. Add the baby bok choy leaves and sliced mushrooms and cook until the bok choy leaves wilt. Stir the hoisin sauce, rice wine, oyster sauce and soy sauce together in a jug. Pour into the wok and heat through.

4 Return the swordfish to the wok and toss. Serve sprinkled with the sesame seeds and drizzled with the sesame oil.

NOTE: You can substitute blue-eye, striped marlin or tuna for the swordfish in this recipe.

BELOW: Swordfish with bok choy

TUNA WITH SORREL HOLLANDAISE

Preparation time: 15 minutes
Total cooking time: 10 minutes
Serves 4

4 tuna steaks (about 150 g/5 oz each)
2 tablespoons olive oil

Sorrel hollandaise

15 young fresh sorrel leaves, stems
   removed
150 g (5 oz) butter
3 egg yolks
1 tablespoon lemon juice

1 Brush the tuna with the oil. Heat a large frying pan and cook the tuna for 2–3 minutes each side over medium heat, or until cooked to your liking. Remove from the pan, cover and keep warm.
2 For the sorrel hollandaise, place the sorrel leaves in a bowl, cover with boiling water, drain and rinse in cold water. Pat the leaves dry with paper towels and chop roughly. Melt the butter in a small pan. Put the egg yolks in a food processor and process for 20 seconds. With the motor running, add the hot butter in a thin steady stream and process until thick and creamy. Add the lemon juice and sorrel, and season, to taste, with salt and black pepper. Process for another 20 seconds.
3 Put the warm tuna on individual plates, spoon sorrel hollandaise over each and serve.
NOTE: You can substitute swordfish, blue-eye, salmon or striped marlin for the tuna.

PAN-FRIED GRAVLAX

Leftover gravlax (see page 62) is just as delicious served hot as it is cold. Cut the gravlax into 4 x 150 g (5 oz) steaks. Heat a little oil in a frying pan and place the portions into the hot oil. Cook for 2–3 minutes, or until lightly browned, then turn and cook the other side. Do not overcook—the salmon should still be slightly pink in the centre. The cooking time will vary according to the thickness of the fillet. Serves 4.

ABOVE: Tuna with sorrel hollandaise

127

SEAFOOD SAUCES
A simple piece of freshly cooked seafood becomes simple perfection when topped with a good spoonful of one of these favourite sauces.

TARTARE SAUCE
Mix 1 tablespoon finely chopped onion, 1 teaspoon lemon juice, 1 tablespoon chopped gherkins, 1 teaspoon drained, chopped capers, 1/4 teaspoon Dijon mustard, 1 tablespoon finely chopped fresh parsley and 1 1/2 cups (375 g/ 12 oz) mayonnaise. Season, to taste. Cover and refrigerate for up to 1 month. Makes about 2 cups.

COCKTAIL SAUCE
Mix 1 cup (250 g/8 oz) whole-egg mayonnaise, 3 tablespoons tomato sauce, 2 teaspoons Worcestershire sauce, 1/2 teaspoon lemon juice and 1 drop of Tabasco sauce. Season with salt and pepper, to taste. Cover and refrigerate for up to 1 month. Makes about 1 cup.

GREEN GODDESS DRESSING
Mix 1 1/2 cups (375 g/12 oz) whole-egg mayonnaise, 4 mashed anchovy fillets, 4 finely chopped spring onions, 1 crushed clove garlic, 3 tablespoons chopped fresh flat-leaf parsley, 3 tablespoons finely chopped chives and 1 teaspoon tarragon vinegar. Cover and refrigerate for up to 1 month. Makes about 2 cups.

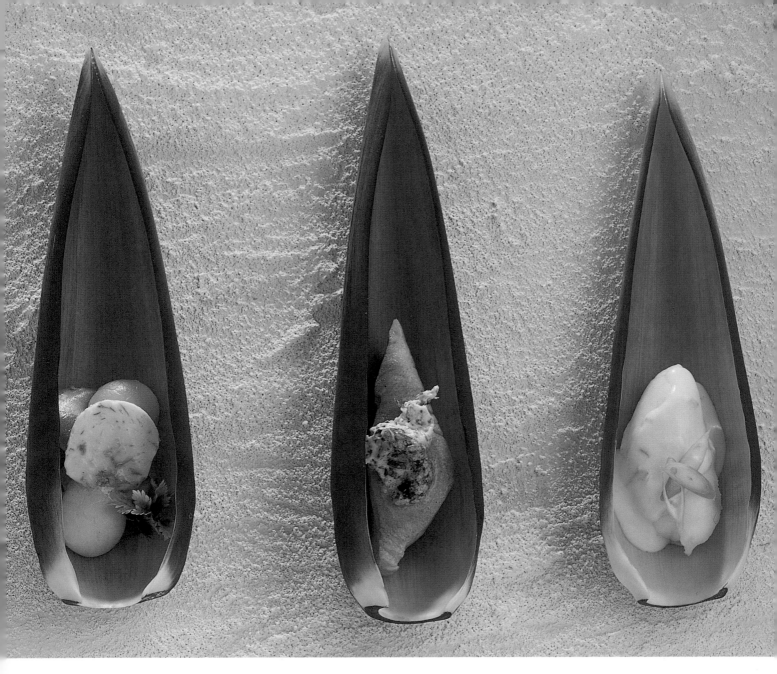

LEMON CAPER BUTTER

Combine 250 g (8 oz) soft butter in a
bowl with 1 tablespoon each of finely
grated lemon rind and juice, 1 crushed
garlic clove and 1 tablespoon drained,
chopped capers. Roll up firmly in foil
to form a roll. Refrigerate for up to
1 month. Cut into rounds for serving.
Serve at room temperature. Makes about
1 cup.

MONTPELLIER BUTTER

Beat 250 g (8 oz) softened butter in a
bowl until creamy. Blanch 100 g (3½ oz)
baby spinach leaves. Drain, refresh in
cold water, then squeeze out as much
water as possible. Chop roughly, then
combine in a food processor with
2 tablespoons chopped fresh parsley
leaves, 1 tablespoon chopped fresh
tarragon, 2 small chopped gherkins,
1 tablespoon drained bottled capers,
2 drained anchovy fillets, 2 hard-boiled
egg yolks, 1 teaspoon lemon juice and
2 tablespoons oil. Process until fine.
Add to the butter, mix well, then season
with cracked black pepper. Cover and
refrigerate for up to 3 days, or freeze.
Serve at room temperature. Portions of
the butter are placed on top of hot
seafood and allowed to melt. Makes
about 1 cup.

WHITE WINE SAUCE

Melt 1 tablespoon butter in a medium
pan, add 1 finely chopped spring onion
and cook, stirring over medium heat
until the onion is soft. Add ½ cup
(125 ml/4 fl oz) white wine, bring to the
boil and simmer for 5 minutes, or until
reduced by half. Add ½ cup (125 ml/
4 fl oz) each of cream and milk and bring
to the boil. Blend 3 teaspoons each of
soft butter and plain flour to form a paste,
then whisk into the boiling liquid and
boil until thick. Season, to taste, with salt
and pepper. If too thick, thin with a little
milk to reach a pouring consistency.
Cover and refrigerate for up to 3 days.
Makes about 1 cup.

*FROM LEFT: Tartare sauce; Cocktail sauce;
Green goddess dressing; Lemon caper
butter; Montpellier butter; White wine sauce*

129

GARLIC AND GINGER
PRAWNS

Gently cut a slit down the
back of each prawn.

Remove the dark vein from
the back of each prawn.

When the veins have been
removed, press the prawns
out flat.

GARLIC AND
GINGER PRAWNS

Preparation time: 25 minutes
Total cooking time: 10 minutes
Serves 4

★

1 kg (2 lb) raw large prawns

2 tablespoons oil

3–4 cloves garlic, finely chopped

5 cm (2 inch) piece fresh ginger, julienned

2–3 small red chillies, seeded and finely chopped

6 fresh coriander roots, finely chopped

8 spring onions, cut diagonally into short lengths

1/2 red pepper (capsicum), thinly sliced

2 tablespoons lemon juice

1/2 cup (125 ml/4 fl oz) white wine

2 teaspoons grated palm sugar or brown sugar

2 teaspoons fish sauce

1 tablespoon fresh coriander leaves, to garnish

1 Peel the prawns, leaving the tails intact. Gently cut a slit down the back of each prawn and remove the dark vein from each. Press each prawn out flat.

2 Heat a wok until very hot, add the oil and swirl it around to coat the side. Stir-fry half of the prawns, garlic, ginger, chilli and coriander root for 1–2 minutes over high heat, or until the prawns have just turned pink, then remove from the wok. Repeat with the remaining prawns, garlic, ginger, chilli and coriander root. Remove all of the prawns from the wok and set aside.

3 Add the spring onion and pepper to the wok. Cook over high heat for 2–3 minutes. Add the combined lemon juice, wine and palm sugar. Boil until the liquid has reduced by two thirds.

4 Return the prawns to the wok and sprinkle with the fish sauce, to taste. Toss until the prawns are heated through. Remove from the heat and serve sprinkled with coriander leaves.

*ABOVE: Garlic
and ginger prawns*

CRUNCHY FISH FILLETS

Preparation time: 10 minutes
Total cooking time: 6 minutes
Serves 4

1/2 cup (75 g/2 1/2 oz) cornmeal
4 firm white fish fillets (eg. snapper, perch,
  John dory, whiting, haddock, cod)
1/4 cup (60 ml/2 fl oz) oil
2/3 cup (170 g/5 1/2 oz) mayonnaise
2 tablespoons chopped fresh chives
1 tablespoon sweet chilli sauce

1 Place the cornmeal on a plate. Cut 4 shallow diagonal slashes in the skin side of each fish fillet, to prevent the fish curling during cooking.
2 Press the fillets into the cornmeal to coat thoroughly. Heat the oil in a frying pan over medium heat. Add the fish and cook skin-side-up for 3 minutes. Turn and cook for another 3 minutes, or until tender and the fish flakes easily when tested with a fork. Remove and drain on crumpled paper towels.
3 Combine the mayonnaise, chives and chilli sauce in a small bowl and serve with the fish.

SPANISH MACKEREL WITH GARLIC BUTTER

Preparation time: 10 minutes
Total cooking time: 15 minutes
Serves 4

2 tablespoons oil
80 g (2 3/4 oz) butter
4 cloves garlic, crushed
4 x 180 g (6 oz) Spanish mackerel cutlets
1/3 cup (30 g/1 oz) flaked almonds
2 tablespoons finely chopped fresh parsley

1 Heat the oil and butter in a pan. Add the garlic and stir over low heat for 2 minutes, or until light golden. Remove from the pan.
2 Add the fish to the pan and cook over high heat for 2–3 minutes, until golden brown on each side and cooked through (the flesh should flake easily when tested with a fork). Remove from the pan, cover and keep warm.
3 Add the almonds to the pan juices and stir until golden brown. Add the parsley and reserved garlic butter and stir for 1 minute.
4 Serve the hot cutlets with the almond and parsley mixture spooned evenly over the top.

JOHN DORY
The French name for this unattractive saltwater fish is Saint-Pierre (St Peter). The John dory has a large head, huge mouth and a deep, thin body. On either side of the body is a fingerprint-shaped impression, the subject of many fanciful legends. One such tale has St Peter leaving the print after throwing a John dory, which was making noises of distress, back into the Sea of Galilee. Another has him throwing it back because it was so ugly. Since this 'sea' is fresh water, the fish could not have been caught there. Despite its ugliness, the fillets yielded from John dory have a most delectable flavour.

LEFT: Crunchy fish fillets

PAN-FRIED CRUSTED FISH CURRY

Preparation time: 30 minutes + 15 minutes
   soaking
Total cooking time: 10 minutes
Serves 4

4 medium dried red chillies
100 g (3½ oz) Asian shallots
3 cloves garlic, chopped
2 stems lemon grass, white part only,
   finely sliced
4 fresh coriander roots
2 teaspoons lime rind
½ teaspoon drained, bottled green
   peppercorns, roughly chopped
½ cup (125 ml/4 fl oz) oil
4 thick skinless fish fillets (eg. blue-eye, snapper,
   ling, gemfish, about 200 g/6½ oz each)
½ cup (125 ml/4 fl oz) coconut milk
1 tablespoon fish sauce
4 kaffir lime leaves, finely shredded
2 tablespoons lime juice

1 Soak the red chillies in a bowl of boiling water for 15 minutes, or until softened. Drain and chop roughly.

2 Process the chillies, shallots, garlic, lemon grass, coriander roots, lime rind and peppercorns in a food processor, until a smooth paste forms. Add 1 tablespoon of the oil to help the processing, and regularly scrape down the sides of the bowl with a rubber spatula. Spread the paste lightly over one side of each fish fillet.

3 Heat the remaining oil in a large heavy-based pan. Cook the fish in a single layer, for 2–3 minutes on each side, until just cooked, turning over carefully with 2 egg slices so the fish doesn't break.

4 Stir together the coconut milk, fish sauce, kaffir lime leaves and lime juice in a small jug. Pour over the fish, reduce the heat and simmer for 3 minutes. Remove the fish from the pan, using an egg slice. Serve the fish drizzled with any pan juices.

BELOW: Pan-fried crusted fish curry

CARAMELIZED PRAWNS

Preparation time: 25 minutes
Total cooking time: 15 minutes
Serves 4

★ ★ ★

500 g (1 lb) raw medium prawns
6 spring onions
4 tablespoons sugar
1 tablespoon oil
3 cloves garlic, finely chopped
1 tablespoon fish sauce
1 tablespoon lime juice
1 tablespoon soft brown sugar
1/2 teaspoon salt
1/4 red pepper (capsicum), cut into
   fine strips

1 Remove the prawn heads but leave the tails, shells and legs intact. Make a small cut in the base of the prawns, three-quarters of the way along. Using a fine needle, lift out the dark veins. Rinse the prawns under running water and pat dry with paper towels.

2 Finely chop half the spring onions. Cut the rest into 4 cm (1 1/2 inch) pieces and finely shred into thin strips.

3 For the caramel sauce, combine the sugar with 3 tablespoons of water in a small pan. Stir over low heat, without boiling, until the sugar has dissolved. Bring to the boil, reduce the heat and simmer gently, without stirring, for 5 minutes, or until the syrup turns dark golden. Take care not to burn it. Remove the pan from the heat and add 4 tablespoons of water—it will spit and sizzle, and the caramel will form hard lumps. Return the pan to low heat and stir until the lumps have dissolved.

4 Heat the oil in a heavy-based frying pan over medium heat. Add the garlic and chopped spring onion. Add the prawns in batches and cook for 3 minutes, tossing the prawns until they turn pink. Drizzle the caramel sauce and fish sauce over the top and continue to cook for 1 minute. Add the lime juice, sugar, salt and the remaining spring onion, then toss well. Serve immediately, garnished with the strips of red pepper.

NOTE: If the prawn shells are tender, they can be eaten. Supply finger bowls and napkins, so people can peel them if they prefer.

GARLIC

Garlic was used as a flavouring as far back as Ancient Egypt and is mentioned in the early history of China. Cloves of garlic are used to create a delicious flavour in many dishes. If the cloves are chopped or mashed, the flavour is more intense than if used whole, or halved and discarded before the dish is served. Raw garlic is believed to have valuable medicinal properties.

ABOVE: Caramelized prawns

FRIED WHITEBAIT

Preparation time: 10 minutes
Total cooking time: 10 minutes
Serves 6

✮✮

500 g (1 lb) whitebait
2 teaspoons sea salt
1/3 cup (40 g/1 1/4 oz) plain flour
1/4 cup (30 g/1 oz) cornflour
2 teaspoons finely chopped fresh flat-leaf parsley
oil, for deep-frying
1 lemon, cut into wedges, for serving

1 Combine the whitebait and sea salt in a bowl and mix well. Cover and refrigerate.
2 Combine the sifted flours and parsley in a bowl and season well with cracked pepper. Fill a deep heavy-based pan one third full of oil and heat to 180°C (350°F), or until a cube of bread dropped into the oil browns in 15 seconds. Toss a third of the whitebait in the flour mixture, shake off the excess flour, and deep-fry for 1 1/2 minutes, or until pale and crisp. Drain well on crumpled paper towels. Repeat with the remaining whitebait, cooking in batches.
3 Reheat the oil and fry the whitebait a second time, in batches, for 1 minute each batch, or until lightly browned. Drain on crumpled paper towels and serve hot with lemon wedges.

DEEP-FRIED SQUID

Preparation time: 30 minutes + 30 minutes chilling
Total cooking time: 5 minutes
Serves 4

✮✮

500 g (1 lb) small squid (about 20)
1/3 cup (40 g/1 1/4 oz) plain flour
oil, for deep-frying
lemon wedges, for serving

1 To clean the squid, gently pull the tentacles away from the hood—the intestines should come away with them. Remove the intestines from the tentacles by cutting under the eyes and remove the beak if it remains in the centre of the tentacles. Pull away the soft bone 'quill' from the hood. Rub the hoods under running water and the skin should come away easily. Wash the hoods and tentacles and drain well. Place in a

bowl and season well with salt. Cover and refrigerate for about 30 minutes.
2 Combine the flour with a pinch each of salt and cracked pepper in a shallow dish. Fill a deep, heavy-based pan one third full of oil and heat to 180°C (350°F), or until a cube of bread browns in 15 seconds. Coat the squid hoods in flour and deep-fry in batches for about 30–60 seconds, or until light brown and tender. Toss the tentacles in the flour and deep-fry for 20–30 seconds, or until lightly browned and tender. Partially cover the deep-fryer while cooking as the squid tends to splatter. Drain on crumpled paper towels, then transfer to a serving platter and sprinkle with salt. Serve hot with lemon wedges.

FISH TEMPURA

Preparation time: 10 minutes
Total cooking time: 20 minutes
Makes 24

✮✮

1 sheet nori (dried seaweed)
3 tablespoons tempura flour
500 g (1 lb) skinless fish fillets (eg. snapper, bream, haddock, John dory, mirror dory, silver dory, ling), cut into bite-sized pieces
1 cup (250 ml/8 oz) iced water
2 cups (250 g/8 oz) tempura flour
oil, for deep-frying

1 Using scissors, cut the nori into tiny squares and combine on a plate with the tempura flour.
2 To make the tempura batter, quickly mix the iced water with the tempura flour. It should still be slightly lumpy. If it is too thick, add more water. Fill a deep, heavy-based pan one third full of oil and heat to 180°C (350°F), or until a cube of bread browns in 15 seconds. The oil is ready when 1/4 teaspoon of batter dropped into the oil keeps its shape, sizzles and rises to the top. Make sure the oil stays at the same temperature and does not get too hot. The fish should cook through as well as browning.
3 Dip the fish, in batches, into the nori and flour, then in the batter. Fry until golden brown, then drain on crumpled paper towels. Season with salt, to taste, and keep warm in a single layer on a baking tray in a very slow 120°C (250°F/Gas 1/2) oven.
NOTE: Buy tempura flour at Asian supermarkets. If unavailable, use 1/2 cup (90 g/3 oz) rice flour and 1 1/2 cups (185 g/6 oz) plain flour.

WHITEBAIT
Whitebait are tiny fish, the young of herrings and sprats. They are plentiful in spring and summer, but are also available frozen all year round. Because whitebait are so small, they are best eaten whole. Usually deep-fried, they can also be used in omelettes, fritters or patties. Refrigerate in a covered container that allows them to drain, for up to 2 days. Excess liquid will cause them to sweat. Avoid placing them in a bag. To freeze, drain them and place in a tightly sealed freezer bag for up to 6 months.

OPPOSITE PAGE: Fried whitebait (top); Deep-fried squid

BALINESE CHILLI SQUID

Preparation time: 30 minutes
Total cooking time: 10 minutes
Serves 4

★ ★

750 g (1 1/2 lb) squid hoods
1/4 cup (60 ml/2 fl oz) lime juice
3 tablespoons oil
1 large fresh red chilli, seeded and
    finely chopped
3 spring onions, sliced
1 tablespoon tamarind concentrate
1 stem lemon grass, white part only,
    finely sliced
1 cup (250 ml/8 fl oz) fish stock
1 tablespoon fresh Thai basil leaves, shredded

Spice paste

2 large fresh red chillies, seeded and chopped
2 cloves garlic, chopped
2 cm (3/4 inch) piece fresh ginger, chopped
2 cm (3/4 inch) piece fresh turmeric, chopped
3 spring onions, chopped
1 ripe tomato, peeled, seeded and chopped
2 teaspoons coriander seeds
1 teaspoon dried shrimp paste

1 Cut each squid hood in half lengthways and open out flat with the inside uppermost. Score a shallow lattice pattern all over the squid, taking care not to cut all the way through. Cut into 4 cm (1 1/2 inch) pieces and mix in a bowl with the lime juice. Season well.
2 For the spice paste, combine the ingredients in a food processor until finely chopped.
3 Heat 2 tablespoons of the oil in a wok or large frying pan. Cook the squid, chilli and spring onion in batches for 2 minutes over medium heat, or until the squid begins to curl. Remove from the wok.
4 Heat the remaining oil in the wok and add the spice paste, tamarind concentrate and lemon grass. Stir over medium heat for 5 minutes, or until fragrant.
5 Return the squid to the wok and add the stock. Season, to taste, with pepper and add the basil. Bring to the boil, then reduce the heat and simmer for 2 minutes.

ABOVE: Balinese chilli squid

CLAMS IN CHILLI PASTE

Preparation time: 15 minutes
Total cooking time: 12–15 minutes
Serves 4

1 kg (2 lb) fresh clams (vongole)
3 cloves garlic, finely sliced
3 small red chillies, seeded and sliced
  lengthways
1 tablespoon light soy sauce
1 cup (250 ml/8 fl oz) fish or chicken stock
5 tablespoons fresh Thai basil leaves

Chilli paste

2 tablespoons oil
2 spring onions, sliced
2 cloves garlic, sliced
1/4 cup (85 g/2³/4 oz) small dried shrimps
6 small fresh red chillies, seeded
2 teaspoons grated palm sugar or
  brown sugar
2 teaspoons fish sauce
2 teaspoons tamarind purée

1 Soak the clams in cold water for 30 minutes. Discard any broken clams or open ones that don't close when tapped on the bench.
2 For the chilli paste, heat the oil in a wok and fry the spring onion, garlic, dried shrimps and chilli over medium heat for about 3 minutes, until golden brown. Remove from the pan with a slotted spoon and reserve the oil.
3 Place the shrimp mixture and sugar in a mortar and pestle or small food processor and grind until well blended. Add the fish sauce, tamarind purée and a pinch of salt. Blend or grind to obtain a finely textured paste.
4 Heat the reserved oil in a wok. Add the garlic, chilli, roasted chilli paste and soy sauce. Mix well, then add the fish or chicken stock and bring just to the boil. Add the clams and cook over medium-high heat for 2–3 minutes. Discard any unopened clams. Stir in the basil and serve immediately with cooked Jasmine rice.
NOTE: Dried shrimp are available in Asian food stores. They are delicious in stir-fries and salads. Store in an airtight container.

BELOW: Clams in chilli paste

WHITEBAIT FRITTERS

Preparation time: 20 minutes + 20 minutes
  standing
Total cooking time: 15 minutes
Makes 10

✷ ✷

¼ cup (30 g/1 oz) self-raising flour
¼ cup (30 g/1 oz) plain flour
½ teaspoon bicarbonate of soda
1 egg, lightly beaten
¼ cup (60 ml/2 fl oz) dry white wine
2 teaspoons chopped fresh flat-leaf parsley
1 clove garlic, crushed
½ small onion, grated
200 g (6½ oz) New Zealand whitebait
olive oil, for shallow-frying
lemon wedges, to serve

1 Sift the flours, bicarbonate of soda, 1 teaspoon
of salt and some freshly ground black pepper into
a large bowl and make a well in the centre.
Gradually add the combined egg and wine,
whisking to make a smooth lump-free batter.
Stir in the parsley, garlic, onion and whitebait.
Cover and leave for 20 minutes.

2 Heat 2.5 cm (1 inch) of oil in a heavy-based
frying pan to 180°C (350°F), or until a cube of
bread dropped into the oil browns in 15 seconds.
Drop tablespoons of batter into the oil, cooking
4 or 5 at a time. When the batter is puffed and
bubbles appear on the surface, carefully turn
with a long-handled slotted metal spoon and
cook the other side. Drain on crumpled paper
towels and repeat with the remaining batter.
Serve with lemon wedges.

LOBSTER AMERICAINE

Preparation time: 30 minutes + cooling
Total cooking time: 40 minutes
Serves 4

✷ ✷ ✷

4 x 500 g (1 lb) lobsters
4 tablespoons olive oil
1 onion, finely chopped
1 carrot, finely chopped
1 celery stick, finely chopped
1 clove garlic, crushed
500 g (1 lb) ripe tomatoes, peeled, seeded
  and chopped

BELOW: Whitebait fritters

2 tablespoons tomato paste

1/2 cup (125 ml/4 fl oz) white wine

2 tablespoons brandy

1 cup (250 ml/8 fl oz) fish stock

60 g (2 oz) butter, softened

3 tablespoons chopped fresh parsley

1 Immobilize the lobsters in the freezer for 1 hour. Cut the heads from the bodies and remove the claws. Heat the oil in a large frying pan and cook the heads, tails and claws in batches over medium heat, until the lobster turns red and the flesh starts to shrink from the shells. Cool slightly before cutting the lobster heads in half and scraping out the red coral and the yellowy substance (liver)—set aside for the sauce.

2 Cut down each side of the tail with scissors and remove the flesh in one piece, reserving the tail shells. Cut the flesh into medallions (rounds).

3 Add the onion to the pan and stir over medium heat for 3 minutes, or until golden. Add the carrot, celery and garlic and cook for 5 minutes, or until soft. Add the tomato, tomato paste, wine, brandy and fish stock and bring to the boil.

4 Arrange the medallions on top of the sauce, cover and cook for 5 minutes or until the lobster is cooked through. Return the medallions to the shells and cook the sauce until reduced by half.

5 Combine the reserved roe and liver with the softened butter and add to the sauce with half the parsley. Season. Spoon the sauce over the lobster and serve sprinkled with parsley.

MARINATED CHILLI SQUID

Preparation time: 10 minutes + 2–3 hours marinating
Total cooking time: 15 minutes
Serves 4

★

500 g (1 lb) squid hoods

1 tablespoon finely chopped fresh ginger

2–3 teaspoons finely chopped fresh red chilli

3 cloves garlic, finely chopped

1/4 cup (60 ml/2 fl oz) oil

2 onions, thinly sliced

500 g (1 lb) baby bok choy, roughly chopped

1 Wash the squid well and pat dry with paper towels. Cut into 1 cm (1/2 inch) rings and place in a shallow glass or ceramic bowl. Combine the ginger, chilli, garlic and oil, pour over the rings and toss well. Cover and refrigerate for 2–3 hours.

2 Drain the rings and reserve the marinade. Heat the wok until very hot and stir-fry the rings over high heat in batches for 1–2 minutes. Remove from the wok as soon as the squid turns white. Do not overcook or the squid will be rubbery. Remove all the rings from the wok and set aside.

3 Heat the reserved marinade in the wok. Add the onion and cook over medium heat for 3–4 minutes, or until it is slightly softened. Add the bok choy and cook, covered, for 2 minutes, or until it has wilted slightly. Return the rings to the wok and toss until well combined. Season well with salt and pepper, to taste. Remove from the wok and serve immediately.

NOTE: Reheat the wok between cooking batches of rings—otherwise the flesh will be tough.

ABOVE: Marinated chilli squid

SKATE WITH
BLACK BUTTER

Cut the fillets from either side of the cartilage with a sharp knife, cutting close to the cartilage.

With the skate skin-side-down, slide a knife between the skin and flesh and, using a sawing action, cut along the length of the wing.

Cut the skate fillets into equal-sized serving pieces. Repeat with the other side.

OPPOSITE PAGE: Skate with black butter (top): Creamy scallops

SKATE WITH BLACK BUTTER

Preparation time: 20 minutes
Total cooking time: 25 minutes
Serves 4

185 g (6 oz) unsalted butter, chopped
1 kg (2 lb) small skate wings
2¹/2 cups (600 ml/20 fl oz) fish stock
¹/3 cup (80 ml/2³/4 fl oz) vinegar
2 tablespoons vinegar, extra
1 tablespoon chopped fresh parsley
2 tablespoons drained bottled capers

1 To clarify the butter, melt it in a pan over low heat, without stirring. Remove from the heat and cool slightly. Skim the foamy mixture from the surface. Pour off the clear yellow liquid and reserve. Discard the milky sediment left behind in the pan.
2 Pat the skate with paper towels. Cut fillets from either side of the cartilage with a sharp knife, cutting close to the cartilage. Place on a board skin-side-down, slide the knife between the skin and flesh and, using a sawing motion, cut along the length of the wing. Cut into equal-sized pieces.
3 Place the stock and vinegar in a large pan and bring to the boil. Add the skate and poach for 8 minutes. Drain well and pat dry with paper towels. Melt a little butter in a frying pan and cook the skate for 1–2 minutes each side, or until tender. Place on a serving dish and keep warm.
4 Heat the clarified butter in a pan until brown and foaming, but not black. Sprinkle the extra vinegar over the skate, then pour the butter over. Sprinkle with the parsley and capers. Serve hot.

CREAMY SCALLOPS

Preparation time: 30 minutes
Total cooking time: 20 minutes
Serves 4

500 g (1 lb) scallops
60 g (2 oz) butter
6 spring onions, white part only, chopped
³/4 cup (185 ml/6 fl oz) dry white wine
2 tablespoons plain flour
1 egg yolk
¹/2 cup (125 ml/4 fl oz) cream

1 Slice or pull off any vein, membrane or hard white muscle from the scallops, leaving any roe attached. Heat half the butter in a pan, add the spring onion and cook until soft. Add the scallops; fry until lightly coloured. Add the wine, salt and white pepper, and water to just cover. Bring to the boil, reduce the heat and cook over low heat for 2–3 minutes, until the scallops are tender.
2 Drain the scallops, reserving the cooking liquid, and divide the scallops among 4 shallow flameproof serving dishes. Keep warm.
3 Melt the remaining butter in a small pan over low heat. Stir in the flour for 2 minutes, or until pale and foaming. Remove from the heat and gradually pour in the strained reserved liquid. Return to the heat and stir constantly until the mixture boils and thickens. Reduce the heat and simmer for 2 minutes. Season, to taste.
4 Preheat a grill. Beat the egg yolk lightly with a fork in a bowl and pour on 2 tablespoons hot sauce, whisking constantly. Return the egg yolk mixture to the saucepan and stir until just heated through. Remove from the heat and add the cream very carefully. Pour the sauce over the scallops and grill until lightly browned.

FRESH TUNA, ALGARVE STYLE

Preparation time: 30 minutes + 4–8 hours chilling
Total cooking time: 8 minutes
Serves 4

4 tuna steaks
¹/2 cup (125 ml/4 fl oz) dry white wine
2 tablespoons fresh lemon juice
2 sprigs fresh parsley
2 tablespoons olive oil
2 cloves garlic, crushed

1 Place the tuna in a shallow non-metallic dish. Mix the wine, lemon juice, parsley and a little salt and pepper in a small bowl. Pour over the fish, cover and refrigerate for 4–8 hours, turning occasionally. Drain the fish, reserving the marinade. Pat the fish dry with paper towels.
2 Heat the oil in a large pan and cook the garlic for 2 minutes on low heat. Add the tuna and cook over medium heat for 3 minutes. Turn and cook for 3 minutes, or until cooked to your liking. Cooking time depends on the thickness of the fish. Do not overcook or the tuna will be dry.
3 Add the marinade to the pan and heat through. Remove the parsley.

ABOVE: Blackened fish

BLACKENED FISH

Preparation time: 5 minutes
Total cooking time: 6–8 minutes
Serves 6

6 large white fish fillets (eg. blue-eye, snapper, ling, warehou, mahi mahi), 2 cm (³/₄ inch) thick
125 g (4 oz) unsalted butter, melted
2 tablespoons Cajun spices (see page 143)
2 teaspoons sweet paprika
lemon wedges or halves, for serving

1 Brush each fish fillet liberally with the butter.
2 Combine the Cajun spices and paprika, then sprinkle thickly over the fish. Use your fingers to rub the spice mix evenly over the fillets.
3 Heat a large frying pan over high heat. Place two fillets in the pan and cook for 1–2 minutes. Turn and cook for another few minutes, until the fish is cooked and flakes easily. The surface should be well charred on each side. Add extra butter if necessary. Cook the remaining fillets.
4 Serve drizzled with any remaining melted butter. The lemon can be served lightly charred.

NEW ORLEANS OYSTERS

Preparation time: 10 minutes
Total cooking time: 4–6 minutes
Serves 4

24 large fresh oysters, shelled
2 teaspoons Cajun spices (see page 143)
¹/₂ teaspoon hot paprika
¹/₄ teaspoon dried basil
¹/₂ cup (60 g/2 oz) plain flour
¹/₂ cup (125 ml/4 fl oz) oil
45 g (1¹/₂ oz) unsalted butter
lemon wedges, for serving
mayonnaise, for serving

1 Dry the oysters on paper towels. In a shallow dish, mix the Cajun spices, paprika and basil. Set aside 2 teaspoons of the mixture. Add the flour to the remaining spice mix and stir thoroughly.
2 Lightly oil 8 thin wooden or metal skewers and thread 3 oysters onto each. Coat with the spiced flour, then shake off any excess.
3 Heat the oil and butter in a large frying pan

wide enough to fit the skewers. Fry the oysters over medium heat until golden brown, turning several times, for about 3–4 minutes. Drain on crumpled paper towel. Sprinkle with the reserved spice mix and serve with the lemon wedges and a dish of mayonnaise.

CAJUN 'POPCORN'

Preparation time: 10 minutes + 30 minutes standing
Total cooking time: 10 minutes
Serves 6

750 g (1 1/2 lb) raw medium prawns
1 egg
1 cup (250 ml/8 fl oz) milk
1/4 cup (35 g/1 1/4 oz) fine cornmeal
3/4 cup (90 g/3 oz) plain flour
1/2 teaspoon baking powder
1 1/2 teaspoons Cajun spices (see recipe on right)
1/4 teaspoon dried basil
1/2 teaspoon celery salt
oil, for deep-frying

1 Peel the prawns and gently pull out the dark vein from each back, starting at the head end. Pat dry with paper towels.
2 Beat the egg and milk together. In a large bowl, combine the cornmeal, flour, baking powder, Cajun spices, basil and celery salt. Make a well in the centre, gradually add half the beaten egg mixture and whisk to form a smooth paste. Add the remaining egg mixture, mix well and leave to stand for 30 minutes.
3 Fill a deep, heavy-based pan one third full of oil and heat to 180°C (350°F), or until a cube of bread dropped in the oil browns in 15 seconds.
4 Dip the prawns in the batter and allow excess to drain off. Cook in small batches in the oil until crisp and lightly golden. Remove with a slotted spoon or strainer and drain on crumpled paper towel. Serve hot with a sauce of your choice.

CAJUN SPICES
Cajun cuisine originated in Louisiana in America. Its distinctive flavour has been influenced by the French, Spanish, Africans and American Indians. The spice mix used in many Cajun recipes is made by mixing 1 tablespoon each of garlic powder and onion powder, 2 teaspoons each of white pepper and cracked black pepper, 1 1/2 teaspoons cayenne pepper, 2 teaspoons dried thyme and 1/2 teaspoon dried oregano. After preparing, it can be stored in an airtight jar for up to 3 months.

LEFT: Cajun 'popcorn'

COATINGS & BATTERS Each of

these mixtures will coat four medium fish fillets (we used snapper). The egg white

batter is enough for six fillets. You can use the mixtures for other seafood as well.

To prepare for all the deep-fried recipes, fill a deep heavy-based saucepan one third full of oil and heat the oil to 180°C (350°F), or until a cube of bread dropped into the oil browns in 15 seconds. Fry the food in batches for even cooking.

BASIC BATTER

Sift 1 cup (125 g/4 oz) self-raising flour into a large bowl, then make a well in the centre. Beat an egg with 1 cup (250 ml/8 fl oz) milk and 1 tablespoon oil in a large jug. Gradually pour into the well, whisking to make a smooth batter. Cover and leave to stand for 10 minutes before using. The mixture should be the consistency of thick cream. Thin with a little extra milk if necessary. Pat the fish dry with paper towel, dust lightly with flour, then dip in the batter, in batches, allowing the excess to drain off. Lower the fish in batches into the oil and deep-fry until golden brown. Drain on crumpled paper towels.

EGG WHITE BATTER

Sift 1 cup (125 g/4 oz) self-raising flour into a large bowl, make a well in the centre and gradually whisk in 1 cup (250 ml/8 fl oz) water to make a smooth batter. Leave to stand for 5 minutes. Beat 2 egg whites in a small clean bowl with electric beaters until stiff peaks form, then fold into the batter in two batches. Use immediately. Pat the fish dry with paper towel, dust lightly with flour, then dip into the batter in batches, allowing the excess batter to drain off. Lower the fish

in batches into the oil and deep-fry until golden brown. Drain well on crumpled paper towels.

BEER BATTER
Sift 1 cup (125 g/4 oz) plain flour into a large bowl, make a well in the centre and gradually whisk in 1 cup (250 ml/8 fl oz) chilled beer. Pat the fish dry with paper towel, dust with flour, then dip into the batter in batches, allowing the excess to drain off. Lower into the oil in batches and deep-fry until golden. Drain on crumpled paper towels. (Soda water can be used instead of beer.)

SESAME SEED COATING
Season some flour with pepper and salt in a shallow bowl. Put 1 cup (155 g/5 oz) sesame seeds in another. Lightly beat an egg in a separate bowl. Pat the fish dry with paper towel, dust lightly with the

flour, then dip in the egg, allowing the excess to drain off. Coat in sesame seeds. Heat 3 cm (1¼ inches) oil in a heavy-based frying pan to 180°C (350°F), or until a cube of bread dropped into the oil browns in 15 seconds. Shallow-fry the fish in batches until golden, turning once. Drain on crumpled paper towels.

NORI AND CRUMB COATING
Place 1½ cups (90 g/3 oz) Japanese breadcrumbs in a bowl. Tear or cut a sheet of nori into small pieces and stir into the crumbs. Season some flour with a little salt and pepper in a shallow bowl. Lightly beat an egg in a separate bowl. Pat the fish fillet dry with paper towel and dust lightly with flour. Dip in the egg, allowing the excess to drain off, then coat in the nori. Deep-fry the fish in batches until golden, then drain on crumpled paper towels.

CHIVE AND LEMON COATING
Combine 1¼ cups (100 g/3½ oz) fresh breadcrumbs with 6 tablespoons finely chopped fresh chives and 1 teaspoon finely grated lemon rind. Season some flour with salt and pepper in a shallow bowl. Lightly beat an egg in a separate bowl. Pat the fillet dry with paper towel and dust lightly with the flour. Dip in the egg, allowing the excess to drain off, then coat in the breadcrumbs. Melt 30 g (1 oz) butter and 2 tablespoons oil in a large frying pan, add the fish in batches and cook over medium heat until golden brown. Turn and cook the other side, adding butter and oil as required.

CLOCKWISE, FROM TOP LEFT:
Basic batter; Beer batter (with prawns);
Nori and crumb coating (with calamari);
Chive and lemon coating; Sesame seed
coating; Egg white batter

ABOVE: Carpetbag steak

1 Trim the meat of excess fat and sinew. With a sharp knife, cut a deep pocket in the side of each steak. Combine the oysters, parsley, lemon juice and a little freshly ground black pepper in a bowl. Spoon evenly into the steak pockets and secure with toothpicks.

2 Heat the oil in a heavy-based pan, add the steaks and cook over high heat for 2 minutes each side, to seal. For rare steaks, cook for another minute each side. For medium and well-done steaks, lower the heat to medium-high and cook for another 2–3 minutes each side for medium, and 4–6 minutes each side for well done. Remove and drain on crumpled paper towels. Cover and keep warm.

3 Bring the stock and sauce to the boil in a pan. Reduce the heat, stir in the butter until melted, then pour over the steaks. Serve with steamed baby snow peas (mangetout) and Brussels sprouts, maybe sprinkled with finely chopped red pepper or chilli. Garnish with thyme.

CALAMARI AND GREEN PEPPERCORN STIR-FRY

Preparation time: 10 minutes + 15 minutes standing
Total cooking time: 10 minutes
Serves 4

500 g (1 lb) calamari rings
2 tablespoons oil
1 tablespoon canned green peppercorns, drained and roughly chopped
4 cloves garlic, chopped
1 teaspoon chopped red chillies
2 tablespoons fish sauce
2 teaspoons soy sauce
fresh basil leaves, to garnish

1 Combine the calamari rings, oil and green peppercorns in a bowl, cover and leave to stand for 15 minutes.

2 Heat a large wok or heavy-based frying pan until very hot, add 2 teaspoons of the oil from the marinating calamari and swirl it around the side. Add the garlic and chilli to the wok or frying pan and cook for 5 seconds. Add the calamari to the pan in batches and stir-fry, tossing constantly, for 2 minutes each batch. Transfer each batch to a plate. Reheat the wok between each batch.

CARPETBAG STEAK

Preparation time: 15 minutes
Total cooking time: 15 minutes
Serves 4

4 rib-eye steaks, each 4 cm (1½ inches) thick
8 fresh oysters, shelled
1 teaspoon chopped fresh parsley
2 teaspoons lemon juice
2 tablespoons oil
1 cup (250 ml/8 fl oz) beef stock
2 teaspoons Worcestershire sauce
60 g (2 oz) butter, chopped

3 Add the fish sauce and soy sauce to the wok and, when bubbling, carefully pour it over the hot calamari. Serve immediately with steamed or boiled rice and perhaps a fresh green salad. Garnish with fresh basil leaves.

SEAFOOD FAJITAS

Preparation time: 30 minutes
Total cooking time: 20 minutes
Serves 4

250 g (8 oz) scallops
300 g (10 oz) raw medium prawns
250 g (8 oz) skinless white fish fillets
  (eg. flake, ling, blue-eye, groper)
3 ripe tomatoes, finely chopped
I small red chilli, finely chopped
2 spring onions, finely sliced
1/3 cup (80 ml/2 3/4 fl oz) lime juice
I clove garlic, crushed
I ripe avocado, sliced
2 tablespoons lemon juice
4 flour tortillas
I onion, thinly sliced
I green pepper (capsicum), cut into
  thin strips

1 Slice or pull off any vein, membrane or white muscle from the scallops, leaving any roe attached.
2 Peel the prawns and gently pull out the dark vein from each prawn back, starting at the head end. Cut the white fish fillets into bite-sized pieces.
3 Preheat the oven to warm 160°C (315°F/ Gas 2–3). Combine the tomato, chilli and spring onion in a bowl and season, to taste, with salt and pepper.
4 Combine the scallops, prawns, fish, lime juice and garlic in a bowl, cover and refrigerate.
5 Slice the avocado and brush with the lemon juice, to prevent browning.
6 Wrap the flour tortillas in foil and heat in the oven for 10 minutes to soften.
7 Heat a lightly oiled chargrill or cast-iron pan to very hot, add the onion and green pepper and cook, turning occasionally, until soft and lightly brown. Push them all over to one side of the pan. Drain the seafood thoroughly and cook briefly until it is seared all over and cooked through.

8 To serve, wrap the seafood, green pepper, onion, sliced avocado and tomato mixture in the tortillas.
NOTE: From Tex-Mex cuisine, fajitas (pronounced *fah-hee-tuhs*) although originally made with meat, are now also made with marinated chicken or seafood, cooked on a sizzling cast-iron plate and wrapped in tortillas with salsa, avocado and other salad ingredients.

PAN-FRIED SALMON WITH GREMOLATA

Combine 4 tablespoons finely chopped fresh parsley, 2 teaspoons each of grated lemon and orange rind and 2 cloves crushed garlic in a small bowl with 3 teaspoons small drained bottled capers. Mix well and set aside. Heat a large frying pan and add 30 g (1 oz) butter and 1 tablespoon olive oil. Add four 200 g (6 1/2 oz) fresh salmon fillets and pan-fry over high heat on both sides for about 2–3 minutes each side, or until cooked as desired. Serve the salmon topped with the gremolata mixture. Serves 4.

BELOW: Seafood fajitas

CHILLI CRAB

Preparation time: 25 minutes + 1 hour freezing
Total cooking time: 25 minutes
Serves 4

★ ★ ★

2 x 1 kg (2 lb) fresh mud crabs
2 tablespoons oil
1 onion, chopped
4 cloves garlic, crushed
3 teaspoons grated fresh ginger
2–3 fresh red chillies, finely chopped
440 g (14 oz) can tomatoes, puréed
1 tablespoon soy sauce
1 tablespoon soft brown sugar
2 teaspoons rice vinegar

1 Freeze the crabs for about 1 hour to immobilize them. Wash well with a stiff brush, then pull the apron back from underneath the crab and separate the shells. Remove the feathery gills and intestines. Twist off the claws. Using a cleaver or a heavy-bladed knife, cut the body in quarters. Crack the claws with a good hit with the back of a cleaver.
2 Heat a wok until very hot, add the oil and swirl to coat the side. Stir-fry the crab in batches for 2–3 minutes, or until bright red. Remove and set aside. Add the onion to the wok and cook for 3 minutes. Add the garlic, ginger and chilli, and cook for 1–2 minutes. Stir in the puréed tomato, soy sauce, sugar, vinegar and 1/2 cup (125 ml/4 fl oz) water. Bring to the boil, then cook for 5 minutes, or until the sauce is slightly thickened.
3 Return the crab to the wok and toss to coat with the sauce. Simmer for 8 minutes, or until the crab is cooked, turning often.

FRESH TUNA AND GREEN BEAN STIR-FRY

Preparation time: 25 minutes
Total cooking time: 10 minutes
Serves 4

★

300 g (10 oz) small green beans
2 tablespoons oil
600 g (1 1/4 lb) fresh tuna, cut into small cubes
250 g (8 oz) small cherry tomatoes
16 small black olives

2–3 tablespoons lemon juice
2 cloves garlic, finely chopped
8 anchovy fillets, rinsed, dried and
   finely chopped
3 tablespoons small fresh basil leaves
   (or roughly torn basil leaves)

1 Trim the beans if necessary and cook in a small pan of boiling water for 2 minutes. Drain and refresh under cold water. Set aside.
2 Heat a wok until very hot, add the oil and swirl it around to coat the side. Stir-fry the tuna in batches for about 5 minutes, or until cooked on the outside but still pink on the inside.
3 Add the cherry tomatoes, olives and beans, and gently toss until heated through. Stir in the lemon juice, garlic and anchovies. Season with salt and black pepper, to taste. Serve scattered with the fresh basil leaves.

CRUMBED ANCHOVIES

Preparation time: 10 minutes
Total cooking time: 15 minutes
Serves 4

★ ★

800 g (1 lb 10 oz) fresh anchovies
2 eggs
dry breadcrumbs, for coating
150 g (5 oz) butter

1 To clean the anchovies, scrape a small knife along the body of each one, starting at the tail end, to remove any scales. This is best done under cold running water. Make a slit along the gut. Cut off the head and pull it away from the body slowly so that the intestines come away with the head. Press open flat on a work surface, press along the backbone with the palm of your hand, then gradually ease out the backbone. Wash the fish briefly and pat dry carefully with paper towel.
2 Beat the eggs with a little salt in a bowl. Dip the anchovies in the egg mixture, drain off the excess, then coat evenly in the breadcrumbs, pressing on gently.
3 Melt the butter in a large frying pan and fry the anchovies in batches until golden brown, turning once. Drain on crumpled paper towel. Sprinkle with salt and serve with lemon wedges.
NOTE: Instead of fresh anchovies, you can use fresh sardines, garfish or red spot whiting, according to availability and your taste.

MUD CRABS
Mud crabs have a delicious moist sweet flesh, especially in their claws. You can buy mud crabs live or cooked. Live ones have a dark brown shell, but once cooked they turn brilliant orange. The live ones should be quite active. Make sure the crabs are securely tied with string. If sluggish, they are near death, after which they deteriorate very quickly. Choose crabs that are heavy in relation to their size to ensure you get plenty of meat. The limbs should be intact and the shell firm, not soft.

OPPOSITE PAGE:
Chilli crab (top);
Fresh tuna and green
bean stir-fry

FISH ROLLS

Preparation time: 45 minutes
Total cooking time: 25 minutes
Makes 12

✹ ✹

500 g (1 lb) black mussels
300 g (10 oz) skinless salmon or ocean trout fillet
300 g (10 oz) raw medium prawns
300 g (10 oz) skinless firm white fish fillets
    (eg. cod, flake, ling, snapper)
1 egg white
1/2 cup (125 ml/4 fl oz) cream
1 tablespoon chopped fresh dill
1 tablespoon chopped fresh chives
80 g (2³/4 oz) butter
1 tablespoon lime juice
1 teaspoon thin strips lime rind
1 tablespoon chopped fresh parsley
2 tablespoons drained bottled baby capers

1 Clean the mussels with a stiff brush and pull out the hairy beards. Discard any broken mussels

ABOVE: Fish rolls

or open ones that don't close when tapped on the bench. Heat 1 cup (250 ml/8 fl oz) water in a saucepan, add the mussels, cover and cook for 4–5 minutes, or until open. Discard any unopened mussels. Remove the meat from the shells, chop roughly, cover and chill until required. Finely chop the salmon, cover and chill.

2 Peel the prawns and gently pull out the dark vein from each prawn back, starting at the head end. Put the prawns, fish and the egg white in a food processor and mix until smooth. Add the cream and process until just combined. Transfer to a large bowl and stir in the mussels, salmon, dill, chives and salt and pepper. To test for seasoning, fry a small amount in a pan. Divide into 12 portions. Place each portion on a sheet of plastic wrap and roll into a log shape. Wrap again in squares of foil, twisting the ends firmly to seal and form a firm log shape. Add the rolls to a pan of simmering water and simmer for 5–8 minutes, or until firm. Remove from the pan and cut the ends off the rolls. Lightly pan-fry or barbecue. Serve on warm plates.

3 Heat the same pan over medium heat, add the butter and swirl until melted. Add the lime juice, rind, parsley and capers, then spoon over the rolls. Can be garnished with extra rind strips.

TROUT WITH ALMONDS

Preparation time: 25 minutes
Total cooking time: 10 minutes
Serves 2

2 rainbow trout, or baby salmon
plain flour, for coating
60 g (2 oz) butter
¼ cup (25 g/¾ oz) flaked almonds
2 tablespoons lemon juice
1 tablespoon finely chopped fresh parsley
lemon or lime wedges, for serving

1 Wash the fish and pat dry with paper towels. Open the fish out skin-side-up. Run a rolling pin along the backbone, starting at the tail, pressing gently down. Turn the fish over and use scissors to cut through the backbone at each end of the fish. Lift out the backbone. Remove any remaining bones. Trim the fins with scissors.
2 Coat the fish with flour. In a large frying pan, heat half the butter and add the fish. Cook for 4 minutes each side, or until golden brown. Remove the fish and place on heated serving plates. Cover with foil.
3 Heat the remaining butter, add the flaked almonds and stir until light golden. Add the juice, parsley, and salt and freshly ground pepper. Stir until the sauce is heated through. Pour over the fish and serve with lemon or lime wedges.

LEMON FLOUNDER

Dust two 375 g (12 oz) flounder or plaice fillets in plain flour and shake off the excess. Heat a little butter in a large frying pan and cook the fish over medium heat, turning once, until lightly browned and cooked through. The fish will flake easily when tested. Transfer to a serving dish and keep hot. Wipe out the pan and melt 60 g (2 oz) butter. Add 1½ tablespoons lemon juice and 2 teaspoons chopped fresh parsley, then season. Cook until foaming, then pour over the fish and sprinkle with parsley. Serves 2.

BELOW: Trout with almonds

JOHN DORY WITH PRAWNS AND CREAMY DILL SAUCE

Preparation time: 15 minutes
Total cooking time: 20 minutes
Serves 4

12 raw large prawns
2½ cups (600 ml/20 fl oz) fish stock
30 g (1 oz) butter
1 clove garlic, finely chopped
2 tablespoons plain flour
2 tablespoons cream
4 x 200 g (6½ oz) John dory fillets
1 tablespoon chopped fresh chives
1 tablespoon chopped fresh dill

1 Peel the prawns and pull out the dark vein from each prawn back, starting at the head end.
2 Heat the stock in a saucepan and bring to the boil. Reduce the heat and simmer for 10 minutes, or until the liquid has reduced. You will need 1½ cups (375 ml/12 fl oz) fish stock.
3 Melt the butter in a small saucepan and add the garlic. Stir in the flour and cook for 1 minute, or until pale and foaming. Remove from the heat and gradually stir in the stock. Return to the heat and stir constantly until the sauce boils and thickens. Reduce the heat and simmer for 1 minute. Remove from the heat and stir in the cream. Season, to taste. Keep warm while you cook the fish and prawns.
4 Heat a little oil in a frying pan and cook the fish fillets over medium heat for 2 minutes each side, or until the fish flakes easily when tested with a fork. Transfer to serving plates.
5 Add the prawns to the same pan (add a little more oil to the pan if necessary) and cook for 2–3 minutes, or until the prawns turn pink and are cooked through.
6 To serve, stir the fresh chives and dill into the hot sauce, then arrange the prawns on top of the fillets and spoon sauce over the top. Each serving can be garnished with strips of fresh chives or sprigs of dill.

RIGHT: John dory with prawns and creamy dill sauce

FISH MEUNIERE

Preparation time: 5 minutes
Total cooking time: 10 minutes
Serves 4

4 thick white fish fillets (eg. blue-eye, warehou, cod, jewfish)
plain flour, for dusting
125 g (4 oz) butter
1–2 tablespoons lemon juice
1 tablespoon chopped fresh parsley

1 Dust the fish lightly with flour and shake off any excess. Heat a little oil in a pan and cook the fish for 5–8 minutes each side, until lightly golden. Transfer to serving plates. Wipe out the pan with paper towel.

2 Heat the pan over high heat, add the butter and swirl quickly to melt (the butter will start to brown). Remove from the heat, immediately add the lemon juice, parsley and some cracked black pepper, then pour over the fish. Serve with extra lemon wedges.

NOTE: The cooking time will depend on the thickness of the fish. This recipe, with its simple sauce, is suitable for most types and cuts of fish.

GRATED POTATO CAKES WITH SALMON

Coarsely grate 1.5 kg (3 lb) peeled waxy potatoes, such as desiree, bintji or pontiac. Rinse in cold water and drain well, squeezing out any excess moisture. Combine in a large bowl with a lightly beaten egg and 1 tablespoon of oil. Season with salt and pepper and stir in 2 tablespoons of plain flour. With floured hands, form into flat patty shapes using 2 tablespoons of mixture for each. Shallow-fry on both sides, in a large pan, until golden brown. Drain on crumpled paper towel. Stack several warm cakes on top of each other on a serving plate, top with a small pile of smoked salmon, a dollop of light sour cream, a few red onion rings and a sprinkle of chopped fresh chives. Serves 4–6.

ABOVE: Fish meunière

FISH BURGERS
AND WEDGES

Pour in enough water to
cover the fish fillets, then
slowly heat the water.

Mix the flaked fish with the
herbs, potato, juice, capers,
gherkin and seasoning.

FISH BURGERS AND WEDGES

Preparation time: 30 minutes + 1 hour chilling
Total cooking time: 25 minutes
Serves 4

★

500 g (1 lb) skinless white fish fillets
   (eg. flake, ling, redfish, warehou)
2 tablespoons finely chopped fresh parsley
2 tablespoons finely chopped fresh dill
2 tablespoons lemon juice
1 tablespoon drained bottled capers, chopped
2 bottled gherkins, finely chopped
350 g (11 oz) potatoes, cooked and mashed
plain flour, for dusting
1 tablespoon olive oil
4 hamburger buns, split into halves
lettuce leaves
2 Roma (egg) tomatoes, sliced
tartare sauce (see page 128)

Crunchy potato wedges

6 potatoes, unpeeled, cut into wedges
1 tablespoon oil
1/2 teaspoon chicken or vegetable stock powder
1/4 cup (25 g/3/4 oz) dry breadcrumbs
2 teaspoons chopped fresh chives
1 teaspoon celery salt
1/4 teaspoon garlic powder
1/2 teaspoon chopped fresh rosemany

1 Place the fish in a frying pan and just cover
with water. Slowly heat, making sure the water
doesn't boil. Cover and cook over low heat until
just cooked. Drain the fish on paper towels,
transfer to a bowl and flake with a fork, removing
any bones. Add the parsley, dill, juice, capers,
gherkins and potato, season with cracked pepper
and salt and mix well. Shape into 4 patties. Dust
with flour and refrigerate on a plate for 1 hour.
2 Heat the oil in a large non-stick frying pan,
add the patties and cook for 5–6 minutes on each
side, or until well browned and cooked through.
3 Grill the buns and butter if you wish. On each
base, put some lettuce, tomato, a patty and some
tartare sauce. Top and serve.
4 For the wedges, preheat the oven to moderately
hot 200°C (400°F/Gas 6). Pat the potato dry
with paper towels and toss with the oil.
Combine the remaining wedge ingredients and
toss with the wedges. Spread on greased baking
trays and bake for 40 minutes, or until golden.

PRAWN BURGERS WITH COCKTAIL SAUCE

Preparation time: 35 minutes + 10 minutes chilling
Total cooking time: 5–10 minutes
Serves 4

★ ★

12 raw large prawns
2 tablespoons lemon juice
1 tablespoon sesame seeds
1 1/2 cups (120 g/4 oz) fresh white breadcrumbs
2 tablespoons chopped fresh coriander
1 egg, lightly beaten
2 teaspoons chilli sauce
plain flour, for dusting
olive oil, for frying
1/3 cup (80 g/2 3/4 oz) whole-egg mayonnaise
1 spring onion, finely chopped
1 tablespoon tomato sauce
1 teaspoon Worcestershire sauce
chilli sauce, to taste, extra
1 tablespoon lemon juice, extra
4 hamburger buns, split into halves
rocket leaves
1 firm ripe avocado, thinly sliced
1 teaspoon cracked pepper

1 Peel the prawns and pull out the dark vein
from each prawn back, starting at the head end.
Flatten slightly to open out. Mix with the juice.
2 Combine the sesame seeds, breadcrumbs and
coriander on a sheet of greaseproof paper.
Combine the egg and chilli sauce in a bowl.
Dust the prawns in the flour and shake off the
excess. Dip in the egg mixture, then press firmly
in breadcrumbs. Place on a tray covered with
baking paper. Cover and chill for 10 minutes.
3 Heat a little oil in a frying pan. Cook the
prawns in batches over medium heat 2–3 minutes
each side, or until crisp and golden brown.
Remove and drain on crumpled paper towels.
4 Combine the mayonnaise, spring onion,
tomato and Worcestershire sauces, extra chilli
sauce and extra lemon juice in a bowl.
5 Grill the buns and butter if you wish. On each
base, put some rocket and avocado. Sprinkle
with cracked pepper. Add prawns, a dollop of
the cocktail sauce and finally, the bun top.

*OPPOSITE PAGE: Fish
burger and wedges*

WHOLE RED MULLET IN TOMATO AND OLIVE SAUCE

Preparation time: 15 minutes
Total cooking time: 35 minutes
Serves 4

8 small whole red mullet (about 1 kg/2 lb),
   cleaned and scaled
2 tablespoons chopped fresh parsley, for serving

Tomato and olive sauce

1 1/2 tablespoons olive oil
1 large onion, sliced
2 cloves garlic, finely chopped
2 x 400 g (13 oz) cans crushed tomatoes
1 1/2 tablespoons red wine vinegar
2 tablespoons tomato paste (tomato purée)
1 tablespoon sugar
1/4 cup (60 ml/2 fl oz) white wine
3/4 cup (185 ml/6 fl oz) fish stock

1 tablespoon chopped fresh oregano
1 tablespoon chopped fresh basil
100 g (3 1/2 oz) black olives

1 Pat the fish dry inside and out with paper towels. Refrigerate until ready to use.
2 Heat the oil in a large deep frying pan large enough to fit the fish in one layer. Cook the onion and garlic over medium heat for 5 minutes, or until softened. Add the remaining sauce ingredients and bring to the boil. Reduce the heat and simmer for 15 minutes, or until the sauce is pulpy and thickened slightly.
3 Add the fish, in a single layer, and cover the pan. Simmer for another 10–12 minutes, or until the fish flakes easily when tested in the thickest part with a fork. As red mullet is a soft-fleshed fish, there is no need to turn it over during cooking (it will fall apart). Serve garnished with parsley if you wish.
NOTES: The sauce can be made in advance and refrigerated, to allow the flavours to develop.

Redfish or garfish can be used in this recipe instead of red mullet.

ABOVE: Whole red mullet in tomato and olive sauce

FISH ON EGGPLANT (AUBERGINE) WITH ROASTED RED PEPPER (CAPSICUM) AIOLI

Preparation time: 15–20 minutes + 20 minutes standing
Total cooking time: 10 minutes
Serves 4

★ ★

8 thick slices of large eggplant (aubergine)
1 large red pepper (capsicum)
2 tablespoons oil
4 x 200 g (6¹/₂ oz) white fish fillets
   (eg. snapper, monkfish, perch, cod),
   each cut diagonally into 6 pieces

Roasted red pepper (capsicum) aioli

2 cloves garlic, roughly chopped
1 egg yolk
2–3 teaspoons lemon juice
¹/₂ cup (125 ml/4 fl oz) olive oil
2 tablespoons chopped fresh parsley

1 Rub some salt into each cut side of the eggplant, place on a plate and set aside for 20 minutes. Rinse off the salt and pat the eggplant dry with paper towels. Set aside.
2 Cut the red pepper into large flattish pieces. Cook, skin-side-up, under a hot grill until the skin blackens and blisters. Cool in a plastic bag, then peel and discard the seeds and membrane. Slice into strips. Reserve half for the aioli.
3 For the roasted red pepper aioli, mix the garlic, egg yolk and juice in a food processor or blender until smooth. With the motor running, pour in half the olive oil in a thin steady stream, blending until the aioli thickens. Add the reserved red pepper and blend until smooth. Transfer to a bowl and season, to taste. Stir in the parsley, cover and refrigerate.
4 Heat a grill to high. Brush the eggplant with half the oil and grill on both sides until brown and tender.
5 Heat the remaining oil in a frying pan and cook the fish for 1–2 minutes each side, or until the fish flakes when tested in the thickest part. Do not overcook or the fish will toughen.
6 To serve, place the eggplant on a plate and top with some sliced roasted pepper. Arrange 3 pieces of fish over the pepper and spoon some aioli over the top.

BELOW: Fish on eggplant with roasted red pepper aioli

SEAFOOD PLATTERS
Presentation is vital when serving seafood platters. Keep the hot and cold seafood separate. Serve with wedges of lemon or lime and the sauces of your choice.

PLANNING AND SERVING
We have suggested quantities of seafood required to assemble platters for 4 people. Most of the preparation can be done before your guests arrive. If it is a hot day, chill the platter you will be using for the cold seafood, or serve it on a bed of crushed ice. Serve the platters with bowls of tartare sauce (see page 128), sour cream mixed with sweet chilli sauce, or

soy sauce mixed with a little honey. And don't forget lime and lemon wedges, finger bowls and maybe wedges or chips.

COLD PLATTER
You will need 500 g (1 lb) cooked tiger prawns, 2 quartered cooked crabs, 12 oysters and 100 g (3½ oz) smoked salmon. If you are feeling extravagant, you could add 2 halved cooked lobsters.

HOT PLATTER
A hot platter can be very simple, using prepared, ready to cook, deep-fried calamari rings, battered fish and crumbed prawn cutlets, found in the freezer at the fishmongers or supermarket. They don't need thawing before cooking. Or, you can stun your guests by combining some of the easy dishes with your choice of the following recipes. For deep-frying, fill a

deep heavy-based saucepan one third full of oil and heat to 180°C (350°F), or until a cube of bread browns in 15 seconds. Don't cook too many pieces at once or the oil temperature will lower and the batter will be soggy. Skim crumbs from the surface as you go.

PRAWNS AND SQUID

Combine 2 cups (120 g/4 oz) Japanese breadcrumbs and 1 tablespoon chopped fresh parsley. Lightly beat 2 eggs and stir in 1 teaspoon sesame oil and 1 crushed garlic clove. Season 1 cup (125 g/4 oz) plain flour. Peel, devein and butterfly 1 kg (2 lb) raw medium prawns and cut 4 squid hoods into calamari rings. Coat the prawns and rings in the seasoned flour. Dip, in batches, into the egg, then

coat in the breadcrumbs, shaking off any excess. Lower batches of prawns into the oil and deep-fry until golden. Drain on paper towels. Repeat with the squid.

JAPANESE OYSTERS

Place 12 fresh oysters in a bamboo steamer, top with thin slivers of spring onion and a little grated fresh ginger. Drizzle with bottled teriyaki marinade. Cover and steam for 4 minutes, or until heated through.

CRISPY LEMON FISH STRIPS

Sift ½ cup (60 g/2 oz) plain flour into a bowl, make a well in the centre and whisk in ½ cup (125 ml/4 fl oz) soda water with the grated rind from 1 lemon. Cut 2 skinless snapper fillets into thin strips. Dust lightly with seasoned flour

and dip, in batches, into the batter, allowing any excess to drip off. Carefully lower into the oil and deep-fry until golden brown. Drain thoroughly on crumpled paper towels.

PROSCIUTTO-WRAPPED SCALLOPS

Rinse 16 cleaned scallops (without roe) and pat dry. Cut 4 thin slices of prosciutto into quarters, each large enough to enclose a scallop. Wrap around the scallops and thread in pairs onto small wooden skewers. Grill under a preheated grill, or on a barbecue for 5 minutes, turning a couple of times during cooking.

FROM LEFT: Cold seafood platter; Hot seafood platter

SALT-AND-PEPPER SQUID

Preparation time: 30 minutes + marinating
Total cooking time: 10 minutes
Serves 6

✷ ✷

1 kg (2 lb) squid hoods, halved lengthways

1 cup (250 ml/8 fl oz) lemon juice

2 cups (250 g/8 oz) cornflour

1¹/2 tablespoons salt

1 tablespoon ground white pepper

2 teaspoons caster sugar

4 egg whites, lightly beaten

oil, for deep-frying

lemon wedges, for serving

fresh coriander leaves, to garnish

1 Open out the squid hoods, wash and pat dry. Lay on a chopping board with the inside facing upwards. Score a fine diamond pattern on the squid, being careful not to cut all the way through. Cut into pieces about 5 x 3 cm (2 x 1¹/4 inches). Place in a flat non-metallic dish and pour the lemon juice over. Cover and refrigerate for 15 minutes. Drain and pat dry.

2 Combine the cornflour, salt, white pepper and sugar in a bowl. Dip the squid into the egg white and dust with the flour mixture, shaking off any excess.

3 Fill a deep heavy-based pan one third full of oil and heat to 180°C (350°F), or until a cube of bread dropped into the oil turns golden brown in 15 seconds. Deep-fry the squid, in batches, for 1–2 minutes, or until the squid turns white and curls. Drain on crumpled paper towels. Serve immediately, with lemon wedges and garnish with coriander leaves or sprigs.

NOTE: This recipe is great served as a starter or, if serving as a main course, cook Asian greens to accompany.

ABOVE: Salt-and-pepper squid

BACALAO CROQUETTES WITH SKORDALIA

Preparation time: 50 minutes + 8–12 hours soaking
Total cooking time: 55 minutes
Makes 24

400 g (13 oz) dried salt cod (bacalao)
300 g (10 oz) floury potatoes, unpeeled
1 small brown pickling onion, grated
2 tablespoons chopped fresh flat-leaf parsley
1 egg, lightly beaten
1/2 teaspoon cracked pepper
oil, for deep-frying

Skordalia

250 g (8 oz) floury potatoes, unpeeled
2 cloves garlic, crushed
1 tablespoon white wine vinegar
2 tablespoons olive oil

1 Put the cod in a large bowl, cover with cold water and soak for 8–12 hours, changing the water three times. This will remove the excess salt from the cod. Drain on paper towels.
2 To make the skordalia, boil or steam the potatoes until tender, remove the peel and mash in a large bowl. Cool and add the garlic, vinegar and oil. Season with salt and cracked black pepper, then mix with a fork. Set aside.
3 Put the cod in a saucepan, cover with water, bring to the boil, then reduce the heat and simmer for 15 minutes. Drain on crumpled paper towels. When cool enough to handle, remove the skin and bones from the cod and flake with your fingers into a large bowl.
4 Meanwhile, boil or steam the potatoes until tender, then peel and mash. Add to the cod with the onion, parsley, egg and pepper. Mix well with a wooden spoon to form a thick mixture. Taste, then season with salt if necessary.
5 Fill a deep heavy-based pan one third full of oil and heat to 180°C (350°F), or until a cube of bread dropped into the oil browns in 15 seconds. Drop level tablespoons of the mixture into the oil and cook in batches for 2–3 minutes, or until well browned. Drain on crumpled paper towels. Serve hot with skordalia.

BELOW: Bacalao croquettes with skordalia

SURF 'N' TURF

Preparation time: 20 minutes
Total cooking time: 15–20 minutes
Serves 4

Lemon mustard sauce

30 g (1 oz) butter
1 spring onion, finely chopped
1 clove garlic, crushed
1 tablespoon plain flour
1 cup (250 ml/8 fl oz) milk
2 tablespoons cream
1 tablespoon lemon juice
2 teaspoons Dijon mustard

1 large or 2 small raw lobster tails
2 tablespoons oil
170 g (5 1/2 oz) fresh or frozen crab meat
4 beef eye fillets (200 g/6 1/2 oz each)

1 For the sauce, melt the butter in a pan, add the onion and garlic and stir over medium heat for 1 minute, or until the onion has softened. Stir in the flour and cook for 1 minute, or until pale and foaming. Remove from the heat and gradually stir in the milk. Return to the heat and stir constantly until the sauce boils and thickens. Reduce the heat and simmer for 2 minutes. Remove from the heat and stir in the cream, lemon juice and mustard; keep warm.

2 Starting at the end where the head was, cut down each side of the lobster shell on the underside with kitchen scissors. Pull back the flap and remove the meat from the shell. Heat half the oil in a frying pan, add the lobster meat and cook over medium heat for 3 minutes each side (longer if using a large tail), or until just cooked through. Remove from the pan and keep warm. Add the crab to the pan and stir until heated through. Remove from the pan; keep warm. Wipe the pan clean.

3 Heat the remaining oil in the pan, add the steaks and cook over high heat for 2 minutes each side to seal, turning once. For rare steaks, cook each side 1 more minute. For medium and well-done steaks, reduce the heat to medium and continue cooking for 2–3 minutes each side for medium or 4–6 minutes each side for well done. To serve, place the steaks on plates. Top with crab followed by slices of lobster. Pour the sauce over the top.

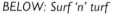

BELOW: Surf 'n' turf

CRISPY FRIED CRAB

Preparation time: 30 minutes + 1 hour freezing
+ overnight marinating
Total cooking time: 15 minutes
Serves 4 as a first course

1 kg (2 lb) fresh mud crab
1 egg, lightly beaten
1 red chilli, finely chopped
1/2 teaspoon crushed garlic
1/2 teaspoon salt
1/4 teaspoon ground white pepper
oil, for deep-frying

Seasoning mix

1/3 cup (40 g/1 1/4 oz) plain flour
1/3 cup (60 g/2 oz) rice flour
3 teaspoons caster sugar
1 teaspoon ground white pepper

1 Freeze the crab for about 1 hour until immobilized. Scrub the crab clean. Pull back the apron and remove the top shell (it should come off easily and in one piece). Remove the intestines and the grey feathery gills. Twist off the legs and claws. Using a sharp, heavy knife, chop the body into 4 pieces.

2 Crack the claws with a good hit with the back of a knife. Beat the egg with the chilli, garlic, salt and pepper in a large bowl. Put the crab pieces in the mixture, cover and refrigerate for 1 hour.

3 Sift the seasoning ingredients together onto a large plate. Dip all the crab segments in the seasoning and dust off any excess.

4 Fill a heavy-based pan one third full of oil and heat to 180°C (350°F), or until a cube of bread dropped into the oil browns in 15 seconds. Carefully cook the claws in batches for 7–8 minutes, the body portions for 3–4 minutes, and the legs for 2 minutes. Drain on crumpled paper towels before serving.

NOTE: Cook the crab just before serving. Eat it with your fingers. You will need a crab cracker to crack the claws so you can remove the flesh. Serve the crab with wedges of lemon.

ABOVE: Crispy fried crab

SALMON CUTLETS WITH FRUIT SALSA

Preparation time: 20 minutes
+ 2 hours marinating
Total cooking time: 10 minutes
Serves 4

4 salmon cutlets
1¹/2 tablespoons seasoned pepper
2 tablespoons lemon juice
¹/2 cup (125 ml/4 fl oz) lime juice
1 tablespoon chopped fresh thyme

Fruit salsa

¹/2 small pawpaw, cut into small cubes
¹/2 small pineapple, cut into small cubes
3 spring onions, chopped
1 tablespoon chopped fresh coriander
2 tablespoons lime juice
3 teaspoons caster sugar

1 Sprinkle the salmon all over with the pepper and place in a shallow non-metal dish. Combine the juices and thyme in a jug and pour over the salmon. Cover and refrigerate for 2 hours.
2 For the fruit salsa, combine the pawpaw, pineapple, spring onion, coriander, lime juice and caster sugar in a bowl. Add salt, to taste.
3 Heat a little oil in a frying pan, add the salmon and brush with any remaining marinade. Cook for 3–5 minutes each side, turning once, until the outside is lightly browned and the flesh is just cooked on the inside. Serve with the fruit salsa.
NOTES: Ocean trout can also be used to make this recipe.

Don't marinate the salmon for more than 2 hours or the citrus juices will begin to 'cook' the fish and turn the flesh opaque. If this should happen, halve the cooking time. The salsa should be made just before serving.

ABOVE: Salmon cutlets with fruit salsa

HONEY PRAWNS

Preparation time: 20 minutes
Total cooking time: 12 minutes
Serves 4

✯ ✯

16 raw large prawns
¹/₂ cup (60 g/2 oz) cornflour
1 cup (125 g/4 oz) self-raising flour
¹/₄ teaspoon lemon juice
1 tablespoon oil
3 tablespoons honey
oil, for deep-frying
3 tablespoons sesame seeds, lightly toasted

1 Peel the prawns and gently pull out the dark vein from each prawn back, starting at the head end. Pat the prawns dry with paper towels, then lightly dust, using half the cornflour.
2 Sift the flour and remaining cornflour into a bowl. Combine the juice and oil with 1 cup (250 ml/8 fl oz) water. Make a well in the flour and gradually add the liquid, beating until smooth.
3 Heat the honey in a large frying pan over very gentle heat. Remove and keep warm.
4 Fill a deep, heavy-based pan one third full of oil and heat to 180°C (350°F), or until a cube of bread browns in 15 seconds. Dip the prawns in batches in the batter and drain any excess. Using tongs or a slotted spoon, lower the prawns, a few at a time, into the hot oil. Cook for 2–3 minutes, or until the prawns are crisp and golden. Drain on crumpled paper towels and keep warm.
5 Add the cooked prawns to the warmed honey and toss gently. Transfer to a serving plate and sprinkle with sesame seeds. Serve immediately.

FRIED HERRINGS IN OATMEAL

Cut the heads off 8 fresh herrings by slicing behind the gills and fins. Cut along the bellies, remove the guts and open out flat. Grasp the bone at the tail and carefully lift out. Use tweezers to remove small bones. Pour ¹/₂ cup (125 ml/4 fl oz) milk into a bowl. Measure 1¹/₂ cups (185 g/6 oz) fine oatmeal onto a plate and season. Dip each fish in the milk, then coat in oatmeal. Heat 3 cm (1¹/₄ inches) oil in a deep frying pan to 180°C (350°F), or until a cube of bread browns in 15 seconds. Cook batches of fish for 3–5 minutes, until golden. Drain on paper towels. Serve with lemon wedges. Makes 8.

TIGER PRAWNS
Tiger prawns are very moist and flavoursome, with a firm texture. They have a spectacular bold 'tiger-like' red or brown stripe on their shells. They are available cooked or raw. Tiger prawns are caught in the wild as well as being farmed. Farming has become quite popular, as this is the only way to supply demand without depleting the oceans. Farmed tiger prawns are more distinctively marked and, once cooked, are a more brilliant colour than wild prawns, but wild prawns are usually larger.

LEFT: Honey prawns

165

FRITTO MISTO DI MARE

Preparation time: 30 minutes
Total cooking time: 12 minutes
Serves 4

★★★

1 cup (125 g/4 oz) self-raising flour
1/4 cup (30 g/1 oz) cornflour
1 tablespoon oil
8 raw large prawns
8 scallops
12 fresh sardines
500 g (1 lb) skinless white fish fillets (eg. perch, snapper, ling, John dory), cut into short strips
1 squid hood, cut into rings
plain flour, for coating
oil, for deep-frying
tartare sauce (see page 128), for serving
lemon wedges, for serving

1 Sift the flour and cornflour, with some salt and pepper, into a bowl and make a well in the centre. Combine the tablespoon of oil with 1 cup (250 ml/8 fl oz) water and gradually whisk into the flour to make a smooth lump-free batter.

2 Peel the prawns and gently pull out the dark vein from each prawn back, starting at the head end. Slice or pull off any vein, membrane or hard white muscle from the scallops.

3 To prepare the sardines, split them open down the belly, remove the gut, then clean with salted water. Cut off the head. Place skin-side-up on a work surface, flatten with the palm of your hand, then turn over and pull out the backbone with your fingers and cut at the tail with scissors.

4 Dry the prepared seafood with paper towels, then dip in flour and shake off the excess.

5 Fill a deep heavy-based pan one third full of oil and heat to 180°C (350°F), or until a cube of bread dropped into the oil browns in 15 seconds. Coat a few pieces of seafood at a time with batter and deep-fry each batch for 2–3 minutes, or until golden brown and crisp. Remove with tongs or a slotted spoon, drain on crumpled paper towels and keep warm. Serve with tartare sauce and lemon wedges.

NOTE: The seafood for this dish can be prepared several hours ahead. Cover and refrigerate.

ABOVE: Fritto misto di mare

SALMON IN NORI WITH NOODLES

Preparation time: 30 minutes
Total cooking time: 10 minutes
Serves 4

2 spring onions, cut into long thin strips

4 salmon cutlets, cut from the centre of the fish

1 sheet nori (dried seaweed)

2 teaspoons oil

250 g (8 oz) somen noodles

Dressing

1/2–3/4 teaspoon wasabi paste

2 tablespoons rice wine vinegar

2 tablespoons mirin

1 tablespoon lime juice

2 teaspoons soft brown sugar

1 tablespoon oil

2 teaspoons soy sauce

2 teaspoons black sesame seeds

1 Put the spring onion in a bowl of cold water. Remove the skin and bones from the salmon, keeping the cutlets in one piece. Cut the nori into strips, the same width as the salmon, and wrap a strip tightly around each cutlet to form a neat circle. Seal the edges with a little water. Season with salt and pepper.

2 Heat a little oil in a frying pan and cook the salmon for 2–3 minutes each side, or until cooked to your liking (ideally, it should be a little pink in the centre).

3 While the salmon is cooking, prepare the dressing and noodles. Combine the dressing ingredients in a jug and mix well.

4 Place the noodles in a large bowl, cover with boiling water and stand for 5 minutes, or until softened. Drain well. Divide the noodles among serving plates, top with salmon and drizzle with the dressing. Drain the spring onion and serve over the top.

NOTES: Ocean trout can also be used.

Sesame seeds come in various colours, ranging from cream to black. The black ones are often used as a garnish. If they are not available at your supermarket, try an Asian speciality food store.

*ABOVE: Salmon
in nori with noodles*

167

POACHED & STEAMED

There is something eminently fitting about returning seafood to its natural element for cooking, almost as if we have gone full circle and admitted that Mother Nature was right all along. Perhaps this is why poached or steamed seafood is always so successful, especially when we have enough confidence in its freshness to prepare it simply. The fish or shellfish that is simmered gently in water or a flavoured broth needs nothing more to recommend it, nothing to hide behind, no fancy cooking flavours or added extras, but its own freshness and delicate succulence.

POACHED ATLANTIC
SALMON

Stud the onions with the
cloves and add to the pan.

Place the whole, cleaned
fish in the fish kettle.

Carefully peel the skin away
from the flesh.

POACHED ATLANTIC SALMON

Preparation time: 50 minutes
Total cooking time: 1 hour
Serves 8–10

2 litres (64 fl oz) good-quality white wine

1/4 cup (60 ml/2 fl oz) white wine vinegar

2 onions

10 whole cloves

4 carrots, chopped

1 lemon, cut in quarters

2 bay leaves

4 sprigs fresh parsley

1 teaspoon whole black peppercorns

2.5 kg (5 lb) Atlantic salmon, cleaned and scaled

Dill mayonnaise

1 egg, at room temperature

1 egg yolk, at room temperature, extra

1 tablespoon lemon juice

1 teaspoon white wine vinegar

1 1/2 cups (375 ml/12 fl oz) light olive oil

1–2 tablespoons chopped fresh dill

1 Put the wine, wine vinegar and 2.5 litres (80 fl oz) water in a large heavy-based pan.
2 Stud the onions with the cloves. Add to the pan with the carrot, lemon, bay leaves, parsley and peppercorns. Bring to the boil, reduce the heat and simmer for 30–35 minutes. Cool. Strain into a fish kettle that will hold the salmon.
3 Place the whole fish in the fish kettle and cover. Bring to the boil, reduce the heat and poach gently for 10–15 minutes, until the fish flakes when tested in the thickest part. Remove from the heat and cool the fish in the liquid.
4 Process the egg, extra yolk, juice and vinegar in a food processor for 10 seconds, or until blended. With the motor running, add the oil in a thin, steady stream, blending until all the oil is added and the mayonnaise is thick and creamy—it should be thick enough to form peaks. Transfer to a bowl and stir in the dill, and salt and pepper.
5 Remove the cold fish from the liquid, place on a work surface or serving platter and peel back the skin. Serve garnished with watercress and lemon slices. Serve with the mayonnaise.
NOTES: Ocean trout, snapper, sea bass or red emperor can also be used.

You can use a baking dish big enough to hold the fish and bake the fish in a moderate 180°C (350°F/Gas 4) oven for 20–30 minutes.

*RIGHT: Poached
Atlantic salmon*

POACHED ATLANTIC SALMON CUTLETS WITH HOLLANDAISE SAUCE

Preparation time: 20 minutes
Total cooking time: 10 minutes
Serves 4

★ ★

1 cup (250 ml/8 fl oz) white wine
2 cups (500 ml/16 fl oz) fish stock
1 tablespoon lemon juice
1 large slice of onion
4 Atlantic salmon cutlets, 2.5 cm (1 inch) thick
fresh dill, to garnish

Hollandaise sauce

3 egg yolks
125 g (4 oz) butter, melted and hot
1/2 teaspoon grated lemon rind
1 tablespoon lemon juice

1 Place the wine, stock, lemon juice and onion slice in a shallow pan and bring to the boil. Reduce the heat so the liquid is just simmering.
2 Place the salmon cutlets in a single layer in the simmering stock. Poach the fish gently for about 7 minutes, or until just cooked. Remove the fish from the pan and drain on crumpled paper towels. Cover with foil to keep warm.
3 For the hollandaise sauce, process the egg yolks in a food processor for 10 seconds. With the motor running, pour hot and bubbling butter in a slow stream onto the egg. Discard any white residue. Add the lemon rind and juice and process for another 30 seconds, or until the sauce thickens. Serve immediately.
4 Arrange the fish on a serving dish. Serve with hollandaise sauce and garnish with fresh dill.
NOTE: You can use blue-eye, warehou or ocean trout cutlets if you wish. You may prefer to use a large salmon fillet or whole salmon, including the head. If using a whole salmon, it is best to skin the fish after poaching. If serving the whole salmon cold, leave in the stock until cooled. Peel away the skin when cool.

HOLLANDAISE SAUCE
This sauce was originally known as *Sauce Isigny*. It was named after a town in Normandy, France, famous for its butter. Butter production in this town ceased during the first world war and butter had to be imported from Holland. Hence the name of the sauce was altered, to indicate the source of the butter. The name was never changed back.

ABOVE: Poached Atlantic salmon cutlets with hollandaise sauce

POACHED WHOLE
SNAPPER

Trim the fins off the fish
with kitchen scissors.

After blanching the lettuce
leaves, use to wrap the fish.

Put the wrapped fish into a
deep-sided baking dish.

POACHED WHOLE SNAPPER

Preparation time: 15 minutes
Total cooking time: 40 minutes
Serves 4-6

★★

10–15 cos lettuce leaves
1.25 kg (2½ lb) whole snapper, gutted
   and scaled
2 onions, thinly sliced
1 lemon, thinly sliced
⅔ cup (170 ml/5½ fl oz) fish stock
⅔ cup (170ml/5½ fl oz) white wine
12 whole black peppercorns
1 bay leaf
155 g (5 oz) unsalted butter, chopped
1 tablespoon lime juice

1 Preheat the oven to moderate 180°C (350°F/ Gas 4). Place the lettuce in a large bowl, cover with boiling water to soften, then drain well and refresh in cold water.
2 Trim the fins off the fish with kitchen scissors. Fill the cavity of the fish with one of the sliced onions and the lemon. Wrap the fish completely in the lettuce leaves and place into a deep-sided baking dish.
3 Pour the stock and wine over the fish. Add the remaining onion, peppercorns and bay leaf to the dish, then dot the lettuce with 30 g (1 oz) of the butter. Cover tightly with foil and bake for 30 minutes, or until the flesh flakes in the thickest part when tested with a fork.
4 Remove the fish from the dish, transfer to a serving dish and keep warm. Strain the liquid into a saucepan, then boil for about 10 minutes, or until reduced by half. Remove from the heat and whisk in the remaining butter a little at a time, whisking constantly until the mixture has thickened slightly. Stir in the lime juice and season, to taste, with salt and pepper. Serve on the side.
NOTE: You can substitute red emperor, coral trout or murray cod for the snapper.

POACHED SNAPPER WITH FRESH TOMATO SAUCE

Preparation time: 20 minutes
Total cooking time: 45 minutes
Serves 4

★★

1 kg (2 lb) whole snapper, gutted and scaled
4 ripe tomatoes
1 onion, finely chopped
4 spring onions, finely sliced
2 tablespoons chopped fresh parsley
1¼ cups (315 ml/10 fl oz) fish stock
60 g (2 oz) butter
1 tablespoon plain flour

1 Preheat the oven to moderately hot 190°C (375°F/Gas 5). Wash the fish in cold water, pat dry inside and out with paper towels.
2 Score a cross in the base of each tomato. Place in a heatproof bowl and cover with boiling water. Leave for 30 seconds, then transfer to cold water. Peel, then cut each in half and remove the core. Scrape out the seeds with a teaspoon and roughly chop the flesh.
3 Lightly grease a baking dish, large enough to hold the fish, with butter. Spread half the tomato, onion and spring onion over the base. Place the fish over the top and cover with the remaining vegetables. Sprinkle with half the parsley, then pour in the stock. Dot the fish with half the butter.
4 Bake for 30 minutes, or until the fish is cooked and flakes easily when tested with a fork.
5 Carefully lift the fish out of the dish, drain well, place on a serving dish and keep warm. Transfer the cooking liquid and vegetables to a small pan. Taste and adjust the seasoning. Bring to the boil and simmer for 5 minutes, or until reduced by a quarter.
6 Make a paste with the remaining butter and the flour in a small bowl. Gradually add to the pan and simmer, whisking until the sauce has thickened. Add salt and pepper, to taste, and pour over the fish. Garnish with the remaining chopped parsley.
NOTE: You can also use red emperor, coral trout or murray cod for this recipe.

OPPOSITE PAGE:
Poached snapper with
fresh tomato sauce (top);
Poached whole snapper

ABOVE: Seafood quenelles

SEAFOOD QUENELLES

Preparation time: 30 minutes + 3 hours
  30 minutes chilling
Total cooking time: 40 minutes
Serves 4

★ ★ ★

Quenelles

200 g (6½ oz) skinless firm white fish fillets
  (eg. pike, cod, ling, monkfish)
150 g (5 oz) scallops, cleaned
150 g (5 oz) raw prawn meat
1 egg white
1 teaspoon finely grated lemon rind
½ cup (125 ml/4 fl oz) cream
3 tablespoons finely chopped fresh chives
1 litre (32 fl oz) fish stock

Tomato coulis

1 tablespoon olive oil
1 clove garlic, crushed
425 g (14 oz) can crushed tomatoes
⅔ cup (170 ml/5½ fl oz) fish stock or water
2 tablespoons cream
2 tablespoons chopped fresh chives

1 For the quenelles, pat the fish and seafood dry with paper towels. Roughly mince the fish in a food processor for 30 seconds, then process the scallops and prawns. Return all the seafood to the processor, add the egg white and lemon rind, and process for about 30 seconds, until finely minced.

2 With the motor running slowly, pour in the cream until the mixture just thickens—do not overprocess. Stir in the chives, then transfer to a bowl. Cover and refrigerate for at least 3 hours.

3 Using two wet tablespoons, mould 2 tablespoons of mixture at a time into egg shapes. Place on a baking tray lined with baking paper. Cover and refrigerate for 30 minutes.

4 For the tomato coulis, heat the oil in a pan, add the garlic and stir over medium heat for 30 seconds. Add the tomatoes, stock or water, and some salt and freshly ground black pepper. Simmer for 30 minutes, stirring occasionally, until thickened and reduced.

5 Push the tomato mixture through a fine sieve, discard the pulp and return the liquid to the cleaned pan. Add the cream and chives and reheat gently, stirring occasionally.

6 In a large frying pan, heat the fish stock until just simmering, but be careful not to allow the stock to boil. Gently lower batches of quenelles into the poaching liquid, then cover the pan, lower the heat and poach each batch for about 5–6 minutes, or until cooked through. Remove with a slotted spoon and drain on crumpled paper towels.

7 Spoon some of the tomato coulis onto each serving plate and top with the seafood quenelles.

BALMAIN BUGS WITH MANGO SAUCE

Preparation time: 10 minutes + 1 hour freezing
Total cooking time: 5 minutes
Serves 4

★★

8 large fresh Balmain bugs or 2 large raw lobster tails
1 large or 2 small mangoes
2–3 tablespoons sour cream
1/4 cup (60 ml/2 fl oz) lemon or lime juice
1 teaspoon soft brown sugar
2–3 teaspoons Thai sweet chilli sauce
1 mango, extra, for serving

1 Immobilize the bugs in the freezer for 1 hour, before cooking. Lower the bugs into a large pan of lightly salted boiling water. Simmer, uncovered, for 4–5 minutes, or until the shells have changed to orange-red. If using lobster, you will need to cook for 8–10 minutes

2 Gently separate the heads from the bodies. To remove the meat, cut down each side of the shell on the soft underside of the bugs. Using kitchen scissors, starting at the head end and working towards the tail, pull back the flap and remove the meat from the shell. Cut each piece of flesh in half lengthways, or the lobster into slices.

3 For the mango sauce, roughly chop the mango flesh and place in a food processor. Add the sour cream, juice, sugar and chilli sauce and mix for 20–30 seconds, or until smooth. Refrigerate, covered, until required. If the sauce is too thick, add a little extra cream or juice.

4 Serve the bug meat on a bed of mixed salad leaves, with extra slices of fresh mango. Drizzle with sauce and serve with the rest on the side.
NOTE: If fresh mango is unavailable for the sauce, you can use canned mango slices, or a 170 g (5½ oz) can of mango purée.

BALMAIN BUGS
Balmain bugs are available raw, frozen or cooked. When buying fresh raw Balmain bugs, look for bugs with limbs intact and tightly curled tails. Ensure there is no dark discolouration around the bellies or legs. The shells should be firm to touch and have a pleasant sea smell. Avoid any that smell 'garlicky', as that is a sign of deterioration.

LEFT: Balmain bugs with mango sauce

175

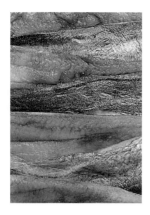

SMOKED HADDOCK

Finnan haddock, the traditional version of smoked haddock, takes its name from Finnan village in Aberdeenshire, Scotland. Originally cured over peat smoke, the heads of the fish were removed, then the fish were gutted and split down the backbones before being soaked in brine. Next, they were threaded onto spears to allow the gloss to develop before being smoked. The smoked haddock sold today is not always prepared this way and sometimes it is dyed, hence the colour variation.

CREAMY SMOKED HADDOCK

Preparation time: 12 minutes
Total cooking time: 20 minutes
Serves 4

1 large onion, thinly sliced
500 g (1 lb) smoked haddock fillets
1²/₃ cups (420 ml/13¹/₂ fl oz) milk
¹/₄ teaspoon cracked black pepper
1¹/₂ teaspoons mustard powder
20 g (³/₄ oz) butter, softened
2 teaspoons plain flour
1 spring onion, finely chopped

1 Spread the onion slices over the base of a large pan. Cut the fish into 2 cm (³/₄ inch) wide pieces and arrange over the top of the onion.
2 Combine the milk, pepper and mustard in a jug and pour over the fish. Bring slowly to the boil, then reduce the heat to low. Cover and simmer for 5 minutes. Uncover and simmer for another 5 minutes.
3 Transfer the fish to a serving dish; keep warm. Simmer the mixture in the pan for another 5 minutes, to reduce, stirring occasionally.

4 Mix the butter and flour to a smooth paste. Whisk into the boiling milk mixture a little at a time. Add the spring onion and stir over low heat until the mixture boils and thickens, then boil for 1–2 minutes. Serve over the fish.

TWEED KETTLE
(POACHED SALMON)

Preparation time: 5 minutes
Total cooking time: 13 minutes
Serves 4

1¹/₂ cups (375 ml/12 fl oz) fish stock
¹/₂ teaspoon cracked black pepper
pinch of ground nutmeg
¹/₂ cup (125 ml/4 fl oz) dry white wine
2 spring onions, finely chopped
4 tail end salmon steaks
3 tablespoons chopped fresh parsley

1 Combine the stock, pepper, nutmeg, wine, spring onion and some salt in a shallow pan and bring slowly to the boil; boil for 1 minute.
2 Place the salmon in the stock in a single layer.

RIGHT: Creamy smoked haddock

Simmer, covered, for 8–10 minutes. Transfer the salmon to serving plates. Keep warm.

3 Boil the stock for another minute. Season, to taste, then add the parsley. Spoon the liquid over the salmon and serve. Garnish with extra parsley.

NOTE: You can also use ocean trout.

SMOKED FISH WITH WHITE SAUCE

Preparation time: 15 minutes
Total cooking time: 8 minutes
Serves 6–8

White sauce

3 cups (750 ml/24 fl oz) milk
1 onion, halved
1 clove
1 bay leaf
60 g (2 oz) butter
1/3 cup (40 g/1 1/4 oz) plain flour
1–2 tablespoons chopped fresh chives or parsley

1 kg (2 lb) smoked cod or haddock fillets
1 cup (250 ml/8 fl oz) milk

1 For the white sauce, combine the milk in a small pan with the onion, clove, bay leaf and a pinch of white pepper. Heat slowly to a simmer, then remove from the heat and allow to stand for 3 minutes before straining into a jug. Melt the butter in a pan over low heat, stir in the flour and cook for 1 minute, or until pale and foaming. Remove from the heat and gradually stir in the milk.

2 Return to the heat and stir constantly until the sauce boils and thickens. Reduce the heat and simmer for 2 minutes. Remove from the heat and season, to taste, with salt and pepper. Stir in the chopped fresh chives or parsley.

3 Cut the fish fillets into serving-sized pieces and place in a large frying pan. Cover with the milk, combined with 1 cup (250 ml/8 fl oz) water. Bring to the boil, reduce the heat to low and gently cook the fish until it flakes easily at the thickest part when tested with a fork. Lift out of the pan with a slotted egg slice. Drain briefly on crumpled paper towel and place on serving plates. Top with the white sauce and garnish with snipped fresh chives.

NOTE: Smoked fish is often very salty. If you want to make it less salty, combine 1/2 cup (125 ml/4 fl oz) each of milk and water in a bowl. Add the fish and soak for several hours before cooking. Discard the soaking liquid.

ABOVE: Smoked fish with white sauce

MUSSELS WITH LEMON GRASS, BASIL AND WINE

Preparation time: 30 minutes
Total cooking time: 15 minutes
Serves 4-6

1 kg (2 lb) small black mussels
1 tablespoon oil
1 onion, chopped
4 cloves garlic, chopped
2 stems lemon grass, white part only, sliced
1–2 fresh red chillies, seeded, chopped
1 cup (250 ml/8 fl oz) white wine or water
1 tablespoon fish sauce
1 cup (50 g/1¾ oz) fresh Thai basil leaves, roughly chopped

1 Scrub the mussels with a stiff brush and pull out the hairy beards. Discard any broken mussels, or open ones that don't close when tapped on the bench. Rinse well.
2 Heat the oil in a large pan. Add the onion, garlic, lemon grass and chilli, and cook for 4 minutes over low heat, stirring occasionally.

Add the wine and fish sauce and continue to cook for 3 minutes.
3 Add the mussels to the pan and toss well. Cover, increase the heat and cook for 4–5 minutes, or until the mussels open. Discard any unopened mussels. Add the basil; toss and serve with rice.

FISH IN GINGER BROTH

Preparation time: 5 minutes
Total cooking time: 15 minutes
Serves 4

1 tablespoon oil
8 spring onions, sliced diagonally
2 tablespoons finely chopped fresh ginger
4 tablespoons fish sauce
4 tablespoons grated palm sugar or brown sugar
4 x 200 g (6½ oz) salmon or ocean trout cutlets or fillets
2 tablespoons lime juice
200 g (6½ oz) frozen baby green peas
fresh coriander leaves, to garnish

ABOVE: Mussels with lemon grass, basil and wine

1 Heat the oil in a large frying pan, add the spring onion and ginger and cook over low heat for 2 minutes, stirring occasionally. Add the fish sauce, sugar and 1.5 litres (48 fl oz) water and bring to the boil. Reduce the heat, add the fish and poach gently for 3–4 minutes, or until the fish is just cooked and flakes easily when tested with a fork. Lift the fish out with a slotted egg slice and put in a warm shallow bowl. Cover with foil to keep warm.

2 Bring the liquid in the pan to the boil, reduce the heat and simmer until reduced by half. Add the lime juice.

3 Cook the baby peas in a pan of boiling water until tender.

4 For serving, put the fish on plates and ladle the broth over the top. Serve with the peas. Garnish the dish with the coriander leaves.

STEAMED FISH CUTLETS WITH GINGER AND CHILLI

Preparation time: 15 minutes
Total cooking time: 10 minutes
Serves 4

4 medium-sized firm white fish cutlets
  (eg. snapper, jewfish, blue-eye, cod)
5 cm (2 inch) piece fresh ginger, shredded
2 cloves garlic, chopped
2 teaspoons chopped fresh red chillies
2 tablespoons chopped fresh coriander stalks
3 spring onions, cut into fine short shreds
2 tablespoons lime juice

1 Line a bamboo steamer basket with banana leaves or baking paper to prevent sticking.

2 Arrange the fish in the basket and top with the ginger, garlic, chilli and coriander stalks. Cover and steam over a wok or pan of boiling water for 8–10 minutes. Sprinkle the spring onion and lime juice over the fish. Cover and steam for 30 seconds, or until the fish flakes easily. Serve.

STEAMING FISH

To prepare for steaming fish, fill a wok or large pan about one third full of water. Before you bring the water to the boil, stand the steamer over the water to check that you have the correct amount. The base of the steamer should not touch the water. If you have too much water, it will boil up into the food. If you have too little, it will boil dry. When the water is boiling, place the steamer with the food in it over the top, cover the wok or pan and maintain the heat so that the water continues to boil rapidly. Be careful when you lift the lid, that you don't get a blast of steam.

LEFT: Steamed fish cutlets with ginger and chilli

179

YUM CHA
A samosa or won ton press saves time and makes sealing wrappers around filling much easier. The presses are available from supermarkets or speciality kitchen stores.

STUFFED CHINESE MUSHROOMS WITH SCALLOPS
Soak 16 Chinese dried mushrooms in boiling water for 30 minutes. Drain and put in a saucepan with 1½ cups (375 ml/ 12 fl oz) water, 2 tablespoons mirin, 2 tablespoons soy sauce and a 5 cm (2 inch) piece roughly chopped fresh ginger. Simmer for 20 minutes. Cool. Discard the stems. Clean 16 scallops and place one in the centre of each mushroom.

Cut a 3 cm (1¼ inch) piece fresh ginger, a spring onion and seeded red chilli into thin strips. Sprinkle over the scallops with 2 teaspoons chopped lemon grass. Steam batches in a bamboo steamer over a large pan of simmering water for 3–5 minutes, or until the scallops are tender. Mix 1 tablespoon each of sweet sherry and oyster sauce with ½ teaspoon each of sesame oil and caster sugar. Drizzle over the scallops. Makes 16.

SEAFOOD POTSTICKERS
Combine 250 g (8 oz) each of chopped scallops and chopped raw prawn meat, 2 finely chopped spring onions, 3 tablespoons roughly chopped water chestnuts, 1 teaspoon sesame oil and 1 tablespoon each of soy sauce and Chinese rice wine. Place 1 tablespoon of the mixture into the centre of a won ton wrapper, brush the edges lightly with water and pleat the edges together with a

samosa or won ton press. Heat 1 tablespoon oil in a frying pan and fry 10 dumplings for 3 minutes, or until golden brown. Add ½ cup (125 ml/4 fl oz) fish stock to the pan, cover and cook for 5 minutes. Uncover and boil until the stock evaporates and the dumplings are crisp. Repeat with the remaining potstickers. Makes 30.

SALMON AND CHILLI PARCELS

Mix 250 g (8 oz) finely chopped, skinless, boneless salmon fillet with 1 chopped spring onion, 3 teaspoons sweet chilli sauce, 1 tablespoon lime juice, 60 g (2 oz) blanched finely chopped baby spinach, 2 tablespoons chopped garlic chives and 1 egg white. Season. Place a teaspoonful onto the centre of a gow gee wrapper, moisten the

edges with water and pleat together to seal, using a samosa or won ton press. Repeat to use all the filling. Steam in batches on a bamboo steamer over a large pan of simmering water for 5–10 minutes, or until cooked. Makes 24.

STEAMED OR DEEP-FRIED PRAWN WON TONS

Soak 15 g (½ oz) sliced dried Chinese mushrooms in boiling water for 5 minutes. Drain and chop finely. Combine with 1 tablespoon each of sake and grated fresh ginger, 1 teaspoon of sesame oil and 2 teaspoons sweet chilli sauce. Peel and devein 24 raw prawns, leaving the tails intact. Cut the prawns in half and set aside the tail sections. Finely chop the remaining prawns and add to the mushrooms. Put a heaped teaspoon of the

mixture in the centre of a gow gee wrapper. Place a prawn tail in the centre, standing up. Brush the edges of the wrapper with water and gather up to form a parcel, leaving the prawn tail exposed. Repeat to make 24. Steam batches in a lightly oiled bamboo steamer for 5 minutes, or until cooked. To make a dipping sauce, stir together ¼ cup (60 ml/2 fl oz) soy sauce, 1 tablespoon each of fish sauce and lime juice and ¼ cup (60 ml/2 fl oz) sweet chilli sauce. These may also be deep-fried. Makes 24.

FROM LEFT: Stuffed Chinese mushrooms with scallops; Seafood potstickers; Salmon and chilli parcels; Steamed or deep-fried prawn won tons

STEAMED SHELLS IN WINE AND GARLIC

Preparation time: 25 minutes + 1 hour soaking
Total cooking time: 5 minutes
Serves 4

1 kg (2 lb) pipis
60 g (2 oz) butter, softened
2 cloves garlic, crushed
2 tablespoons chopped fresh dill
2 tablespoons chopped fresh chives
1 teaspoon chopped fresh thyme leaves
2 tablespoons toasted pine nuts
1/4 teaspoon cracked black pepper
1 small ripe tomato
1/2 cup (125 ml/4 fl oz) white wine
1 small onion, finely chopped

BELOW: Steamed shells in wine and garlic

1 Soak the pipis for 1 hour to remove any sand. Discard any open pipis that do not close when tapped on the bench.
2 Beat the butter and garlic in a bowl with a wooden spoon until well combined and light in colour. Beat in the herbs, pine nuts and pepper.
3 Cut a cross in the base of the tomato. Place the tomato in a heatproof bowl and cover with boiling water. Leave for 30 seconds, plunge into cold water, then peel away from the cross. Remove the core and finely chop the flesh.
4 Place the wine, onion and 1/2 cup (125 ml/4 fl oz) water in a large saucepan and bring to the boil. Add the pipis, cover and cook over high heat, shaking the pan occasionally, for 3–5 minutes, or until the pipis have opened.
5 Add the herb and garlic butter and the tomato to the pan and stir well until the butter has melted. Spoon into serving bowls and serve immediately with lots of crusty bread to soak up the juices. Discard any unopened pipis.

SCALLOP TIMBALES WITH OYSTER CREAM SAUCE

Preparation time: 20 minutes
Total cooking time: 35 minutes
Serves 6

★ ★

400 g (13 oz) scallops
200 g (6¹/₂ oz) skinless white fish fillets
  (eg. snapper, bream, pike, flathead)
2 egg whites
1 teaspoon grated lemon rind
³/₄ cup (185 ml/6 fl oz) cream

Oyster cream sauce

15 g (¹/₂ oz) butter
¹/₂ carrot, very finely diced
¹/₂ stick celery, very finely diced
2 spring onions, finely chopped
1 bay leaf
¹/₄ cup (60 ml/2 fl oz) white wine
¹/₂ cup (125 ml/4 fl oz) fish stock
¹/₂ cup (125 ml/4 fl oz) cream
1 teaspoon butter
1 teaspoon flour
18 fresh oysters, removed from the shells
2 tablespoons sour cream
1 teaspoon chopped fresh dill

1 Slice or pull off any vein, membrane or hard white mussel from the scallops. Process the scallops and fish in a food processor until smooth. Add the egg whites, rind and salt and white pepper, and process until combined. Pour in the cream and process quickly until only just combined. Do not overprocess or the mixture will curdle. To test for seasoning, poach a small amount of mixture in simmering water.
2 Preheat the oven to warm 170°C (325°F/ Gas 3). Lightly oil six ¹/₂ cup (125 ml/4 fl oz) capacity timbales. Spoon the scallop mixture into each mould, tapping firmly on a work surface to remove any air bubbles, then cover the tops loosely with lightly greased foil. Place in a baking tray and add boiling water to come halfway up the sides of the moulds. Bake for 15–20 minutes, or until cooked through. A knife inserted into the centre of the scallop mixture should come out clean.
3 While the timbales are cooking, prepare the oyster cream sauce. Melt the butter in a small saucepan, add the vegetables and bay leaf and stir for 5 minutes, until softened but not brown. Add the wine and simmer for 1 minute. Add the fish stock and cream, bring to the boil, reduce the heat and simmer for 5 minutes. Blend the butter and flour into a paste, add to the pan and whisk until the sauce boils and thickens. Stir in the oysters and any of their juices, the sour cream, dill and salt and cracked black pepper, to taste.
4 Drain off any liquid and turn the moulds out onto serving plates. Spoon some of the sauce over each timbale.

ABOVE: Scallop timbales with oyster cream sauce

183

INDIAN STEAMED FISH

Trim off the fins and tail with scissors.

Make several deep cuts through the thickest part of the fish on both sides.

OPPOSITE PAGE: Red emperor poached in coconut milk

INDIAN STEAMED FISH

Preparation time: 20 minutes
Total cooking time: 20 minutes
Serves 2–4

500 g (1 lb) whole white-fleshed fish (eg. bream, ocean perch, whiting, snapper), cleaned, scaled
15 g (1/2 oz) toasted almonds
2 bay leaves
1/2 green pepper (capsicum), sliced
1 tablespoon oil
1 1/4 cups (315 g/10 oz) natural yoghurt
1/2 teaspoon garam masala
1/2 teaspoon sugar

1 Wash the fish and pat dry inside and out with paper towels. Trim off the fins and tail with scissors. Make several deep diagonal cuts through the thickest part of the flesh on both sides, then place in a steamer lined with banana leaves or baking paper.
2 Combine the remaining ingredients and spoon over the fish. Steam the fish over a saucepan of simmering water for 20 minutes, or until the fish flakes easily when tested with a fork.

RED EMPEROR POACHED IN COCONUT MILK

Preparation time: 20 minutes
Total cooking time: 30–40 minutes
Serves 4

1 litre (32 fl oz) coconut milk
2 teaspoons grated fresh ginger
3 small red chillies, finely chopped
1 tablespoon chopped coriander roots and stems
6 Asian shallots, finely chopped
6 kaffir lime leaves, shredded
2 stems lemon grass, white part only, sliced
2 teaspoons grated lime rind
2 cups (500 ml/16 fl oz) fish stock
1/3 cup (80 ml/2 3/4 fl oz) fish sauce
1/3 cup (80 ml/2 3/4 fl oz) lime juice, strained
4 x 250 g (8 oz) red emperor fillets, skin on
coriander leaves, to garnish
1 small red chilli, cut in long strips, to garnish
2 kaffir lime leaves, shredded, to garnish

1 Bring the coconut milk to the boil in a saucepan and boil for 3 minutes. Add the ginger, chilli, coriander roots and stems, shallots, kaffir lime leaves, lemon grass and lime rind and bring back to the boil. Add the fish stock and fish sauce and simmer for 15 minutes. Pass through a fine strainer and add the lime juice. Taste and add extra fish sauce if necessary.
2 Heat the sauce in a wide-based frying pan and when it comes to the boil add the fish, then reduce the heat and simmer very gently for 10–15 minutes, or until just cooked through.
3 Carefully transfer the fish to a serving platter. Serve with some of the liquid and a sprinkling of coriander, chilli and shreds of kaffir lime leaf.
NOTE: You can also use coral trout, snapper or murray cod.

POACHED FILLETS IN DILL SAUCE

Preparation time: 15 minutes
Total cooking time: 20 minutes
Serves 4

500 g (1 lb) skinless fish fillets (eg. groper, ocean perch, snapper, blue-eye)
1 onion, sliced
1 small bay leaf
1 tablespoon butter
1 tablespoon plain flour
1/2 cup (125 ml/4 fl oz) sour cream
2 tablespoons chopped fresh dill

1 Remove any bones from the fish. Combine 2 1/2 cups (625 ml/20 fl oz) water with the onion and bay leaf in a large frying pan. Bring to the boil and reduce the heat to low. Add the fish and poach over gentle heat for 5 minutes, or until cooked and the fish flakes easily when tested with a fork. Remove the fish with a fish slice and keep warm on a serving dish.
2 Strain the cooking liquid and reserve 1 cup (250 ml/8 fl oz). Melt the butter in a small pan over low heat. Stir in the flour and cook for 1 minute, or until pale and foaming. Remove from the heat and gradually stir in the reserved stock. Return to the heat and stir until the sauce boils and thickens. Reduce the heat and simmer for 2 minutes. Remove from the heat and stir in the sour cream and dill. Add salt and white pepper. Serve the sauce over fish, with extra dill.

JAPANESE-STYLE SALMON PARCELS

Cut the celery sticks into short lengths, then cut into thin strips.

Arrange celery and spring onion strips, then ginger slices, on top of the fish.

Wrap the salmon in baking paper, tightly folding the sides to seal in the juices.

JAPANESE-STYLE SALMON PARCELS

Preparation time: 40 minutes
Total cooking time: 20 minutes
Serves 4

2 teaspoons sesame seeds

4 x 150 g (5 oz) salmon cutlets or fillets

2.5 cm (1 inch) piece fresh ginger

2 sticks celery

4 spring onions

1/4 teaspoon dashi granules

1/4 cup (60 ml/2 fl oz) mirin

2 tablespoons tamari

1 Cut baking paper into four squares large enough to enclose the salmon steaks. Preheat the oven to very hot 230°C (450°F/Gas 8). Stir the sesame seeds over low heat in a small pan until lightly browned, then remove from the pan.

2 Wash the salmon and pat dry with paper towels. Place a salmon cutlet in the centre of each paper square.

3 Cut the ginger into paper-thin slices. Slice the celery and spring onions into long thin strips. Arrange a bundle of the prepared strips and several slices of ginger on each salmon steak.

4 Combine the dashi granules, mirin and tamari in a small saucepan. Stir gently over low heat until the granules dissolve. Drizzle over each parcel, sprinkle with sesame seeds and carefully wrap the salmon, folding in the sides to seal in all the juices. Arrange the parcels in a bamboo steamer over a pan of simmering water and steam for about 15 minutes. (The paper will puff up when the fish is cooked.) Serve immediately with boiled rice.

NOTES: You can use ocean trout as a substitute for this recipe.

Dashi, mirin and tamari are all available from Japanese food stores.

ABOVE: Japanese-style salmon parcels

STEAMED SCALLOPS

Preparation time: 20 minutes
Total cooking time: 10 minutes
Serves 4

1 small red pepper (capsicum)
90 g (3 oz) butter
1 tablespoon chopped fresh chives
2 teaspoons Dijon mustard
1/4 teaspoon cracked black pepper
2 teaspoons lime juice
24 scallops on the shell
6 spring onions, cut into long thin strips

1 Cut the red pepper into quarters and remove the seeds and membrane. Cook, skin-side-up, under a hot grill until the skin blackens and blisters. Cool in a plastic bag, then peel. Purée the flesh until smooth.
2 Beat the butter in a small bowl until light, then beat in the chives, mustard, pepper, lime juice and red pepper purée. Set aside.
3 Remove the scallops and slice or pull off any vein, membrane or hard white mussel from each. Place a few strips of spring onion over each shell and top with the scallop. Place the scallops in a single layer in a bamboo or metal steamer. Place over a large pan of simmering water and steam in batches for 2–3 minutes. Transfer to a warmed serving platter while cooking the remaining scallops. Top with a dollop of butter. The butter will melt from the heat of the scallops. Serve.

STEAMED PRAWN ROLLS

Unroll 4 fresh rice noodle rolls (available from Asian supermarkets in packs of 4–6, they roll out into a long sheet) and use a sharp knife to cut each in half. Peel and devein 24 raw prawns. Place 3 prawns, a sprinkle of finely chopped fresh ginger and garlic and some strips of spring onion and shredded Chinese broccoli leaves on one long edge. Fold in the ends and roll up like a spring roll. Line a bamboo steamer with baking paper and steam 3–4 rolls over simmering water for 7–10 minutes, or until the prawns are pink and cooked through. Cover with foil while cooking the remaining rolls. Serve with a bowl of light soy sauce for dipping. Serves 4.

BELOW: Steamed scallops

STEAMED TROUT WITH LIME BUTTER

Preparation time: 15 minutes
Total cooking time: 15 minutes
Serves 2

Lime butter

90 g (3 oz) butter, softened
1 teaspoon finely grated lime rind
1 tablespoon lime juice

2 small fresh rainbow trout, washed
    and dried
4 tablespoons lime juice
pinch of mixed dried herbs (thyme,
    rosemary, marjoram and oregano)

1 Put the butter in a small bowl and beat with a wooden spoon until smooth. Add the lime rind and juice and beat together thoroughly. Transfer to a serving bowl and set aside until needed.

2 Cut two 30 cm (12 inch) squares (depending on the size of the fish) of foil and grease lightly. Place a trout on each piece of foil and spoon 1 teaspoon of lime butter inside each fish. Sprinkle some lime juice over both the fish, then sprinkle with herbs (see Note below) and some black pepper. Wrap the foil around the trout to enclose. Place in a bamboo or metal steamer over a pan of simmering water and steam for about 15 minutes, or until the fish flakes easily when tested with a fork. Serve with the remaining lime butter. Lime wedges can also be served with the fish.

NOTES: This recipe is equally delicious made with baby salmon or ocean trout steaks or cutlets. Follow the same preparation and dollop the fish with the butter. Wrap firmly in foil and steam for 15 minutes.

If fresh herbs are available, you can substitute, using twice the quantity of fresh herbs as dried.

BELOW: Steamed trout with lime butter

POACHED FLOUNDER FILLETS WITH WINE AND OYSTER SAUCE

Preparation time: 10 minutes
Total cooking time: 15 minutes
Serves 4

2 teaspoons butter
1 French shallot, finely chopped
1/2 cup (125 ml/4 fl oz) sparkling wine
1 tablespoon white wine vinegar
1/2 cup (125 ml/4 fl oz) fish stock
1 teaspoon sugar
150 g (5 oz) unsalted butter, chopped, extra
2 teaspoons chopped fresh dill
2 bay leaves
whole black peppercorns
4 x 150 g (5 oz) flounder fillets
12 fresh oysters
lemon wedges, for serving

1 Melt the butter in a small saucepan and cook the shallot over medium heat for 1 minute, or until softened. Add the sparkling wine, vinegar and fish stock and bring to the boil. Reduce the heat and simmer until the liquid has reduced to 3 tablespoons. Stir in the sugar, then remove from the heat.

2 Whisk in the extra butter until it has melted and the sauce has thickened slightly. Add the chopped dill and salt and pepper, to taste. Keep warm while you cook the fish.

3 Put 2 1/2 cups (600 ml/20 fl oz) water, the bay leaves and peppercorns in a frying pan large enough to fit the fillets. Bring to the boil, reduce the heat and add the fillets. Simmer for about 3 minutes, or until the fish flakes easily when tested with a fork.

4 Just before serving, place the oysters in the wine sauce to heat through. Serve the fish on serving plates with wine and oyster sauce spooned over the top and a wedge of lemon on the side.

NOTE: You can make this recipe using sole, plaice or John dory instead of flounder.

BELOW: Poached flounder fillets with wine and oyster sauce

189

ABOVE: Sole veronique

SOLE VERONIQUE

Preparation time: 45 minutes
Total cooking time: 20 minutes
Serves 4

12 sole fillets or 3 whole sole, filleted
   and skinned
1 cup (250 ml/8 fl oz) fish stock
1/4 cup (60 ml/2 fl oz) white wine
1 French shallot, thinly sliced
1 bay leaf
6 black peppercorns
2 sprigs fresh parsley
3 teaspoons butter
3 teaspoons flour
1/2 cup (125 ml/4 fl oz) milk
1/4 cup (60 ml/2 fl oz) cream
125 g (4 oz) seedless white grapes,
   peeled

1 Preheat the oven to moderate 180°C (350°F/ Gas 4). Roll the fillets into coils with the skin side on the inside. Secure the coils with toothpicks and place side-by-side in a well-greased shallow ovenproof dish.
2 Combine the stock, wine, shallot, bay leaf, peppercorns and parsley in a jug and pour over the fish. Cover with greased foil and bake for 15 minutes, or until the fish flakes when tested with a fork. Carefully lift the rolls out of the liquid with a slotted spoon and transfer to another dish. Cover and keep warm.
3 Pour the cooking liquid into a saucepan and boil for about 2 minutes, or until reduced by half, then strain through a fine strainer.
4 In a clean pan, melt the butter, add the flour and stir for 1 minute, or until pale and foaming. Remove from the heat and gradually stir in the combined milk, cream and reduced cooking liquid. Return to the heat and stir until the mixture boils and thickens. Season, to taste, add the grapes, then stir until heated through. Serve the sauce over the fish.
NOTE: You can substitute flounder for the sole.

GEFILTE FISH

Preparation time: 5 minutes
Total cooking time: 1 hour 35 minutes
Serves 4

 ✿ ✿

1 kg (2 lb) firm white fish fillets (eg. cod, redfish, pike, haddock), with skin and bones

2 sticks celery, chopped

2 onions, chopped

2 carrots, sliced

1 tablespoon chopped fresh parsley

2 tablespoons ground almonds

2 eggs, beaten

matzo meal (see Note)

1 Remove the skin and bones from the fish and place the skin and bones in a large pan with the celery, half the onion and half the carrot. Add 3 cups (750 ml/24 fl oz) water, bring to the boil and simmer for 20 minutes. Strain the stock.

2 Chop the fish roughly and combine in a food processor with the remaining onion and parsley. Process until fine, add the ground almonds, eggs, a little salt and pepper and sufficient matzo meal to bind. The amount of matzo meal will vary according to the texture of the fish. Roll the mixture into 8 balls with floured hands.

3 Simmer the remaining sliced carrot in the fish stock for 10 minutes, then remove. Add the fish balls to the stock, cover and simmer gently for 1 hour. Remove the fish balls with a slotted spoon and place on a serving plate. Top each with a slice of carrot.

4 Strain the fish stock and spoon a little over each fish ball.

NOTES: Matzo meal (pictured in margin) is finely crushed unleavened crispbreads that are made from flour and water. It is available in some supermarkets.

The remaining stock can be chilled until set to a jelly. Chop the jelly and use to garnish the fish balls if you like.

GEFILTE FISH

This famous Jewish dish is traditionally served as a first course at meals on the Sabbath and holidays. *Gefilte* means stuffed. Originally, chopped freshwater fish was made into a forcemeat and used to stuff the empty skin of a pike or carp. In some places, such as Poland, the dish was made with a distinctly sweet flavour. The recipe has evolved and the forcemeat is now made into fish balls poached in fish stock. In many places, saltwater fish is now used instead of the freshwater fish.

LEFT: Gefilte fish

GRILLS & BARBECUES

For seafood lovers, the barbecue is a fabulous opportunity to indulge. From spicy Thai flavours to citrus marinades, juicy fish steaks and aromatic lemon grass skewers, seafood can hold its own on the barbecue and beat the rest hands down. Quicker to cook than a steak and a million times more exciting than sausages, fresh fish is the perfect companion for the quick and ready heat of the grill or hotplate. For the lucky fisherman, or woman, cooking the catch over an open fire is the most perfect ending to a day. The rest of us can visit the fishmonger, fire up the grill and talk about the one that got away.

BARBECUED ASIAN-STYLE PRAWNS

Preparation time: 10 minutes + 3 hours marinating
Total cooking time: 5 minutes
Serves 4

500 g (1 lb) large raw prawns

Marinade

2 tablespoons lemon juice

2 tablespoons sesame oil

2 cloves garlic, crushed

2 teaspoons grated fresh ginger

1 Peel the prawns, leaving the tails intact. Gently pull out the dark vein from each prawn back, starting at the head end. Make a cut along the back of each prawn, slicing three-quarters of the way through the flesh.
2 Mix the lemon juice, sesame oil, garlic and ginger in a bowl. Add the prawns and gently stir to coat the prawns. Cover and refrigerate for at least 3 hours.
3 Heat the barbecue. Cook the prawns on a hot, lightly greased barbecue plate for 3–5 minutes, or until pink and cooked through. Brush frequently with marinade while cooking. Serve immediately.
NOTES: Alternatively the prawns can be threaded onto bamboo skewers. Soak the skewers in cold water for about 30 minutes, or until they sink. This will prevent the skewers burning during cooking. After marinating, thread the prawns evenly onto the skewers and cook as stated, turning and basting occasionally during cooking.

This recipe is also nice using both scallops and prawns, halving the quantity of prawns.

The amount of garlic can be altered, according to taste. For a stronger flavour, double the quantity of garlic and omit the ginger. For a spicy dish, substitute 2 finely chopped fresh chillies for the garlic.

RIGHT: Barbecued Asian-style prawns

CITRUS FISH WITH AVOCADO SALSA

Preparation time: 25 minutes + 5 minutes
    marinating
Total cooking time: 10 minutes
Serves 4

4 firm fish cutlets (eg. snapper, salmon, jewfish,
    blue-eye), about 185 g (6 oz) each
3 teaspoons finely grated orange rind
3 teaspoons finely grated lemon rind
1 tablespoon lime juice
2 tablespoons olive oil

Avocado salsa

1 small fresh red chilli
1½ teaspoons ground cumin
1 large avocado, finely chopped
1 red onion, very finely chopped
2 teaspoons lemon juice
2 teaspoons olive oil

1 Place the fish in a shallow, non-metallic dish. Combine the orange and lemon rind, lime juice and olive oil in a small bowl and season with freshly ground black pepper. Pour over the fish and set aside to marinate for about 5 minutes.
2 Lightly oil a preheated chargrill pan or barbecue and cook the fish for 3–5 minutes on each side, or until lightly browned and cooked through. The fish will flake easily when tested with a fork.
3 For the avocado salsa, discard the seeds from the chilli and finely chop the flesh. Fry the cumin in a dry frying pan for about 40 seconds, shaking the pan constantly until fragrant. Combine the cumin with the avocado, onion, chilli, lemon juice and olive oil in a bowl.
4 Serve the fish steaks with the avocado salsa. The fish is delicious served with grilled halved cherry tomatoes, steamed snow peas (mangetout) and steamed baby potatoes.
NOTE: Prepare the avocado salsa close to serving time so the avocado doesn't discolour. If you would like your salsa a bit hotter, leave the seeds in the chilli.

LIMES
Limes grow in tropical and sub-tropical regions and can be used instead of lemons in many dishes. Use less than you would lemon because limes have a more sour taste. Choose firm limes that are heavy for their size and have unmottled skin.

LEFT: Citrus fish with avocado salsa

1 Sprinkle the fish fillets with the lemon pepper and place in a shallow non-metallic dish. Mix the dill with the lemon juice, then pour over the fish, cover and refrigerate for several hours.
2 Heat the barbecue and cook the fish on a hot lightly greased barbecue flatplate for 2–3 minutes each side, or until the flesh flakes easily when tested with a fork.
3 For the lemon butter sauce, simmer the lemon juice in a small pan until reduced by half. Stir in the cream. Remove from the heat and whisk in the butter a little at a time until all the butter has melted. Stir in the chives.
4 Serve the fish with the lemon butter sauce poured over the top. The fish can be garnished with fresh dill sprigs and perhaps served with barbecued citrus slices and fresh bread.

CHILLI PEPPER YABBIES

Preparation time: 10 minutes + 1 hour marinating
Total cooking time: 15 minutes
Serves 6

12 raw yabbies or scampi
2 fresh red chillies, seeded and chopped
1/2 cup (125 ml/4 fl oz) tomato passata
2 cloves garlic, crushed
6 spring onions, thinly sliced
2 tablespoons chopped fresh basil
3 teaspoons cracked black pepper

1 Fill a large bowl with plenty of ice, some water and a pinch of salt. Submerge the live yabbies for 20–30 minutes. Remove and make a small slit on the underside of each tail, to allow the flesh to absorb the marinade.
2 For the marinade, combine the chopped chilli, tomato passata, garlic, spring onion, fresh basil and cracked pepper in a large bowl and mix well. Add the yabbies, cover and refrigerate for 1 hour.
3 Heat a chargrill pan or barbecue plate and cook the yabbies, with their marinade, for 10–15 minutes, or until the flesh is just tender. Delicious served with a crisp leafy salad. Provide your guests with crab/lobster crackers (or nutcrackers) and finger bowls.
NOTE: Bottled passata, from supermarkets, is cooked, finely chopped tomato and onion.

DILL FISH WITH LEMON BUTTER SAUCE

Preparation time: 10 minutes + 3 hours marinating
Total cooking time: 10 minutes
Serves 4

4 skinless fish fillets (eg. perch, snapper, jewfish, red mullet, ocean trout, John dory)
1 1/2 tablespoons lemon pepper
1–2 tablespoons chopped fresh dill
1/3 cup (80 ml/2 3/4 fl oz) lemon juice

Lemon butter sauce

2 tablespoons lemon juice
1/2 cup (125 ml/4 fl oz) cream
40 g (1 1/4 oz) butter, chopped
2 tablespoons chopped fresh chives

ABOVE: Dill fish with lemon butter sauce

SWEET AND SOUR FISH KEBABS

Preparation time: 20 minutes + 3 hours marinating
Total cooking time: 10 minutes
Makes 12 skewers

★

750 g (1 1/2 lb) skinless thick fish fillets
(eg. ling, cod, blue-eye, striped marlin)
225 g (7 oz) can pineapple pieces
1 large red pepper (capsicum)
3 teaspoons soy sauce
1 1/2 tablespoons soft brown sugar
2 tablespoons white vinegar
2 tablespoons tomato sauce

1 Soak 12 wooden skewers in cold water for 30 minutes, or until they sink. This is to ensure they don't burn during cooking.

2 Meanwhile, cut the fish into 2.5 cm (1 inch) cubes. Drain the pineapple, reserving 2 tablespoons of liquid. Cut the pepper into 2.5 cm (1 inch) pieces. Thread the pepper, fish and pineapple alternately onto skewers.

3 Place the kebabs in a shallow non-metallic dish. Combine the soy sauce, reserved pineapple juice, sugar, vinegar and tomato sauce in a small bowl. Mix well and pour over the kebabs. Cover and refrigerate for 3 hours.

4 Preheat the barbecue. Barbecue the kebabs on a lightly greased barbecue, brushing frequently with the marinade, for 2–3 minutes each side, or until just cooked through. Serve immediately with cooked noodles and a dressed green salad.

NOTE: Do not marinate the kebabs for more than 3 hours or the vinegar in the marinade will start to 'cook' the fish. This method of cooking the fish with acid, vinegar or lemon/lime juice is used in many recipes.

COD

Saltwater fish (such as cod and tuna) have larger and heavier bone structures than freshwater fish (such as trout), making the bones easier to see and lift out. This makes cod a popular fish among those who are finicky about picking lots of tiny bones out of their food. Cod has lean, white, firm meat with a low oil content. Fish oil is now recognised as being high in Omega-3, which has many beneficial properties for humans. The oil in lean fish is stored in the liver rather than the flesh—hence the fact that a spoonful of cod liver oil can do you a power of good.

LEFT: Sweet and sour fish kebabs

HONEYED PRAWN AND SCALLOP SKEWERS

Preparation time: 15 minutes + 3 hours marinating
Total cooking time: 5 minutes
Makes 8

500 g (1 lb) raw medium prawns
250 g (8 oz) scallops

Marinade

1/4 cup (60 ml/2 fl oz) honey
2 tablespoons soy sauce
1/4 cup (60 ml/2 fl oz) bottled barbecue sauce
2 tablespoons sweet sherry

1 Soak 8 wooden skewers in water for 30 minutes, or until they sink. This will ensure they don't burn during cooking.
2 Meanwhile, peel the prawns, leaving the tails intact. Gently pull out the dark vein from each prawn back, starting at the head end.
3 Slice or pull off any vein, membrane or hard white muscle from the scallops, leaving any roe attached.
4 Thread the prawns and scallops alternately onto the skewers (about 2 prawns and 3 scallops per skewer). Place in a shallow non-metallic dish. Combine the honey, soy sauce, barbecue sauce and sherry in a jug and pour over the skewers. Cover and marinate in the refrigerator for 3 hours, or overnight.
5 Preheat the barbecue. Cook the skewers on a lightly greased barbecue flatplate, turning several times, for 5 minutes, or until cooked through. Brush frequently with marinade while cooking.
NOTE: You can substitute cubes of firm-fleshed fish for the prawns or scallops.

PRAWNS WITH LIME AND SWEET CHILLI

Remove the heads from 24 raw large prawns, cut in half lengthways and devein. Combine 2 crushed garlic cloves, 2 tablespoons sweet chilli sauce, 2 tablespoons lime juice and 1 tablespoon olive oil. Add the prawns and toss well to coat. Cover and refrigerate for 30 minutes. Remove the prawns and barbecue or grill until cooked through, brushing with some of the remaining marinade. Makes 48.

FISH PATTIES

Preparation time: 25 minutes + 15 minutes chilling
Total cooking time: 10 minutes
Makes 8–10

750 g (1 1/2 lb) skinless firm fish fillets (eg. flake, haddock, cod, pike), cut into cubes
1 cup (80 g/2 3/4 oz) stale white breadcrumbs
3 spring onions, chopped
1/4 cup (60 ml/2 fl oz) lemon juice
2 teaspoons seasoned pepper
1 tablespoon chopped fresh dill
2 tablespoons chopped fresh parsley
90 g (3 oz) Cheddar, grated
1 egg
plain flour, for dusting

Herbed mayonnaise

1/2 cup (125 g/4 oz) good-quality mayonnaise
1 tablespoon chopped fresh parsley
1 tablespoon chopped fresh chives
2 teaspoons drained, bottled capers, chopped

1 Heat the barbecue. Process the fish in a food processor for 20–30 seconds, until smooth. Transfer to a large bowl.
2 Add the breadcrumbs, spring onion, juice, pepper, herbs, cheese and egg to the fish. Mix well, divide into 8–10 portions and shape into round patties. Place on a tray and refrigerate for 15 minutes, or until firm.
3 Toss the patties in flour and shake off any excess. Cook on a hot lightly greased barbecue flatplate for 2–3 minutes each side, until browned and cooked through.
4 For the herbed mayonnaise, combine the mayonnaise, herbs and capers in a small bowl and mix well.
5 Serve the hot patties with the herbed mayonnaise and a salad.
NOTE: These fish patties can be prepared up to 3 hours ahead and stored, covered, in the refrigerator. Cook just before serving.

CAPERS
These are the unopened buds of a bush native to the Mediterranean region. Picked while still firm, they are pickled or salted and used as a flavouring, especially in sauces, as well as a garnish. Salted capers should be rinsed before you use them.

OPPOSITE PAGE: Honeyed prawn and scallop skewers (top); Fish patties

GARLIC SQUID WITH PARMESAN

Preparation time: 30 minutes + 10 minutes marinating
Total cooking time: 5 minutes
Serves 2–4

350 g (11 oz) squid hoods
4 cloves garlic, chopped
2 tablespoons olive oil
2 tablespoons finely chopped fresh parsley
1 large tomato
25 g ($^3/_4$ oz) Parmesan, grated

1 Cut the squid hoods in half lengthways, wash and pat dry. Score a shallow lattice pattern all over the fleshy side of the squid, taking care not to cut right through. Lay them flat, with the fleshy side facing upwards, and cut into rectangles, about 6 x 2.5 cm (2½ x 1 inch).
2 Mix the garlic, oil, half the parsley, and salt and pepper, in a bowl. Add the squid and refrigerate for at least 10 minutes.
3 Score a cross in the base of the tomato. Place in a heatproof bowl, cover with boiling water for 30 seconds, then transfer to a bowl of cold water. Drain and peel away from the cross. Scoop out the seeds with a teaspoon, then chop the flesh.
4 Heat a lightly oiled chargrill pan or barbecue hotplate until very hot. Cook the squid in 2 batches, tossing regularly, until the squid curls and turns white. Add the chopped tomato and toss through to just heat.
5 Arrange the squid on a plate and scatter the grated Parmesan and remaining parsley over the top.

FISH KEBABS WITH CORN SALSA

Soak 8 bamboo skewers in cold water for 30 minutes. Combine $^1/_2$ cup (125 ml/4 fl oz) lemon juice, 1 tablespoon each of chopped fresh parsley and coriander with a crushed garlic clove in a bowl. Mix half in a bowl with 500 g (1 lb) cubed firm-fleshed fish (hake or salmon). Thread onto skewers and barbecue on an oiled flatplate, turning once or twice, for 5 minutes, or until tender. Drain a 270 g (9 oz) can corn kernels and mix with a diced avocado and tomato, 2 sliced spring onions and remaining lemon mixture. Serve with the fish. Serves 4.

BELOW: Garlic squid with Parmesan

GLAZED GRILLED FISH FILLETS

Preparation time: 10 minutes + 1 hour
  marinating
Total cooking time: 8 minutes
Serves 4

2 tablespoons olive oil
2 tablespoons lemon juice
2 tablespoons fruit chutney
1 tablespoon honey
1 tablespoon chopped fresh coriander
2 cloves garlic, crushed
4 firm-fleshed white fish fillets
    (eg. snapper, flounder, John dory,
    bream, leatherjacket)

1 Combine the olive oil, lemon juice, fruit
chutney, honey, fresh coriander and garlic in
a small bowl.
2 Place the fish fillets in a flat non-metallic dish
and pour the oil mixture over the fish. Cover
and refrigerate for 1 hour.
3 Preheat the grill to high and place the fish
fillets on a lightly oiled grill tray. Cook the fish
fillets, brushing with the remaining marinade
occasionally, for about 4–6 minutes each side,
or until the flesh flakes easily when tested with
a fork.

BARBECUED SALMON CUTLETS WITH SWEET CUCUMBER DRESSING

Preparation time: 15 minutes
Total cooking time: 5 minutes
Serves 4

2 small Lebanese cucumbers, peeled, seeded
    and finely diced
1 red onion, finely chopped
1 fresh red chilli, finely chopped
2 tablespoons pickled ginger, shredded
2 tablespoons rice wine vinegar
1/2 teaspoon sesame oil
4 salmon cutlets
1 sheet toasted nori (dried seaweed), cut into
    thin strips

1 Combine the cucumber, onion, chilli, ginger,
rice wine vinegar and sesame oil in a medium
bowl, cover and stand at room temperature
while cooking the salmon.
2 Preheat a barbecue flatplate and lightly brush
with oil. Cook the salmon on the barbecue for
about 2 minutes on each side, or until cooked as
desired. Be careful you do not overcook the fish
or it will be dry—it should be still just pink in the
centre. Serve the salmon topped with the
cucumber dressing. Sprinkle the top with strips
of toasted nori.
NOTES: Ocean trout cutlets can also be used in
this recipe.
    An easy way to cut the nori into thin strips is
to cut it with clean, dry scissors.

*ABOVE: Glazed grilled
fish fillets*

BARRAMUNDI

Barramundi is considered one of the finest eating fish in Australia. As an estuarine fish, it is found in bays and tidal lakes, harbours, lagoons and large rivers. It is such a popular catch among holiday anglers in northern Australia that some now pay huge amounts of money to be taken by helicopter to inaccessible regions where barramundi can be found. The name is aboriginal, meaning 'river fish with large scales'.

ABOVE: Piri piri prawns

PIRI PIRI PRAWNS

Preparation time: 20 minutes + 3 hours marinating
Total cooking time: 10 minutes
Serves 4

6 tablespoons oil
2 teaspoons dried chilli flakes, or 1–2 red bird's eye chillies, finely chopped
4 large cloves garlic, crushed
1 teaspoon salt
1 kg (2 lb) raw medium prawns
75 g (2 1/2 oz) butter
1/4 cup (60 ml/2 fl oz) lemon juice

1 Place the oil, chilli flakes, garlic and salt in a large glass bowl and mix well. Peel the prawns, leaving the tails intact. Gently pull the dark vein from each prawn back, starting at the head end. Stir into the chilli mixture, cover and refrigerate for 3 hours, stirring and turning occasionally.
2 Preheat the grill to very hot. Place the prawns in a single layer on a baking tray and brush with any of the remaining oil and chilli mixture. Grill for about 5 minutes, or until tender.

3 Meanwhile, melt the butter with the lemon juice in a small pan and pour into a serving jug. Serve the prawns hot, drizzled with lemon butter.

BARRAMUNDI KEBABS

Preparation time: 20 minutes + 1 hour marinating
Total cooking time: 30 minutes
Serves 4

Marinade

2 tablespoons oil
large pinch of dried thyme
large pinch of dried marjoram
1/2 cup (125 ml/4 fl oz) lemon juice
2 bay leaves
1 teaspoon chopped fresh parsley

8 pickling onions, peeled
500 g (1 lb) skinless barramundi fillets, cut into 2.5 cm (1 inch) cubes
12 button mushrooms
1 red pepper (capsicum), cut into squares

1 Combine all the ingredients for the marinade in a shallow non-metallic dish.

2 Add the onions to a small pan of boiling water and simmer for 15 minutes. Thread the fish onto skewers, alternately with the onions, mushrooms and red pepper. Put the kebabs in the marinade, toss to coat the fish, then cover and refrigerate for 1 hour, turning often.

3 Preheat the grill to high. Grill the kebabs for 10–15 minutes, turning once or twice.

BARBECUED FISH WITH ONIONS AND GINGER

Preparation time: 25 minutes + 20 minutes
  marinating
Total cooking time: 25 minutes
Serves 4-6

1 kg (2 lb) small, firm, white-fleshed whole fish
  (eg. red emperor, bream, snapper),
  cleaned and scaled

2 teaspoons drained, bottled green
  peppercorns, finely crushed

2 teaspoons chopped red chillies

3 teaspoons fish sauce

3 tablespoons oil

2 onions, finely sliced

4 cm (1 1/2 inch) piece fresh ginger, thinly sliced

3 cloves garlic, cut into very thin slivers

2 teaspoons sugar

4 spring onions, finely shredded

Lemon and garlic dipping sauce

1/4 cup (60 ml/2 fl oz) lemon juice

2 tablespoons fish sauce

1 tablespoon sugar

2 small fresh red chillies, finely chopped

3 cloves garlic, chopped

1 Wash the fish and pat dry inside and out. Cut 2 or 3 diagonal slashes into the thickest part on both sides. In a food processor, process the peppercorns, chillies and fish sauce to a paste and brush over the fish. Refrigerate for 20 minutes.

2 Heat a grill or barbecue hotplate until very hot and brush with 1 tablespoon of oil. Cook the fish for 8 minutes each side, or until the flesh flakes easily. If grilling, don't cook too close to the heat.

3 While the fish is cooking, heat the remaining oil in a pan and stir the onion over medium heat, until golden. Add the ginger, garlic and sugar and cook for 3 minutes. Serve over the fish. Sprinkle with spring onion.

4 Stir all the dipping sauce ingredients in a bowl until the sugar has dissolved. Serve with the fish.

*BELOW: Barbecued fish
with onions and ginger*

MARINADES & BASTES

Add a little extra zest to your barbecued seafood by using one of these tangy

marinades or spicy bastes.

SPICED YOGHURT MARINADE
(For firm-fleshed skinless fish fillets—
snapper, bream, ocean perch, flake.)
Combine 400 g (13 oz) natural yoghurt,
1 tablespoon each of grated fresh ginger,
ground cumin, ground cinnamon,
ground coriander and ground mace, add
1–2 tablespoons each of grated lime rind
and juice and 2 tablespoons chopped
fresh mint. Add 1 kg (2 lb) fish fillets,

cover and refrigerate for 3 hours. Cook
on a preheated barbecue hotplate until
tender. Serves 4–6.

**SWEET AND SPICY
BASTING SAUCE**
(For yabbies, bugs and scampi.)
Combine 1 cup (250 ml/8 fl oz) sweet
chilli sauce, 2 crushed cloves garlic,
1–2 tablespoons lemon juice, 1 tablespoon

peanut oil, 50 g (1¾ oz) melted butter
and 2 tablespoons chopped fresh coriander
in a large jug. Toss 1 kg (2 lb) yabby, bug
or scampi meat in 1 tablespoon oil and
cook in batches on a preheated barbecue
hotplate, turning and basting frequently
with the sauce. Serve with any leftover
sauce. Serves 4–6.

LIME AND PEPPERCORN MARINADE

(For prawns, fish steaks and cutlets—tuna, swordfish, blue-eye, salmon.)

Stir-fry 1 cup (60 g/2 oz) Szechwan or black peppercorns in a wok until fragrant. Transfer to a mortar and pestle or spice grinder, add 4 chopped Asian shallots and crush together. Transfer to a shallow glass dish and add ⅓ cup (80 ml/2¾ fl oz) lime juice, 1 tablespoon salt, 1 teaspoon sesame oil and ¼ cup (60 ml/2 fl oz) peanut oil. Add 1 kg (2 lb) firm white fish fillets or 1 kg (2 lb) peeled, deveined prawns with tails intact. Cover; chill for 3 hours. Cook on a preheated barbecue hotplate in batches until the seafood is cooked through. If you are using tuna or salmon, don't overcook it or it will be dry. Serves 4–6.

GARLIC MARINADE

(For prawns and fish.)

Combine 6 crushed cloves garlic, 1 cup (250 ml/8 fl oz) extra virgin olive oil, 1 tablespoon lemon juice and chopped fresh dill in a shallow dish. Add 1 kg (2 lb) cubed firm white fish or 1 kg (2 lb) peeled, deveined prawns. Coat in the marinade, cover and chill overnight. Return to room temperature, thread onto skewers and cook on a hot barbecue grill or hotplate until cooked through. Serves 4–6.

THAI MARINADE

(For octopus.)

Combine ½ cup (125 ml/4 fl oz) fish sauce, 4 finely shredded kaffir lime leaves, 2–3 tablespoons grated palm sugar or brown sugar, juice and rind of 2 limes and 1 teaspoon sesame oil. Add 1 kg (2 lb) cleaned octopus and marinate overnight. Drain well. Cook over very high heat on a barbecue grill, turning frequently, for 3 minutes or until cooked. Serves 4–6.

TEXAN BARBECUE BASTING SAUCE

(For all shellfish.)

Combine 1 cup (250 ml/8 fl oz) tomato sauce, 6 splashes of Tabasco, 3 chopped rehydrated chipotle chillies, 1 tablespoon each of vinegar and oil in a bowl. Use to baste while cooking 1 kg (2 lb) prawns, bugs or yabbies. Serves 4–6.

CLOKWISE, FROM TOP LEFT: Spiced yoghurt marinade; Lime and peppercorn marinade; Thai marinade; Texan barbecue basting sauce; Garlic marinade; Sweet and spicy basting sauce

TUNA STEAKS WITH TAPENADE

Preparation time: 15 minutes + 10 minutes marinating
Total cooking time: 6 minutes
Serves 4

2 tablespoons tapenade (olive paste)
2 tablespoons olive oil
2 cloves garlic, finely chopped
2 teaspoons finely grated lemon rind
4 tuna steaks
spring onion, diagonally sliced, to garnish

1 Combine the tapenade, oil, garlic, lemon rind and some black pepper. Spread over both sides of the tuna and refrigerate for 10 minutes.
2 Place the tuna on a heated and lightly oiled chargrill pan, barbecue grill or flatplate and cook, turning once, for about 3 minutes each side. When cooked, the steak should still be pink in the centre. Sprinkle with the slices of spring onion.
NOTE: Instead of tuna, you can use swordfish, kingfish, warehou or blue-eye.

SPICY FISH KEBABS

Preparation time: 15 minutes + 1 hour marinating
Total cooking time: 5–6 minutes
Serves 6

1 kg (2 lb) skinless firm fish fillets
   (eg. swordfish, blue-eye, striped marlin)
2 cloves garlic, crushed
2/3 cup (170 g/5 1/2 oz) natural yoghurt
1 teaspoon chopped fresh ginger
1 fresh red chilli, finely chopped
2 teaspoons garam masala
1 tablespoon chopped fresh coriander

1 Soak 12 wooden skewers for 30 minutes, to prevent them burning during cooking. Cut the fish into 3 cm (1 1/4 inch) cubes.
2 Mix the garlic, yoghurt, ginger, chilli, garam masala and coriander in a small bowl.
3 Thread the fish onto skewers and place in a shallow dish. Spoon the marinade over the fish, cover and marinate in the refrigerator for 1 hour.
4 Preheat the grill or barbecue to high. Grill or barbecue the skewers for 5–6 minutes, turning occasionally. The fish is cooked when it flakes easily when tested with a fork. Delicious served with bread and green salad.

RIGHT: Tuna steaks with tapenade

ROSEMARY TUNA KEBABS

Preparation time: 20 minutes
Total cooking time: 20 minutes
Serves 4

3 tomatoes
1 tablespoon olive oil
2–3 small fresh red chillies, seeded and chopped
3–4 cloves garlic, crushed
1 red onion, finely chopped
1/4 cup (60 ml/2 fl oz) white wine or water
2 x 300 g (10 oz) cans chickpeas
3 tablespoons chopped fresh oregano
4 tablespoons chopped fresh parsley
lemon wedges, for serving

Tuna kebabs

1 kg (2 lb) tuna fillet, cut into 4 cm (1 1/2 inch)
   cubes
8 stalks of fresh rosemary, about 20 cm (8 inch)
   long, with leaves
cooking oil spray

1 Cut the tomatoes into halves or quarters and use a teaspoon to scrape out the seeds. Roughly chop the flesh.
2 Heat the oil in a large non-stick frying pan. Add the chilli, garlic and red onion and stir over medium heat for 5 minutes, or until softened. Add the chopped tomato and the white wine or water. Cook over low heat for 10 minutes, or until the mixture is soft and pulpy and most of the liquid has evaporated.
3 Stir in the rinsed chickpeas with the fresh oregano and parsley. Season with salt and pepper, to taste.
4 Heat a grill or barbecue plate. Thread the tuna onto the rosemary stalks, lightly spray with oil, then cook, turning, for 3 minutes. Do not overcook or the tuna will be dry and fall apart. Serve with the chickpeas and lemon wedges.
NOTE: Swordfish, striped marlin or salmon are also suitable for this recipe.

ABOVE: Rosemary tuna kebabs

LOBSTER THERMIDOR

Use a sharp knife to cut the lobster in half lengthways through the shell.

Pull the meat out of the shell and wash the head and shell halves.

Cut the lobster meat into bite-sized pieces after patting dry.

Place the prepared lobster under the grill until lightly browned.

OPPOSITE PAGE:
Lobster thermidor (top);
Lobster mornay

LOBSTER THERMIDOR

Preparation time: 25 minutes
Total cooking time: 5–10 minutes
Serves 2

 ✳ ✳

1 cooked medium lobster
80 g (2³/₄ oz) butter
4 spring onions, finely chopped
2 tablespoons plain flour
¹/₂ teaspoon dry mustard
2 tablespoons white wine or sherry
1 cup (250 ml/8 fl oz) milk
¹/₄ cup (60 ml/2 fl oz) cream
1 tablespoon chopped fresh parsley
60 g (2 oz) Gruyère cheese, grated

1 Using a sharp knife, cut the lobster in half lengthways through the shell. Lift the meat from the tail and body. Remove the cream-coloured vein and soft body matter and discard. Cut the meat into 2 cm (³/₄ inch) pieces, cover and refrigerate. Wash the head and shell halves, then drain and pat dry.
2 In a frying pan, heat 60 g (2 oz) of the butter, add the spring onion and stir for 2 minutes. Stir in the flour and mustard and cook for 1 minute, or until pale and foaming. Remove from the heat and gradually stir in the wine and milk. Return to the heat and stir constantly until the mixture boils and thickens. Reduce the heat and simmer for 1 minute. Stir in the cream, parsley and lobster meat, then season with salt and pepper, to taste. Stir over low heat until the lobster is heated through.
3 Heat the grill. Spoon the mixture into the lobster shells, sprinkle with cheese and dot with the remaining butter. Place under the grill for 2 minutes, or until lightly browned. Serve with mixed salad leaves and lemon slices.

LOBSTER MORNAY

Preparation time: 25 minutes + 15 minutes
  standing
Total cooking time: 5–10 minutes
Serves 2

✳ ✳

1 cooked medium lobster
1¹/₄ cups (315 ml/10 fl oz) milk
1 slice of onion
1 bay leaf
6 black peppercorns
30 g (1 oz) butter
2 tablespoons plain flour
2 tablespoons cream
pinch of nutmeg
60 g (2 oz) Cheddar, grated
pinch of paprika, to garnish

1 Using a sharp knife, cut the lobster in half lengthways through the shell. Lift the meat from the tail and body. Remove the cream-coloured vein and soft body matter and discard. Cut the meat into 2 cm (³/₄ inch) pieces, cover and refrigerate. Wash the head and shell halves, then drain and pat dry. Set aside.
2 Heat the milk, onion, bay leaf and peppercorns in a small pan. Bring to the boil. Remove from the heat, cover and leave for 15 minutes. Strain.
3 Melt the butter in a large pan, stir in the flour and cook for 1 minute, or until pale and foaming. Remove from the heat and gradually stir in the milk. Return to the heat and stir constantly until the mixture boils and thickens. Reduce the heat and simmer for 1 minute. Stir in the cream. Season with the nutmeg and salt and pepper, to taste.
4 Fold the lobster meat through the sauce. Stir over low heat until the lobster is heated through. Spoon the mixture into the shells and sprinkle with cheese. Heat the grill and place the lobster under the grill for 2 minutes, or until the cheese is melted. Sprinkle with paprika. Can be served with thick potato chips.

FISH WITH RICE STUFFING

Preparation time: 20 minutes
Total cooking time: 12–15 minutes
Serves 4

8 large garfish or whiting, scaled and cleaned
2 teaspoons oil
1 small onion, finely chopped
1 clove garlic, crushed
1 tomato, finely chopped
1 tablespoon tomato paste (tomato purée)
1/4 green pepper (capsicum), finely chopped
3/4 cup (140 g/4 1/2 oz) cold cooked rice
2 teaspoons soy sauce

1 Wash the fish thoroughly and pat dry inside and out with paper towels.
2 Heat the oil in a pan, add the onion and garlic and stir over medium heat for 2–3 minutes. Add the tomato, tomato paste, green pepper, rice and soy sauce and stir over medium heat for 2 minutes. Transfer to a bowl and cool slightly.
3 Heat the grill to high. Fill the cavity of each fish with the stuffing and secure with toothpicks. Grill on a greased baking tray for 3–4 minutes each side, or until the fish is cooked and flakes easily. Remove the toothpicks before serving.
NOTE: You will need to cook 1/4 cup (55 g/ 2 oz) raw white rice for this recipe.

CHARGRILLED SCALLOPS WITH LIME HOLLANDAISE

Preparation time: 20 minutes
Total cooking time: 15 minutes
Serves 4-6

500 g (1 lb) scallops
2 tablespoons olive oil
2 teaspoons cracked black pepper

Lime hollandaise

185 g (6 oz) butter
3 egg yolks
2 teaspoons finely grated lime rind
1 tablespoon lime juice

ABOVE: Fish with rice stuffing

1 Soak twelve wooden skewers in water for 30 minutes, or until they sink, to prevent them burning during cooking.

2 Meanwhile, slice or pull off any vein, membrane or hard white muscle from the scallops, leaving any roe attached. Thread onto the skewers. Drizzle with the oil, sprinkle with pepper and refrigerate until required.

3 For the lime hollandaise, melt the butter in a small saucepan over low heat, without stirring. Allow to cool slightly. Skim the foam from the surface, then pour off the clear yellow liquid, being careful to leave the milky sediment behind in the pan. Discard the sediment. Place the egg yolks and 3 tablespoons water in a heatproof bowl and whisk to combine. Place the bowl over a pan of simmering water and whisk for about 3 minutes, until the egg mixture is thick. Remove the bowl from the heat and gradually and slowly whisk in the butter. Stir in the lime rind and juice, a few drops at a time, until the mixture starts to thicken. Add salt and pepper, to taste.

4 Preheat a grill or barbecue and cook the scallops until browned all over and just cooked through. Be careful not to overcook or the scallops will go rubbery. Serve with lime hollandaise on the side.

RED MULLET IN CORN HUSKS

Preparation time: 10 minutes
Total cooking time: 5–6 minutes
Serves 6

6 small red mullet, cleaned and scaled
12 sprigs fresh lemon thyme
1 lemon, sliced
2 cloves garlic, sliced
12 large corn husks
olive oil
cracked black pepper

1 Wash the fish and pat dry inside and out with paper towels. Fill each fish cavity with thyme, lemon and garlic, then place each in a corn husk. Drizzle with oil and sprinkle with pepper, then top each fish with another husk. Tie each end of the husks with string to enclose.

2 Place on coals or on a barbecue and cook, turning once, for 6–8 minutes, or until the fish is cooked and flakes easily when tested with a fork.
NOTE: You can also use redfish to make this recipe.

BELOW: Red mullet in corn husks

LEMON AND HERB RAINBOW TROUT

Preparation time: 20 minutes
Total cooking time: 15 minutes
Serves 4

3 tablespoons chopped fresh dill
2 tablespoons chopped fresh rosemary
4 tablespoons coarsely chopped fresh
  flat-leaf parsley
2 teaspoons fresh thyme leaves
1 1/2 tablespoons crushed green peppercorns

BELOW: Lemon and herb rainbow trout

1/3 cup (80 ml/2 3/4 fl oz) lemon juice
1 lemon
4 whole fresh rainbow trout
1/3 cup (80 ml/2 3/4 fl oz) dry white wine
1 lime, sliced, to garnish

Horseradish cream

1 tablespoon horseradish cream
1/2 cup (125 g/4 oz) sour cream
2 tablespoons cream

Lemon sauce

150 g (5 oz) butter
2 egg yolks
3–4 tablespoons lemon juice

1 Prepare and heat the barbecue. Cut 8 sheets of foil large enough to wrap the fish. Place 4 on top of the others, so you'll have double thickness, and lightly grease the top ones.
2 Mix the herbs, peppercorns, juice and salt and pepper, to taste, in a bowl. Cut the lemon into slices and put some in each fish cavity. Wipe any slime off the fish with paper towel. Spoon the herb mixture into the fish cavities.
3 Place each fish on the foil and sprinkle each with 1 tablespoon of wine. Fold the foil to form parcels. Cook on the barbecue for 10–15 minutes, or until the fish is just cooked through. (Test for doneness. The fish will flake easily when tested with a fork.) Leave the wrapped fish for 5 minutes, then serve with horseradish cream and lemon sauce.
4 For the horseradish cream, mix the creams in a bowl and season with salt and pepper, to taste.
5 For the lemon sauce, melt the butter in a small saucepan over low heat, without stirring. Skim the foam off the surface and pour off the clear yellow liquid, leaving the milky sediment behind. Discard the sediment. Blend the egg yolks in a food processor for 20 seconds. With the motor running, add the butter slowly in a thin, steady stream. Continue processing until all the butter has been added and the mixture is thick and creamy. Add the juice and season with salt and pepper. Garnish the fish with lime slices and perhaps some strips of chives.
NOTE: If small trout are unavailable, choose baby salmon or Atlantic salmon steaks. They have a similar oily flesh and flavour to the trout. Place the salmon on a bed of the lemon slices and spread the herb mixture over the top, or cut a slit through the centre of the steak and fill with the lemon and herb mixture. Cook as above.

OCEAN TROUT WITH LEEK AND CAPER SAUCE

Preparation time: 10 minutes
Total cooking time: 10 minutes
Serves 4

45 g (1½ oz) butter, melted
4 thick skinless ocean trout fillets (about 150 g/
    5 oz each)

Leek and caper sauce

50 g (1¾ oz) butter
1 leek, white part only, chopped
1 cup (250 ml/8 fl oz) white wine
2 tablespoons bottled capers, drained
1 tablespoon chopped fresh flat-leaf parsley

1 Brush a baking tray with melted butter, put the trout on the tray and brush with melted butter. Grill under moderate heat, without turning, until the fish is just cooked and flakes easily when tested with a fork. Remove and cover loosely with foil to keep warm.

2 For the sauce, melt the butter in a small pan over low heat and cook the leek until soft, but not brown. Add the wine and simmer for 3–4 minutes. Stir in the capers and parsley and salt and pepper, to taste.

3 Spoon the hot sauce over the fish and serve immediately with steamed baby potatoes.

NOTE: You can use salmon fillets or cutlets or any thick white fish instead of trout.

TANDOORI FISH SKEWERS

Soak wooden skewers in cold water for 30 minutes. Combine 1 cup (250 g/8 oz) natural yoghurt, 2 crushed cloves garlic and 2 teaspoons each of ground turmeric, garam masala and grated fresh ginger in a bowl. Transfer to a shallow rectangular dish. Cut 500 g (1 lb) firm white fish (ling, shark or hake), into 3 cm (1¼ inch) cubes, and a red pepper (capsicum) and 1 onion into the same size. Thread alternately onto skewers. Add to the marinade and coat. Cover and chill for 1 hour. Heat a barbecue or grill. Cook the fish for 5–10 minutes, turning, until browned and cooked. Serves 4–6.

ABOVE: Ocean trout with leek and caper sauce

INTERNATIONAL BARBECUED SHELL PLATTER

Preparation time: 40 minutes + 1 hour freezing
Total cooking time: 30 minutes
Serves 6

6 raw Balmain bugs
30 g (1 oz) butter, melted
1 tablespoon oil
12 black mussels
12 scallops on their shells
12 oysters
18 raw large prawns, unpeeled

Salsa verde, for scallops

1 tablespoon finely chopped preserved lemon
  (see Note)
1 cup (20 g/³/₄ oz) fresh parsley leaves
1 tablespoon drained bottled capers
1 tablespoon lemon juice
3 tablespoons oil, approximately

Vinegar and shallot dressing, for mussels

¹/₄ cup (60 ml/2 fl oz) white wine vinegar
4 French shallots, finely chopped
1 tablespoon chopped fresh chervil

Pickled ginger and wasabi sauce, for oysters

1 teaspoon soy sauce
¹/₄ cup (60 ml/2 fl oz) mirin
2 tablespoons rice wine vinegar
¹/₄ teaspoon wasabi paste
2 tablespoons finely sliced pickled ginger

Sweet balsamic dressing, for Balmain bugs

1 tablespoon olive oil
1 tablespoon honey
¹/₂ cup (125 ml/4 fl oz) balsamic vinegar

Thai coriander sauce, for prawns

¹/₂ cup (125 ml/4 fl oz) sweet chilli sauce
1 tablespoon lime juice
2 tablespoons chopped fresh coriander

1 Freeze the bugs for 1 hour to immobilize. Cut each bug in half with a sharp knife, then brush the flesh with the combined butter and oil. Set aside while you prepare the rest of the seafood.
2 Scrub the mussels with a stiff brush and pull out the hairy beards. Discard any broken mussels, or open ones that don't close when tapped on the bench. Rinse well.
3 Slice or pull off any vein, membrane or hard white muscle from the scallops, leaving any roe attached. Brush the scallops with the combined butter and oil.
4 Remove the oysters from the shells, then rinse the shells under cold water. Pat the shells dry and return the oysters to their shells. Cover and refrigerate all the seafood while you make the dressings.
5 For the salsa verde, combine all the ingredients in a food processor and process in short bursts until roughly chopped. Transfer to a bowl and add enough oil to moisten the mixture. Season with salt and pepper. Serve a small dollop on each cooked scallop.
6 For the vinegar and shallot dressing, whisk the vinegar, shallots and chervil in a bowl until combined. Pour over the cooked mussels.
7 For the pickled ginger and wasabi sauce, whisk all the ingredients in a bowl until combined. Spoon over the cooked oysters.
8 For the sweet balsamic dressing, heat the oil in a pan, add the honey and vinegar and bring to the boil, then boil until reduced by half. Drizzle over the cooked bugs.
9 For the Thai coriander sauce, combine all the ingredients in a jug or bowl and drizzle over the cooked prawns.
10 Cook the seafood in batches on a preheated barbecue grill and flatplate. If necessary, do this in batches, depending on the size of your barbecue. The Balmain bugs will take the longest time to cook, about 5 minutes—they are cooked when the flesh turns white and starts to come away from the shells. The mussels, scallops, oysters and prawns all take about 2–5 minutes to cook.

NOTES: To prepare the preserved lemon, remove the flesh and discard. Wash the skin to remove excess salt and then chop finely.

Mirin, rice wine vinegar and pickled ginger are all available from Asian food speciality stores.

OYSTERS
Oysters are sold freshly shucked on the half shell, in bottles of salted water, or alive and unshucked. Shucked oysters are also sold canned, dried and frozen. When buying fresh shucked oysters, look for a plump moist oyster. The flesh should be creamy with a clear liquid (oyster liquor) surrounding it. Oysters should smell like the fresh sea and have no traces of shell particles. If you prefer to shuck them yourself, look for tightly closed, unbroken shells.

OPPOSITE PAGE:
International barbecued shell platter

BALMAIN BUGS WITH
LIME AND CORIANDER
BUTTER

Spoon the lime and
coriander butter onto a
piece of foil.

Wrap the butter, roll into a
log shape and twist the
ends tightly.

BALMAIN BUGS WITH LIME AND CORIANDER BUTTER

Preparation time: 10 minutes + refrigeration
Total cooking time: 5–6 minutes
Serves 4-6

90 g (3 oz) butter, softened
2 teaspoons finely grated lime rind
2 tablespoons lime juice
3 tablespoons chopped fresh coriander
1 teaspoon cracked black pepper
1 kg (2 lb) raw Balmain bugs
3 cloves garlic, crushed
2 tablespoons oil

1 Mix the butter, lime rind and juice, coriander and pepper in a bowl. Put in the centre of a piece of foil and roll into a log shape. Twist the ends tightly, then refrigerate until firm.
2 Fill a large bowl with plenty of ice, some water and a pinch of salt. Submerge the live Balmain bugs for 20–30 minutes.
3 Heat the barbecue. Place the bugs, garlic and oil on the barbecue plate and toss for 5–6 minutes, or until the bugs turn deep orange and the flesh turns white and starts to come away from the shell. Cut the butter into rounds and serve on the hot bugs.

CRUMBED FISH

Heat the grill. Place 4 skinless John dory, snapper, leatherjacket, whiting or flounder fillets, on a lightly oiled baking tray and grill for 3–4 minutes, or until nearly cooked. Mix 1 cup (80 g/2¾ oz) fresh breadcrumbs, 2 chopped hard-boiled eggs, 2 chopped spring onions, 50 g (1¾ oz) melted butter and 1 tablespoon chopped fresh parsley in a bowl. Season, to taste. Sprinkle some of the mixture over each fish fillet, pressing on lightly. Grill for 1–2 minutes, or until cooked through and lightly golden. Serves 4.

RIGHT: Balmain bugs with lime and coriander butter

BARBECUED PRAWNS WITH SWEET CUCUMBER VINEGAR

Preparation time: 30 minutes
Total cooking time: 5 minutes
Serves 4

1/4 cup (60 ml/2 fl oz) white wine vinegar
1/3 cup (90 g/3 oz) caster sugar
2 tablespoons lime juice
2 tablespoons fish sauce
1 long red chilli, seeded, thinly sliced
1 long green chilli, seeded, thinly sliced
2 spring onions, diagonally sliced
1 Lebanese cucumber, peeled, halved, seeded and thinly sliced
2 tablespoons chopped fresh coriander
24 raw prawns

1 Combine the white wine vinegar and caster sugar in a pan and bring to the boil. Stir, remove from the heat and cool. Stir in the lime juice, fish sauce, chilli, spring onion, cucumber and coriander.
2 Cook the unpeeled prawns on a chargrill or barbecue plate over medium heat for 1–2 minutes each side, or until pink and cooked through. Pour the sauce over the prawns.
NOTE: You can also use yabbies for this recipe. They will take a little longer to cook.

HERBED SCAMPI WITH SWEET CIDER SAUCE

Preparation time: 15 minutes + 1 hour freezing
  + 1 hour marinating
Total cooking time: 5–10 minutes
Serves 4

12 raw scampi or Balmain bugs
1/4 cup (60 ml/2 fl oz) olive oil
1/2 cup (125 ml/4 fl oz) lemon juice
2 cloves garlic, crushed
5 tablespoons finely chopped fresh flat-leaf parsley
2 tablespoons finely chopped fresh dill
1/4 cup (60 ml/2 fl oz) apple cider
30 g (1 oz) butter

1 Freeze live bugs for 1 hour to immobilize, then cut bugs or scampi in half lengthways. Place in a single layer in a shallow non-metallic dish. Combine the olive oil, lemon juice, garlic, parsley and dill, and pour over the seafood. Cover and refrigerate for at least 1 hour.
2 Cook the seafood on a chargrill or barbecue plate, shell-side-down, for 2 minutes. Turn and cook for another 2 minutes, or until tender. (Bugs may take longer to cook.) Transfer to a serving platter.
3 Simmer the apple cider in a small saucepan until reduced by two thirds. Reduce the heat and add the butter, stirring until melted. Remove from the heat, pour over the scampi and serve.

ABOVE: Barbecued prawns with sweet cucumber vinegar

BARBECUED SQUID

Gently pull the tentacles away from the squid hoods.

Cut under the eyes to remove the intestines.

Rub the hoods under cold running water and remove the skin.

BARBECUED SQUID

Preparation time: 40 minutes + 30 minutes chilling
Total cooking time: 10 minutes
Serves 6

✷ ✷

500 g (1 lb) small squid (see Note)
1/4 teaspoon salt

Picada dressing

2 tablespoons extra virgin olive oil
2 tablespoons finely chopped fresh
  flat-leaf parsley
1 clove garlic, crushed
1/4 teaspoon cracked black pepper

1 To clean the squid, gently pull the tentacles away from the hood (the intestines should come away at the same time). Remove the intestines from the tentacles by cutting under the eyes, then remove the beak, if it remains in the centre of the tentacles, by using your fingers to push up the centre. Pull away the soft bone.

2 Rub the hoods under cold running water and the skin should come away easily. Wash the hoods and tentacles and drain well. Place in a bowl, add the salt and mix well. Cover and refrigerate for about 30 minutes.
3 Heat a lightly oiled barbecue hotplate or preheat a grill to its highest setting.
4 For the picada dressing, whisk together the olive oil, parsley, garlic, pepper and some salt in a small jug or bowl.
5 Cook the squid hoods in small batches on the barbecue hotplate, or under the grill, for about 2–3 minutes, or until the hoods are white and are tender. Barbecue or grill the squid tentacles, turning to brown them all over, for 1 minute, or until they curl up. Serve hot, drizzled with the picada dressing.
NOTES: Bottleneck squid is the name given to the small variety of squid used in this recipe. If unavailable, choose the smallest squid you can find. You can also use cuttlefish, octopus, prawns, or even chunks of firm white fish fillet, instead of the squid.

Make the picada dressing as close to serving time as possible so the parsley doesn't discolour.

ABOVE: Barbecued squid

CHARGRILLED BABY OCTOPUS

Preparation time: 15 minutes + 3 hours marinating
Total cooking time: 5 minutes
Serves 4

★★

1 kg (2 lb) baby octopus
3/4 cup (185 ml/6 fl oz) red wine
2 tablespoons balsamic vinegar
2 tablespoons soy sauce
2 tablespoons hoisin sauce
1 clove garlic, crushed

1 Wash the octopus thoroughly and wipe dry with paper towel. Use a small sharp knife to cut off the heads. Discard the heads. If the octopus are large, cut the tentacles in half.
2 Put the octopus in a large bowl. Combine the wine, vinegar, sauces and garlic in a jug and pour over the octopus. Stir to coat thoroughly, then cover and marinate in the refrigerator for several hours, or overnight.

3 Heat the grill or barbecue hotplate to high. Drain the octopus, reserving the marinade. Cook the octopus, in batches, on a lightly greased hotplate for 3–5 minutes, until the octopus flesh turns white. Brush the reserved marinade over the octopus during cooking. Serve warm or cold.

LEMON GRASS PRAWN SKEWERS

Peel and devein 400 g (13 oz) raw medium prawns. Combine 1 1/2 tablespoons each of soft brown sugar and lime juice, 2 teaspoons green curry paste and 2 finely shredded kaffir lime leaves in a bowl. Add the prawns and chill for several hours. Cut 2 lemon grass stems into 20 cm (8 inch) lengths, leaving the root attached, then cut lengthways into four 'skewers'. Slit the prawns and thread onto the lemon grass. Grill or barbecue until cooked. Serve with a salsa made with a finely chopped mango, 2 teaspoons lime juice, 1 teaspoon lime rind and 1/2 teaspoon grated palm sugar or brown sugar. Serves 4.

BARBECUING SEAFOOD
Prepare the barbecue for seafood well in advance. The temperature must be very hot for octopus and shellfish and a medium heat for fish. A good test is to hold your hand above the barbecue plate and if you can hold it there for more than 2–3 seconds for very hot, or 3–4 seconds for medium, the barbecue is not yet hot enough. For recipes such as marinated octopus, drain the octopus well so that it cooks quickly and doesn't stew in the marinade. If necessary, barbecue seafood in batches so that it isn't too crowded on the barbecue plate and the temperature remains high.

ABOVE: Chargrilled baby octopus

SMOKED SEAFOOD
There are two methods of smoking seafood. Hot smoking can be done at home, whereas cold is reserved for commercial purposes. Smoked fish can be kept for 3–5 days.

Cold smoking is the commercial method used to produce smoked salmon. The fish is smoked at a low temperature and not actually cooked.

Hot smoking is the method described here, using a kettle barbecue. This method is particularly suitable for whole trout and mackerel. The fish is simultaneously smoked and cooked on the hot barbecue.

BRINING
All fish for smoking must first be soaked in a brine solution (salted water), or salted by rubbing generous quantities of salt into the skin. This helps preservation and improves the flavour. To determine the strength of the brine solution, see if a potato will float. If it doesn't, keep adding and dissolving more salt until the potato floats. If it does, add the whole

fish and leave it for 3 hours, or 2 hours if gutted. Fish fillets will only need 30 minutes. Next, clean the fish and gut, if necessary. If you don't have time to brine the fish, you can leave this step out, but the fish won't keep after smoking and you will have to eat it straight away. Ungutted fish are the most suitable to use for hot smoking, so ask your fishmonger for advice on types.

TYPE OF WOOD TO USE

The recommended smoking woodchips are hickory, oak, apple, red gum, or any hardwood, available from barbecue and related speciality stores. Resinous woods, including pine, should never be used as they tend to taint the fish with an antiseptic flavour. Adding some herbs such as thyme, rosemary or bay leaves will infuse aromatic flavours into the fish.

TO SMOKE WHOLE FISH

The first thing you will need if you want to smoke fish at home is a covered kettle barbecue or a smoke box. We have given a recipe for use with a kettle barbecue as these are more popular.

1 Place a cupful of smoking chips (apple, hickory or oak) in a non-reactive bowl,

add ½ cup (125 ml/4 fl oz) white wine or water, and allow to stand for 1 hour. Drain well.

2 Meanwhile, light your coals and leave them until they turn white.

3 Fill the cavities of 4 whole rainbow trout with thin slices of lime and red onion. Tie a small bunch of fresh herbs around each tail. Suitable fresh herbs include bay leaves, sprigs of dill, lemon thyme and parsley.

4 Carefully lift the sides of the rack and scatter the chips over the coals.

5 Place the rainbow trout directly on the lightly greased rack or a double layer of foil. Spray lightly with olive oil, and season generously with sea salt and cracked black pepper. Cover and smoke for 7–15 minutes, or until the fish flakes

easily when tested with the tip of a knife. The cooking time will vary, depending on the size of the fish.

TO SMOKE FISH FILLETS

Fish fillets or butterflied fish can be smoked in the same way, but the cooking time will depend on the size of the fillet. Oily fish, including salmon, mackerel, tailor or warehou, are best.

TO SMOKE MUSSELS

Mussels do not require soaking. Thoroughly scrub the mussels and pull out the hairy beards. Discard any that do not close when tapped on the bench. Put the mussels in a baking dish in the prepared barbecue. Cover and cook for 3–5 minutes.

SCALLOPS EN BROCHETTE

Preparation time: 25 minutes
Total cooking time: 15 minutes
Serves 4-6

★★

36 scallops
3/4 cup (185 ml/6 fl oz) white wine
1 tablespoon lemon juice
1 cup (20 g/3/4 oz) parsley sprigs
2 cloves garlic, chopped
4 rashers rindless bacon, cut into
    5 cm (2 inch) strips
30 g (1 oz) butter, melted
1 small onion, finely chopped
2 tablespoons white wine vinegar
1/3 cup (80 ml/2 3/4 fl oz) cream
1/2 teaspoon cornflour

1 You will need 12 metal or wooden skewers. Soak wooden skewers in water for 30 minutes, to prevent burning. Slice or pull off any vein, membrane or hard white muscle from the scallops, leaving any roe attached. In a small pan, heat the wine and lemon juice. Add the scallops and simmer for 1 minute, until just turning opaque. Drain and reserve the poaching liquid.
2 Process the parsley and garlic in a food processor for 30 seconds, or until finely chopped. Spread onto a plate. Roll the scallops in the parsley mixture until completely covered.
3 Thread 3 scallops, alternating with pieces of rolled bacon, onto the skewers. Brush the brochettes with melted butter, then season with salt and pepper.
4 In a small pan, heat the onion, vinegar and 1/3 cup (80 ml/2 3/4 fl oz) of the reserved poaching liquid. Boil for 5 minutes, or until the liquid is reduced to 2 tablespoons. Blend the cream and cornflour in a small bowl and add to the mixture. Stir over low heat until the mixture boils and thickens. Set aside and keep warm.
5 Preheat the grill or barbecue to medium and grill the brochettes for 4–5 minutes, turning frequently, until the bacon is cooked. Serve immediately with pasta, or on a bed of rice. Accompany with warm sauce in a serving jug.
NOTE: Brochettes and sauce can be prepared several hours ahead and refrigerated. Reheat the sauce gently when required. Cook the brochettes just prior to serving. You can use cubed firm white-fleshed fish instead of scallops.

SCALLOPS

Scallops are sold fresh both on and off the shell, or frozen off the shell. When buying fresh, look for plump, moist scallops with a creamy-white translucent flesh. Some are sold without roe but, if it is attached, the roe should be plump and brightly coloured. Don't buy scallops that are sitting in a tray of water as they can absorb the water and so be more expensive if bought by weight. The water can also come out during cooking, resulting in the scallops stewing and becoming tough. Cook scallops quickly over high heat until they just turn white—do not overcook. Though fresh scallops are more expensive, they have a beautiful mild flavour and are well worth the cost.

RIGHT: Scallops en brochette

BARBECUED SARDINES

Preparation time: 25 minutes + 2 hours
  marinating
Total cooking time: 6 minutes
Serves 4

8 large fresh sardines
8 sprigs fresh lemon thyme
3 tablespoons extra virgin olive oil
2 cloves garlic, crushed
1 teaspoon finely grated lemon rind
2 tablespoons lemon juice
1 teaspoon ground cumin
lemon wedges, for serving

1 Carefully slit the sardines from head to tail and remove the gut. Rinse, then pat dry inside and out with paper towels. Place a sprig of fresh lemon thyme in each fish cavity and arrange the fish in a shallow non-metallic dish.
2 Combine the olive oil, garlic, lemon rind, lemon juice and cumin in a small bowl and pour over the fish. Cover and refrigerate for 2 hours.
3 Cook on a preheated barbecue hotplate for 2–3 minutes each side, basting frequently with the marinade, or until the flesh flakes easily when tested with a fork. Alternatively, barbecue in a sardine cooking rack until tender. Serve with lemon wedges.

SCALLOPS WITH LEMON HERB BUTTER

Beat together 60 g (2 oz) softened butter, 1 teaspoon grated lemon rind, 1 tablespoon each of chopped fresh chervil and fresh chives and 1 tablespoon lemon juice in a bowl. Place 24 scallops in the shell face down on a heated barbecue and cook until lightly golden. Turn, dollop with the lemon herb butter and cook until the butter is sizzling and the scallops are just cooked. To serve, sprinkle the tops with some chopped fresh herbs and serve with extra wedges of lemon. Serves 4–6.

ABOVE: Barbecued sardines

223

CAJUN SWORDFISH

Preparation time: 15 minutes
Total cooking time: 10 minutes
Serves 4

1 tablespoon garlic powder

1 tablespoon onion powder

2 teaspoons white pepper

2 teaspoons cracked black pepper

2 teaspoons dried thyme

2 teaspoons dried oregano

1 teaspoon cayenne pepper

4 swordfish steaks

oil, for cooking

lime wedges, for serving

yoghurt, optional, for serving

1 Mix all the dried spices and herbs in a bowl.
2 Pat the swordfish steaks dry with paper towels, then coat both sides of each steak in the spice mixture, shaking off any excess.
3 Heat a barbecue hotplate and drizzle with a little oil. Cook the swordfish steaks for about 3–5 minutes each side, depending on the thickness of each steak. Serve with wedges of lime and yoghurt, if desired.
NOTE: You can use tuna, mahi mahi, kingfish or striped marlin instead of the swordfish.

TANDOORI FISH CUTLET

Preparation time: 15 minutes + overnight
   marinating
Total cooking time: 8 minutes
Serves 4

4 fish cutlets (eg. blue-eye, snapper, warehou)

1/4 cup (60 ml/2 fl oz) lemon juice

1 onion, finely chopped

2 cloves garlic, crushed

1 tablespoon grated fresh ginger

1 fresh red chilli

1 tablespoon garam masala

1 teaspoon paprika

1/4 teaspoon salt

2 cups (500 g/1 lb) Greek-style
   thick natural yoghurt

red and yellow food colouring

1 Pat the fish cutlets dry with paper towels and arrange in a shallow non-metallic dish. Drizzle the lemon juice over the fish and turn to coat the cutlets with the juice.
2 Blend the onion, garlic, ginger, chilli, garam masala, paprika and salt in a blender until smooth. Transfer to a bowl and stir in the yoghurt and enough food colouring to give an authentic tandoori colour (deep orange). Spoon the marinade over the fish and turn the fish to coat thoroughly. Cover and refrigerate overnight.
3 Heat the barbecue hotplate. Remove the cutlets from the marinade and allow any excess to drip off. Cook the cutlets on the barbecue, or under a grill, for 3–4 minutes each side, or until the fish flakes easily when tested with a fork. Delicious served with extra yoghurt and baby spinach leaves.

GRILLED FISH

Preparation time: 5 minutes
Total cooking time: 5–10 minutes
Serves 4

30 g (1 oz) butter, melted

4 skinless white fish fillets (eg. perch, snapper,
   cod, bream, whiting, flathead, John dory)

lemon wedges, for serving

1 Preheat the grill and cover the tray with foil. Brush lightly with a little of the melted butter.
2 Place the fish fillets on the grill tray, brush with the remaining butter and lightly sprinkle the fish with salt and pepper.
3 Grill the fish for about 5–10 minutes, or until the flesh flakes easily when tested in the thickest part with a fork. The cooking time will vary according to the thickness of the fish fillet. Serve with lemon wedges.
NOTE: If you prefer, drizzle with a little lemon juice during cooking.

SWORDFISH
This fish is named for the swordlike projection from its upper jaw. It is found around the world in temperate waters. The swordfish's mild-flavoured flesh and very 'meaty' texture make it ideal for more 'robust' recipes with stronger flavours, such as Cajun or Indian.

OPPOSITE PAGE: Cajun swordfish (top); Tandoori fish cutlet

Dill mayonnaise

3/4 cup (185 g/6 oz) whole-egg mayonnaise
2 tablespoons chopped fresh dill
1 1/2 tablespoons lemon juice
1 gherkin, finely chopped
1 teaspoon drained bottled capers, chopped
1 clove garlic, crushed

1 For the marinade, combine the olive oil, lemon juice, mustard, honey and fresh dill in a bowl, pour over the unpeeled prawns and coat well. Cover and refrigerate for at least 2 hours, turning occasionally.
2 For the dill mayonnaise, whisk together the mayonnaise, dill, lemon juice, gherkin, capers and garlic in a small bowl, then cover and chill.
3 Lightly oil a heated chargrill pan or barbecue grill or hotplate. Add the drained prawns and cook in batches over high heat for 4 minutes, turning frequently until pink and cooked through. Serve with the dill mayonnaise.

TUNA WITH SOY AND HONEY

Preparation time: 15 minutes + 1 hour chilling
Total cooking time: 8–10 minutes
Serves 4

4 tuna steaks
10 cm (4 inch) piece of peeled fresh ginger, cut into julienne strips
2 spring onions, finely sliced
2 tablespoons honey
2 tablespoons balsamic vinegar
1/2 cup (125 ml/4 fl oz) low-salt soy sauce

1 Place the tuna, ginger and spring onion in a shallow non-metallic dish.
2 Stir the honey, balsamic vinegar and soy sauce together in a small bowl. Pour over the tuna steaks and turn them to coat in the marinade. Cover and refrigerate for 1 hour.
3 Heat the barbecue grill. Cook on the barbecue for 3–4 minutes each side, or until cooked to your liking. The cooking time will depend on the thickness of the tuna.
NOTE: Swordfish, striped marlin and kingfish are all just as suitable as the tuna steaks for making this recipe.

PRAWNS WITH DILL MAYONNAISE

Preparation time: 15 minutes + 2 hours marinating
Total cooking time: 10–15 minutes
Serves 4

Marinade

1/2 cup (125 ml/4 fl oz) olive oil
1/3 cup (80 ml/2 3/4 fl oz) lemon juice
2 tablespoons wholegrain mustard
2 tablespoons honey
2 tablespoons chopped fresh dill

20 raw large prawns

ABOVE: Prawns with dill mayonnaise

SALMON WITH DILL CREAM

Preparation time: 25 minutes
Total cooking time: 25 minutes
Serves 4

4 baby salmon
4 cloves garlic, peeled
2 lemons, sliced
8 fresh bay leaves
8 sprigs fresh flat-leaf parsley
8 sprigs fresh thyme
olive oil, for brushing

Dill cream

90 g (3 oz) butter
1 cup (250 ml/8 fl oz) fish stock
1 1/2 teaspoons wholegrain mustard
1 cup (250 ml/8 fl oz) cream
2 tablespoons lemon juice
3 tablespoons chopped fresh dill

1 Preheat a barbecue or chargrill pan to hot. Wash the fish and pat dry inside and out with paper towels. Place a clove of garlic, a few slices of lemon and a bay leaf in the cavity of each fish. Bundle together 1 sprig of parsley and thyme and tie a bundle with string onto each fish, near the tail. Reserve the other sprigs. Brush both sides of the fish with a little of the olive oil.

2 For the dill cream, melt the butter in a pan and add the fish stock, mustard and cream. Bring to the boil, then reduce the heat and simmer for 15 minutes, or until the sauce is slightly thickened. Stir in the lemon juice and dill. Set aside and keep warm. Season, to taste, with salt and pepper.

3 While the dill cream is cooking, barbecue or chargrill the fish for 3–6 minutes on each side, turning carefully, or until cooked through. Discard the herbs. For serving, bundle together a fresh parsley sprig, a thyme sprig and a bay leaf, and tie a bundle near each fish tail. Serve warm with the dill cream.

NOTE: Rainbow trout is also a suitable fish for this recipe.

BELOW: Salmon with dill cream

SEAFOOD WITH PASTA, RICE & NOODLES

We've come a long way since our ancestors foraged for grains, hunted for fish and delved for clams but probably never considered combining the flavours in their stone bowls. And certainly not with a squeeze of lemon juice, or a hint of that fresh dill growing nearby! It is only natural that today, when we no longer eat merely for sustenance, but for life-enhancing enjoyment, creative cooks mingle flavours and textures and mix staples such as pasta and rice with seafood.

SEAFOOD RISOTTO

Thoroughly scrub the mussels, then pull away the hairy beards.

Stir a little of the stock at a time into the rice until it is all absorbed.

Put the mussels in a pan of boiling water, then cover the pan and cook the mussels until they open.

Stir the herbs and grated Parmesan through the cooked risotto.

RIGHT: Seafood risotto

SEAFOOD RISOTTO

Preparation time: 25 minutes
Total cooking time: 45–50 minutes
Serves 4

★★

8–10 black mussels

8 raw medium prawns

150 g (5 oz) skinless white fish fillet
    (eg. coley, blue-eye, ling, cod) cubed

1.75 litres (56 fl oz) fish or chicken stock

2 tablespoons oil

2 onions, finely chopped

2 cloves garlic, finely chopped

1 stick celery, finely chopped

2 cups (440 g/14 oz) arborio rice

2 tablespoons chopped fresh parsley

1 tablespoon chopped fresh oregano

1 tablespoon chopped fresh thyme

2 tablespoons freshly grated Parmesan

1 Scrub the mussels with a stiff brush and pull out the hairy beards. Discard any broken mussels, or open ones that don't close when tapped on the bench. Rinse well. Refrigerate.

2 Peel the prawns, leaving the tails intact. Gently pull out the dark vein from each prawn back, starting at the head. Put the prawns and fish in a bowl, cover and refrigerate.

3 Put the stock in a saucepan and bring to the boil. Reduce the heat until just simmering; cover.

4 Heat a little oil in a large saucepan over medium heat. Add the onion, garlic and celery and cook for 2–3 minutes. Add 2 tablespoons water, cover and cook for 5 minutes, or until the vegetables soften. Add the rice and cook, stirring, over medium heat for 3–4 minutes, or until the rice grains are well coated.

5 Gradually add 1/2 cup (125 ml/4 fl oz) of the hot stock to the rice, stirring over low heat with a wooden spoon, until all the stock has been absorbed. Repeat, adding 1/2 cup (125 ml/4 fl oz) stock each time until only a small amount of stock is left and the rice is just tender.

6 Meanwhile, bring 1/4 cup (60 ml/2 fl oz) water to the boil in a saucepan. Add the mussels, cover and cook for about 4–5 minutes, shaking the pan occasionally, until the mussels have opened. Drain; discard any unopened ones. Set aside.

7 Add the fish, prawns and the remaining hot stock to the rice; stir well. Cook for 5–10 minutes, or until the seafood is just cooked and the rice is tender and creamy. Remove from the heat, stir in the mussels, cover and set aside for 5 minutes. Stir the herbs and Parmesan through the risotto, then season, to taste. Serve immediately.

PRAWN RAVIOLI WITH BASIL BUTTER

Preparation time: 30 minutes + 30 minutes chilling
Total cooking time: 20 minutes
Serves 4

★★

500 g (1 lb) raw medium prawns
1 tablespoon chopped fresh chives
1 egg white, lightly beaten
1 1/3 cups (350 ml/11 fl oz) cream
200 g (6 1/2 oz) packet gow gee wrappers
1 egg, lightly beaten

Basil butter

90 g (3 oz) butter
1 clove garlic, crushed
15 g (1/2 oz) fresh basil leaves, finely shredded
40 g (1 1/4 oz) pine nuts

1 Peel the prawns and gently pull out the dark vein from each prawn back, starting at the head end. Put the prawns in a food processor with the chives and egg white and process until smooth. Season with salt and pepper. Add the cream, being careful not to overprocess or the mixture will curdle. Transfer to a bowl, cover and chill for 30 minutes.

2 Place 2–3 teaspoons of the prawn mixture in the centre of half the gow gee wrappers. Brush the edges with beaten egg, then cover with the remaining wrappers. Press the edges to seal. Add in batches to a large pan of boiling water and cook each batch for 4 minutes. Drain, taking care not to damage the ravioli, and divide among 4 warm serving plates.

3 For the basil butter, melt the butter gently in a pan, add the garlic and stir until fragrant. Add the shredded basil, pine nuts and a little freshly ground black pepper, and cook until the butter turns a nutty brown colour. Drizzle the butter over the pasta. Serve immediately.

NOTE: Buy the gow gee wrappers from Asian food speciality stores.

PINE NUTS
These are harvested from the stone pine, a native of the Mediterranean region. Pine nuts contain a lot of natural oils and are used extensively in cookery in the Mediterranean and in the Middle East. For maximum flavour, toast lightly before use. Pine nuts are processsed with basil and garlic to make pesto and these flavours marry well in other recipes as well.

ABOVE: Prawn ravioli with basil butter

ABOVE: Seafood lasagne

2 cups (500 ml/16 fl oz) milk
2 cups (500 ml/16 fl oz) dry white wine
125 g (4 oz) Cheddar, grated
1/2 cup (125 ml/4 fl oz) cream
60 g (2 oz) Parmesan, grated
2 tablespoons chopped fresh parsley

1 Preheat the oven to moderate 180°C (350°F/ Gas 4). Line a greased shallow ovenproof dish (about 30 cm/12 inches square) with lasagne sheets, gently breaking them to fill any gaps. Set aside.
2 Slice or pull off any vein, membrane or hard white muscle from the scallops, leaving any roe attached.
3 Peel the prawns and gently pull out the dark vein from each prawn back, starting at the head end. Chop the seafood into even-sized pieces.
4 Melt the butter in a large pan over low heat, add the leek and cook, stirring over medium heat for 1 minute, or until starting to soften. Stir in the flour and cook for 1 minute, or until pale and foaming. Remove from the heat and gradually stir in the combined milk and wine. Return to the heat and stir constantly over medium heat until the sauce boils and thickens. Reduce the heat and simmer for 2 minutes. Add the seafood and simmer for 1 minute. Remove from the heat and stir in the cheese and some salt and pepper.
5 Spoon half the seafood mixture over the lasagne sheets in the dish, then top with another layer of lasagne sheets. Spoon the remaining seafood mixture over the lasagne sheets, then cover with another layer of lasagne sheets.
6 Pour the cream over the top, then sprinkle with the combined Parmesan and parsley. Bake, uncovered, for 30 minutes, or until bubbling and golden brown.

SEAFOOD LASAGNE

Preparation time: 15 minutes
Total cooking time: 45 minutes
Serves 4-6

250 g (8 oz) instant lasagne sheets
125 g (4 oz) scallops
500 g (1 lb) raw medium prawns
500 g (1 lb) skinless white fish fillets (eg. hake, snapper, flake, gemfish, ling)
125 g (4 oz) butter
1 leek, white part only, thinly sliced
2/3 cup (85 g/3 oz) plain flour

SQUID INK SPAGHETTI

Preparation time: 20 minutes
Total cooking time: 20 minutes
Serves 4-6

500 g (1 lb) small squid hoods
375 g (12 oz) spaghetti
4 tablespoons extra virgin olive oil
3 cloves garlic, crushed
1 onion, finely chopped
1/3 cup (80 ml/2 3/4 fl oz) white wine
3 x 4 g sachets squid ink

1 Cut the squid hoods in half and then cut into thin strips.
2 Cook the spaghetti in a large pan of rapidly boiling water until *al dente*. Drain; keep warm.
3 Heat 2 tablespoons of the oil in a large deep frying pan, add the garlic and onion and stir over medium heat until golden. Add the wine, bring to the boil and boil for 5 minutes, or until half the liquid has evaporated. Reduce the heat and stir in the squid ink. Add to the spaghetti and toss. Season well with salt and pepper. Divide among warmed serving bowls
4 Heat the remaining oil and stir-fry the squid in batches, over high heat, for 1 minute, or until white and tender. Serve over the pasta.

FARFALLE WITH TUNA, MUSHROOMS AND CREAM

Preparation time: 10 minutes
Total cooking time: 15 minutes
Serves 4

60 g (2 oz) butter
1 tablespoon olive oil
1 onion, chopped
1 clove garlic, crushed

125 g (4 oz) button mushrooms, sliced
1 cup (250 ml/8 fl oz) cream
450 g (14 oz) can tuna in brine, drained and flaked
1 tablespoon lemon juice
1 tablespoon chopped fresh parsley
500 g (1 lb) farfalle

1 Heat the butter and olive oil in a large frying pan. Add the onion and garlic to the pan and stir over low heat for 3–5 minutes, until the onion is soft.
2 Add the mushrooms to the pan and cook for 2 minutes. Pour in the cream, bring to the boil, then reduce the heat and simmer until the sauce begins to thicken. Add the tuna, lemon juice and parsley and stir until heated through. Add salt and pepper, to taste.
3 While the sauce is cooking, add the farfalle to a large pan of rapidly boiling water and cook until *al dente*. Drain thoroughly, then return to the pan. Add the sauce to the farfalle and toss to combine. Serve immediately.
NOTES: You can use a can of salmon, drained and flaked, instead of tuna.

Farfalle, attractive pasta made into the shape of a bow or butterfly, comes in various sizes, as well as flavours other than the plain, such as tomato or spinach.

SQUID INK
Squid and octopus use ink as a means of defence and escape from predators. The squid fires ink into the water, forming a cloud about the same size as its own body. It then speeds away, leaving this decoy behind to confuse the predator. Squid ink is today popular as a dye for pasta. However, sepia, the pigment extracted from the ink sacs, has been used as a drawing ink since ancient Roman times.

LEFT: Farfalle with tuna, mushrooms and cream

SALMON AND PASTA FRITTATA

Preparation time: 25 minutes
Total cooking time: 35–40 minutes
Serves 6

150 g (5 oz) spaghettini (see Note)
300 g (10 oz) frozen broad beans
415 g (13 oz) can red salmon, drained
30 g (1 oz) butter
1 leek, white part only, thinly sliced
6 eggs, lightly beaten
1/2 cup (125 ml/4 fl oz) cream
3/4 cup (185 ml/6 fl oz) milk

1 Add the pasta to a large pan of boiling water and boil until *al dente*; drain. Put the broad beans in a large bowl, cover with boiling water and leave for 10 minutes. Drain, then remove and discard the outer skins. Remove and discard any skin and bones from the salmon and roughly flake the flesh.
2 Melt the butter in a saucepan, add the leek and cook, stirring over medium heat until soft, but not browned. In a large bowl, mix the pasta, broad beans, leek, salmon, eggs, cream and milk. Season, to taste, with salt and cracked black pepper.
3 Pour the mixture into a lightly greased heated frying pan 25 cm (10 inches) across the base. Cover with foil or a lid and cook over low heat for 25 minutes, or until nearly set.
4 Meanwhile, heat the grill. Place the frying pan under the grill (wrap the handle with foil to protect it from the heat) and grill until the top has set. Set aside for 5 minutes. Gently ease the frittata away from the edges of the pan, then hold a large plate over the top and turn the pan over to release the frittata onto the plate or cut into wedges directly from the pan. Serve with a leafy green salad.
NOTES: Spaghettini is a thin version of spaghetti.
 Canned pink salmon or canned tuna can also be used in this recipe. Choose a good-quality tuna that isn't too dry.

SALMON WITH LEMON CANNELLONI

Preparation time: 25 minutes
Total cooking time: 40 minutes
Serves 4-6

Filling

415 g (13 oz) can pink salmon
250 g (8 oz) ricotta cheese
1 tablespoon lemon juice
1 egg yolk, lightly beaten
2 tablespoons finely chopped onion

Sauce

125 g (4 oz) butter
2/3 cup (85 g/3 oz) plain flour
23/4 cups (685 ml/23 fl oz) milk
1 teaspoon finely grated lemon rind
1/4 teaspoon ground nutmeg

16 cannelloni tubes
1–2 tablespoons chopped fresh dill, to garnish

1 Drain the salmon, reserving the liquid for the sauce. Remove and discard the skin and bones. Flake the salmon flesh and mix with the ricotta, lemon juice, egg yolk and onion in a bowl. Add a little salt and pepper, to taste.
2 For the sauce, melt the butter in a saucepan over low heat. Stir in the flour and cook for 1 minute, or until pale and foaming. Remove from the heat and gradually stir in the milk. Return to the heat and stir constantly until the sauce boils and thickens. Reduce the heat and simmer for 2 minutes. Add the reserved salmon liquid, lemon rind, nutmeg and salt and pepper, to taste. Set aside to cool.
3 Preheat the oven to moderate 180°C (350°F/Gas 4). Fill the cannelloni tubes with filling, using a small spoon or piping bag. Spread one third of the sauce over the bottom of a shallow ovenproof dish, then sit the cannelloni tubes in the dish side-by-side. Pour the remaining sauce over the top, covering all the exposed pasta. Bake for about 30 minutes, until bubbly. Serve garnished with the dill.

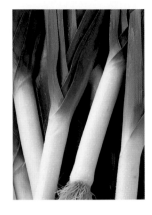

SALMON
Salmon is an anadromous creature, meaning it makes a yearly journey upriver from its saltwater habitat to spawn in freshwater. There is something heroic about the famed Scottish salmon who battle their way courageously up rocky streams to lay their eggs. The American Indians viewed the salmon with superstitious respect, forbidding certain tribe members to eat the fish in case they angered its spirit causing it to desert their waters.

OPPOSITE PAGE:
Salmon and pasta frittata (top); Salmon with lemon cannelloni

PRAWN SAFFRON RISOTTO

Preparation time: 20 minutes
Total cooking time: 40 minutes
Serves 4

1/4 teaspoon saffron threads
500 g (1 lb) raw medium prawns
1/4 cup (60 ml/2 fl oz) olive oil
2 cloves garlic, crushed
3 tablespoons chopped fresh parsley
1/4 cup (60 ml/2 fl oz) dry sherry
1/4 cup (60 ml/2 fl oz) white wine
1.5 litres (48 fl oz) fish stock
1 onion, chopped
2 cups (440 g/14 oz) arborio rice

1 Soak the saffron threads in a small bowl with 3 tablespoons hot water. Peel the prawns, leaving the tails intact. Gently pull out the dark vein from each prawn back, starting at the head end.

2 Heat half the olive oil in a medium pan. Add the garlic, parsley and prawns and season with salt and pepper. Cook for 2 minutes, then add the sherry, wine and saffron threads with their liquid. Remove the prawns with a slotted spoon and set aside. Simmer until the liquid has reduced by half. Pour in the fish stock and 1 cup (250 ml/8 fl oz) water, cover and leave to simmer.

3 In a separate large, heavy-based pan, heat the remaining oil. Add the onion and cook for 3 minutes, or until golden. Add the rice and stir over medium heat for 3 minutes.

4 Keep the pan of stock constantly at simmering point. Add 1/2 cup (125 ml/4 fl oz) hot stock to the rice mixture and stir constantly over low heat, with a wooden spoon, until all the liquid has been absorbed. Add 1/2 cup (125 ml/4 fl oz) stock and repeat the process until all the stock has been added and the rice is tender and creamy—this will take 25–30 minutes. Add the prawns and stir until heated through. Season, to taste, with salt and cracked black pepper and serve immediately.

ARBORIO RICE
This is the best type of rice for making risotto because it absorbs the cooking liquid and still holds its shape without softening too much. When cooked, it has a creamy texture. The grain is medium-sized and plump and is translucent at the edges. The core is hard and white.

RIGHT: Prawn saffron risotto

FUSILLI WITH TUNA, CAPERS AND PARSLEY

Preparation time: 15 minutes
Total cooking time: 10 minutes
Serves 4

425 g (14 oz) can tuna in spring water, drained

2 tablespoons olive oil

2 cloves garlic, finely chopped

2 small red chillies, finely chopped

3 tablespoons drained bottled capers

1/2 cup (30 g/1 oz) chopped fresh parsley

1/4 cup (60 ml/2 fl oz) lemon juice

375 g (12 oz) fusilli

1/2 cup (125 ml/4 fl oz) hot chicken stock

1 Place the drained tuna in a bowl and flake lightly with a fork. In a small bowl, combine the oil, garlic, chilli, capers, parsley and lemon juice. Pour over the tuna and mix lightly. Season well with salt and freshly ground black pepper.

2 Meanwhile, cook the pasta in a large pan of rapidly boiling salted water for 10 minutes, or until *al dente*. Drain. Toss the tuna mixture through the pasta, adding enough of the hot chicken stock to give a moist consistency. Serve immediately.

SMOKED SALMON WITH FETTUCINE

Cook 500 g (1 lb) dried fettucine in a large pan of boiling water until *al dente*. Drain. Melt 30 g (1 oz) butter in a saucepan, add 1 finely sliced leek and cook, stirring over low heat until soft but not browned. Stir in 300 g (10 oz) sour cream, 1/2 cup (125 ml/ 4 fl oz) chicken stock and 300 g (10 oz) sliced smoked salmon, cut into strips. Stir until heated through, but do not boil. Stir through the hot pasta with 1–2 tablespoons each of chopped fresh dill and chives. Season, to taste, with salt and cracked black pepper. Serves 4.

ABOVE: Fusilli with tuna, capers and parsley

20 black mussels
200 g (6¹/2 oz) raw medium prawns
¹/4 cup (60 ml/2 fl oz) white wine
¹/4 cup (60 ml/2 fl oz) fish stock
1 clove garlic, crushed
375 g (12 oz) spaghetti
30 g (1 oz) butter
125 g (4 oz) calamari rings
125 g (4 oz) skinless fish fillets
  (eg. blue-eye, groper, striped marlin), cubed
¹/2 cup (10 g/¹/4 oz) fresh parsley, chopped
200 g (6¹/2 oz) can clams, drained

1 For the tomato sauce, heat the olive oil in a pan, add the onion and carrot and stir over medium heat for 10 minutes, or until the vegetables are lightly browned. Add the garlic, tomato, white wine and sugar, bring to the boil, reduce the heat and gently simmer for 30 minutes, stirring occasionally.

2 Scrub the mussels with a stiff brush and pull out the hairy beards. Discard any broken mussels, or open ones that don't close when tapped on the bench. Rinse well.

3 Peel the prawns and gently pull out the dark vein from each prawn back, starting at the head end.

4 Heat the wine together with the stock and garlic in a large pan. Add the unopened mussels. Cover the pan and shake it over high heat for 4–5 minutes. After 3 minutes, start removing any opened mussels and set them aside. After 5 minutes, discard any unopened mussels and reserve the liquid.

5 Cook the spaghetti in a large pan of rapidly boiling salted water until *al dente*. Drain and keep warm.

6 Meanwhile, melt the butter in a frying pan, add the calamari rings, fish and prawns in batches and stir-fry for 2 minutes, or until just cooked through. Remove from the heat and add the reserved liquid, mussels, calamari, fish, prawns, parsley and clams to the tomato sauce and stir gently until heated through. Gently combine the sauce with the pasta and serve at once.

SPAGHETTI MARINARA

Preparation time: 40 minutes
Total cooking time: 50 minutes
Serves 6
★ ★

Tomato sauce
2 tablespoons olive oil
1 onion, finely chopped
1 carrot, sliced
2 cloves garlic, crushed
425 g (14 oz) can crushed tomatoes
¹/2 cup (125 ml/4 fl oz) white wine
1 teaspoon sugar

ABOVE: Spaghetti marinara

SINGAPORE NOODLES

Preparation time: 35 minutes
Total cooking time: 15 minutes
Serves 2–4

300 g (10 oz) dried rice vermicelli
300 g (10 oz) raw medium prawns
2 tablespoons oil
2 cloves garlic, finely chopped
350 g (11 oz) pork loin, cut into strips
1 large onion, cut into thin wedges
1–2 tablespoons Asian curry powder (see Note)
150 g (5 oz) green beans, cut into
   short lengths
1 large carrot, sliced
1 teaspoon sugar
1 teaspoon salt
1 tablespoon soy sauce
200 g (6½ oz) bean sprouts
1 spring onion, cut into fine strips,
   to garnish

1 Soak the vermicelli in boiling water for about 5 minutes, or until soft. Drain well. Cut into short lengths.
2 Peel the prawns and pull out the dark vein from each prawn back, starting at the head end.
3 Heat half the oil in a wok over high heat and add the garlic, pork and prawns in batches. Stir-fry for 2 minutes, or until the mixture is just cooked. Remove from the wok and set aside.
4 Reduce the heat to medium. Add the remaining oil and stir-fry the onion and curry powder for 2–3 minutes. Add the beans, carrot, sugar and salt, sprinkle with a little water and stir-fry for 2 minutes.
5 Toss the vermicelli and soy sauce through the mixture. Add the bean sprouts, prawn and pork mixture to the wok. Season, to taste, with salt and pepper. Toss well and garnish with the spring onion.
NOTE: There are many varieties of Asian curry powder, each with a blend of spices designed to match the meat, chicken or seafood it is cooked with. Here we have used Asian fish curry powder, available from Asian food speciality stores. Commercial brands are not suitable for this recipe.

RICE VERMICELLI
Commonly used fresh in rice-growing areas in southern China, rice vermicelli (or rice noodles) are usually sold elsewhere in dried bundles. Before using in recipes, they need to be soaked in boiling water to soften them. They can be deep-fried in hot oil instead of soaking, to create crispy noodles.

LEFT: Singapore noodles

SPAGHETTI AND MUSSELS IN TOMATO AND FRESH HERB SAUCE

Preparation time: 15 minutes
Total cooking time: 30 minutes
Serves 4

1.5 kg (3 lb) black mussels
2 tablespoons olive oil
1 onion, finely sliced
2 cloves garlic, crushed
425 g (14 oz) can crushed tomatoes
1 cup (250 ml/8 fl oz) white wine
1 tablespoon chopped fresh basil
2 tablespoons chopped fresh parsley
500 g (1 lb) spaghetti

1 Scrub the mussels with a stiff brush and pull out the hairy beards. Discard any broken mussels or open ones that don't close when tapped on the bench. Rinse well, then refrigerate.
2 Heat the oil in a large pan, add the onion and garlic and stir over low heat for 5 minutes, or until the onion is tender. Add the tomato and wine and season, to taste. Bring to the boil, then reduce the heat and simmer for 15–20 minutes, or until the sauce begins to thicken.
3 Add the mussels to the pan, cover and simmer for 4–5 minutes, shaking the pan occasionally until the mussels are cooked. Discard any unopened mussels. Stir in the basil and parsley. While the sauce is cooking, add the spaghetti to a large pan of rapidly boiling water and cook until *al dente*. Drain immediately. Serve the mussels and sauce over the pasta.

SPAGHETTI ALLE VONGOLE

Preparation time: 30 minutes
Total cooking time: 30 minutes
Serves 4-6

750 g (1 1/2 lb) vongole (clams)
2 tablespoons olive oil
1/2 cup (125 ml/4 fl oz) white wine
1 onion, finely chopped
1–2 cloves garlic, finely chopped
2 zucchini (courgettes), finely chopped
8 ripe tomatoes, peeled and chopped

RIGHT: Spaghetti and mussels in tomato and fresh herb sauce

2 tablespoons tomato paste (tomato purée)
1 teaspoon caster sugar
500 g (1 lb) spaghetti
4 tablespoons chopped fresh flat-leaf parsley

1 Scrub the clams thoroughly, discarding any open or broken ones. Soak in cold water for 5 minutes to remove any sand. Heat half the oil in a large heavy-based pan. Add the clams, white wine and ½ cup (125 ml/4 fl oz) water. Cover and cook for 3–4 minutes, shaking the pan occasionally, until the shells have opened. Transfer the clams to a side plate, discarding any that have unopened shells. Strain and reserve the cooking liquid.

2 Heat the remaining oil in the same pan. Add the onion, garlic and zucchini and cook for 3–4 minutes, or until the onion has softened. Add the tomato, tomato paste, sugar and reserved cooking liquid. Cook for 20 minutes, or until thickened. Season, to taste.

3 Remove about two-thirds of the clams from their shells and discard the shells.

4 While the sauce is cooking, cook the spaghetti in a large pan of boiling water until *al dente*. Drain thoroughly.

5 Return all the shelled and unshelled clams to the sauce and heat for 2 minutes. Toss the sauce and clams through the spaghetti. Sprinkle with the fresh parsley and serve immediately.

SMOKED SALMON AND PASTA

Preparation time: 10 minutes
Total cooking time: 10 minutes
Serves 4

1 tablespoon olive oil
1 clove garlic, crushed
1½ cups (375 ml/12 fl oz) cream
3 tablespoons chopped fresh chives
¼ teaspoon mustard powder
200 g (6½ oz) smoked salmon, cut into strips
2 teaspoons lemon juice
500 g (1 lb) fettucine
3 tablespoons sun-dried tomatoes, chopped
2 tablespoons grated Parmesan, for serving

1 Heat the oil in a pan and cook the garlic briefly over low heat. Add the cream, chives and mustard powder. Season, to taste, and bring to the boil. Reduce the heat and stir until the sauce thickens.

2 Add the salmon and lemon juice and stir until heated through. Meanwhile, add the fettucine to a large pan of rapidly boiling water and cook until *al dente*. Drain well and return to the same pan. Toss the sauce through the pasta. Top with the tomato, Parmesan and extra chives.

NOTE: You can also use smoked trout.

ABOVE: Smoked salmon and pasta

241

SEAFOOD
CANNELLONI

Cut all the seafood into pieces small enough to fit in the cannelloni tubes.

Drain the seafood through a strainer, reserving the liquid.

Use a teaspoon to spoon the seafood mixture into the cannelloni tubes.

OPPOSITE PAGE:
Seafood cannelloni

SEAFOOD CANNELLONI

Preparation time: 30 minutes
Total cooking time: 1 hour 55 minutes
Serves 6

★ ★

1 onion, sliced
1 carrot, sliced
1 stick celery, cut in half
1 bouquet garni
1 cup (250 ml/8 fl oz) white wine
4 whole black peppercorns
300 g (10 oz) scallops
500 g (1 lb) raw medium prawns
300 g (10 oz) skinless fish fillets (eg. flathead,
    flake, hake, ling, cod), boned and chopped
60 g (2 oz) butter
1 onion, finely chopped
200 g (6½ oz) button mushrooms, finely chopped
2 x 400 g (13 oz) cans tomatoes, finely chopped
2 tablespoons chopped fresh parsley
2 tablespoons chopped fresh basil
2 tablespoons cream
15 cannelloni tubes
125 g (4 oz) Cheddar, grated

Bechamel sauce

60 g (2 oz) butter
2 tablespoons flour
3 cups (750 ml/24 fl oz) milk

1 Preheat the oven to moderate 180°C (350°F/ Gas 4). Combine the onion, carrot, celery, bouquet garni and 2 cups (500 ml/16 fl oz) water in a large pan and bring to the boil. Reduce the heat and simmer for 15 minutes. Add the wine and peppercorns and simmer for 15 minutes. Strain, discard the vegetables and reserve the liquid.
2 Meanwhile, slice or pull off any vein, membrane or hard white muscle from the scallops, leaving any roe attached. Dice the scallops. Peel the prawns and gently pull out the dark vein from each prawn back, starting at the head end, and roughly dice the prawn meat. Cut the seafood small enough to fit in the cannelloni tubes.
3 Put the reserved liquid in a clean pan and bring to the boil. Add the seafood. Reduce the heat and simmer for 3 minutes, or until tender. Strain and reserve the liquid.
4 Melt the butter in a large frying pan, add the onion and cook over medium heat until golden brown. Add the mushrooms and cook until tender. Add ¼ cup (60 ml/2 fl oz) of the reserved liquid, the tomato and herbs and bring to the boil. Reduce the heat and simmer for 30 minutes, or until the sauce thickens slightly. Stir in the seafood and cream and season, to taste.
5 For the bechamel sauce, melt the butter in a saucepan, add the flour and stir for 1 minute, or until pale and foaming. Remove from the heat and gradually stir in the milk. Return to the heat and stir until the sauce boils and thickens.
6 Spoon the seafood mixture into the cannelloni tubes and place in a greased 3 litre (96 fl oz) capacity ovenproof dish. Pour the sauce over and sprinkle with the grated cheese. Bake for 40 minutes, or until the cannelloni tubes are tender.

FRIED RICE

Preparation time: 15 minutes
Total cooking time: 10 minutes
Serves 4

★

250 g (8 oz) cooked small prawns
2 eggs, lightly beaten
2 tablespoons oil
1 onion, cut into wedges
250 g (8 oz) sliced leg ham, cut into thin strips
4 cups (740 g/1½ lb) cold, cooked rice
¼ cup (40 g/1¼ oz) frozen peas
2 tablespoons soy sauce
4 spring onions, cut diagonally into short lengths

1 Peel the prawns and gently pull out the dark vein from each prawn back, starting at the head end. Season the eggs with salt and pepper.
2 Heat 1 tablespoon of the oil in a wok or large frying pan and add the eggs, pulling the set egg towards the centre and tilting the pan to let the unset egg run to the edges. When almost set, break up into large pieces, to resemble scrambled eggs. Transfer to a plate and set aside.
3 Heat the remaining oil in the wok, swirling to coat the base and side. Add the onion and stir-fry over high heat until it starts to turn opaque. Add the ham and stir for 1 minute. Add the rice and peas and stir for 3 minutes, or until heated through. Add the eggs, soy sauce, spring onion and prawns, and stir until heated through. Serve.
NOTES: Cook 1⅓ cups (275 g/9 oz) raw rice a day in advance. Drain, cover and chill.
    You can use barbecued pork, Chinese sausage or bacon instead of the leg ham.

BLACK MUSSELS

Sometimes referred to as 'poor man's oyster' or 'blue mussel', the mussel is full of flavour. Mussels attach themselves to rocks or, if farmed, onto bags or ropes, with the tough brown fibres we call the 'beard'. Farmed mussels take 18 months to 2 years to mature. When buying mussels, avoid any with broken shells. Use soon after purchasing, or keep in a very cool place in a small amount of water, covered with a damp hessian bag. When you come to cook the mussels, if any of them have open shells, tap them on the bench and if they don't close, they are dead and should be thrown away. When mussels are cooked, the shells should open. Any that haven't opened by the end of cooking time (usually 3–5 minutes) should be thrown away.

ABOVE: Paella

PAELLA

Preparation time: 30 minutes
    + 2 hours soaking
Total cooking time: 45 minutes
Serves 4

12 raw medium prawns
12–16 black mussels
1/2 cup (125 ml/4 fl oz) white wine
1 small red onion, chopped
1/2 cup (125 ml/4 fl oz) olive oil
1 small chicken breast fillet, cut into
    bite-sized cubes
100 g (3 1/2 oz) calamari rings
100 g (3 1/2 oz) skinless white fish fillet
    (eg. cod, ling, mahi mahi, blue-eye, monkfish),
    cut into bite-sized cubes
1/2 small red onion, extra, finely chopped
1 rasher bacon, finely chopped
4 cloves garlic, crushed
1 small red pepper (capsicum), finely chopped

1 ripe tomato, peeled and chopped
90 g (3 oz) chorizo or pepperoni, thinly sliced
pinch of cayenne pepper
1 cup (200 g/6 1/2 oz) long-grain rice
1/4 teaspoon saffron threads
2 cups (500 ml/16 fl oz) chicken stock, heated
1/2 cup (80 g/2 3/4 oz) fresh or frozen peas
2 tablespoons finely chopped fresh parsley

1 Peel the prawns and pull out the dark vein from each prawn back, starting at the head end.
2 Scrub the mussels with a stiff brush and pull out the hairy beards. Discard any broken mussels, or open ones that don't close when tapped on the bench.
3 Heat the wine and onion in a large pan. Add the mussels, cover and gently shake the pan for 4–5 minutes over high heat. After 3 minutes, start removing opened mussels and set aside. At the end of 5 minutes, discard any unopened mussels. Reserve the cooking liquid.
4 Heat half the oil in a large frying pan. Pat the chicken dry with paper towels, then cook the chicken for 5 minutes, or until golden brown. Remove from the pan and set aside. Add the

prawns, calamari and fish to the pan and cook for 1 minute. Remove from the pan; set aside.

5 Heat the remaining oil in the pan, add the extra onion, bacon, garlic and red pepper and cook for 5 minutes, or until the onion is soft. Add the tomato, chorizo and cayenne. Season, to taste. Stir in the reserved cooking liquid, then add the rice and mix well.

6 Blend the saffron with ½ cup (125 ml/4 fl oz) of stock, then add with the remaining stock to the rice and mix well. Bring slowly to the boil. Reduce the heat to low and simmer, uncovered, for 15 minutes, without stirring.

7 Place the peas, chicken, prawns, calamari and fish on top of the rice. Using a wooden spoon, push pieces into the rice, cover and cook over low heat for 10–15 minutes, or until the rice is tender and the seafood cooked. Add the mussels for the last 2 minutes to heat. If the rice is not quite cooked, add a little extra stock and cook for a few more minutes. Serve sprinkled with parsley.

LEMONY HERB AND FISH RISOTTO

Preparation time: 20 minutes
Total cooking time: 30 minutes
Serves 4

✩ ✩

60 g (2 oz) butter
400 g (13 oz) skinless white fish fillets
  (eg. coley, cod, blue-eye, ling), cut
  into 3 cm (1¼ inch) cubes
1.25 litres (40 fl oz) fish stock
1 onion, finely chopped
1 clove garlic, crushed
1 teaspoon ground turmeric
1½ cups (330 g/11 oz) arborio rice
2 tablespoons lemon juice
1 tablespoon chopped fresh parsley
1 tablespoon chopped fresh chives
1 tablespoon chopped fresh dill

1 Melt half the butter in a pan. Add the fish in batches and fry over medium–high heat for 3 minutes, or until the fish is just cooked through. Remove from the pan and set aside.

2 Pour the fish stock into another pan, bring to the boil, cover and keep at simmering point.

3 To the first pan, add the remaining butter, onion and garlic and cook over medium heat for 3 minutes, or until the onion is tender. Add the turmeric and stir for 1 minute. Add the rice and stir to coat, then add ½ cup (125 ml/4 fl oz) of the fish stock and cook, stirring constantly, over low heat until all the stock has been absorbed. Continue adding ½ cup (125 ml/4 fl oz) of stock at a time until all the stock has been added and the rice is translucent, tender and creamy.

4 Stir in the lemon juice, parsley, chives and dill. Add the fish and stir gently. Serve, maybe garnished with slices of lemon or lime and fresh herb sprigs.

NOTE: The rice must absorb the stock between each addition—the whole process will take about 20 minutes. If you don't have time to make your own stock, you can buy fresh or frozen fish stock from delicatessens, some seafood outlets and most supermarkets.

BELOW: Lemony herb and fish risotto

KEDGEREE

Preparation time: 10 minutes
Total cooking time: 15 minutes
Serves 4

⭐

600 g (1¼ lb) smoked cod fillets

3 slices lemon

1 bay leaf

4 eggs, hard-boiled

60 g (2 oz) butter

1 small onion, finely chopped

1–2 tablespoons mild curry paste

4 cups (740 g/24 fl oz) cooked long-grain rice

1 tablespoon finely chopped fresh parsley

²/₃ cup (170 ml/5½ fl oz) cream

1 Put the cod in a deep frying pan with the lemon and bay leaf, cover with water and simmer for 6 minutes, or until cooked through. Remove the fish with a slotted spoon and break into flakes. Discard any bones.

2 Finely chop 2 eggs. Cut the other 2 eggs into quarters and set aside to use as garnish.

3 Melt the butter in a frying pan over medium heat. Add the onion and cook for 3 minutes, or until soft. Add the curry paste and cook for another 2 minutes. Add the rice and carefully stir through, cooking for 2–3 minutes, or until heated through. Add the parsley, fish, chopped egg and cream and stir until heated through.

4 Serve immediately with toast, garnishing each portion with egg quarters.

BELOW: Kedgeree

CREAMY SEAFOOD RAVIOLI

Preparation time: 45 minutes + 30 minutes
   standing
Total cooking time: 15 minutes
Serves 4

⭐ ⭐ ⭐

Pasta

2 cups (250 g/8 oz) plain flour

3 eggs

1 tablespoon olive oil

1 egg yolk, extra

Filling

100 g (3½ oz) scallops

50 g (1¾ oz) butter, softened

3 cloves garlic, finely chopped

2 tablespoons chopped fresh flat-leaf parsley

100 g (3½ oz) raw prawn meat,
   finely chopped

Knead the dough on a lightly floured surface until smooth and elastic.

Place a teaspoon of filling at intervals down one side of the pasta.

Cut between each mound of filling with a sharp knife.

Sauce

60 g (2 oz) butter

1/4 cup (30 g/1 oz) plain flour

1 1/2 cups (375 ml/12 fl oz) milk

300 ml (10 fl oz) cream

1/2 cup (125 ml/4 fl oz) white wine

50 g (1 3/4 oz) Parmesan, grated

2 tablespoons chopped fresh flat-leaf parsley

1 Sift the flour and a pinch of salt into a bowl and make a well. Whisk the eggs, oil and 1 tablespoon water in a jug, add gradually to the flour and mix to a firm dough. Gather into a ball. (This can also be done in a food processor.)

2 Knead on a lightly floured surface for 5 minutes, or until smooth and elastic. Place in a lightly oiled bowl, cover with plastic wrap and set aside for at least 30 minutes.

3 For the filling, slice or pull off any vein, membrane or hard white muscle from the scallops, leaving any roe attached. Chop finely. Stir together the butter, garlic, parsley, scallops and prawn meat in a bowl. Set aside.

4 Roll out a quarter of the pasta dough at a time on a lightly floured surface, or use a pasta machine, until very thin (each portion should be roughly 10 cm/4 inches wide when rolled). Place 1 teaspoon of filling at 5 cm (2 inch) intervals down one side of each strip. Whisk the extra egg yolk with 3 tablespoons water. Brush along one side of the dough and between the filling. Fold the dough over the filling to meet the other side. Repeat with the remaining filling and dough. Press the edges together firmly to seal.

5 Cut between the mounds with a knife or fluted pastry cutter. Cook batches in a large pan of rapidly boiling water for 6 minutes. Drain well and return to the pan to keep warm.

6 For the sauce, melt the butter in a pan over low heat. Stir in the flour and cook for 1 minute, or until pale and foaming. Remove from the heat and gradually stir in the combined milk, cream and white wine. Return to the heat and stir constantly until the sauce boils and thickens. Reduce the heat and simmer for 2 minutes. Add the grated Parmesan and chopped parsley and stir. Season, to taste. Remove from the heat, add to the ravioli in the pan and toss gently to coat.

*ABOVE: Creamy
seafood ravioli*

TAGLIATELLE WITH PRAWNS AND CREAM

Preparation time: 30 minutes
Total cooking time: 20 minutes
Serves 4

500 g (1 lb) raw medium prawns
500 g (1 lb) fresh tagliatelle
60 g (2 oz) butter
6 spring onions, finely chopped
1/4 cup (60 ml/2 fl oz) brandy
1 1/4 cups (315 ml/10 fl oz) thick (double) cream
1 tablespoon chopped fresh thyme
1/2 cup (15 g/1/2 oz) finely chopped fresh
   flat-leaf parsley
grated Parmesan, for serving

1 Peel the prawns, leaving the tails intact. Gently pull out the dark vein from each prawn back, starting at the head end.
2 Cook the pasta in a large pan of boiling water until *al dente*. Drain thoroughly.
3 Meanwhile, melt the butter in a large heavy-based pan, add the spring onion and stir for 2 minutes. Add the prawns and stir for 2 minutes, or until the prawns just start to change colour. Remove the prawns from the pan and set aside.
4 Add the brandy to the pan and boil for 2 minutes, or until the brandy is reduced by half. Stir in the cream and add the thyme and half the parsley. Season with freshly ground black pepper. Simmer for 5 minutes, or until the sauce begins to thicken. Return the prawns to the sauce and cook for 2 minutes. Season well.
5 Toss the sauce through the pasta. If you prefer a thinner sauce, add a little hot water or milk. Sprinkle with the remaining fresh parsley and grated Parmesan.
NOTE: You can use sherry or white wine instead of brandy, if preferred.

SEAFOOD SPAGHETTI PAPER PARCELS

Preparation time: 20 minutes
Total cooking time: 35 minutes
Makes 6

185 g (6 oz) thin spaghetti
4 ripe Roma (egg) tomatoes
1 tablespoon olive oil
4 spring onions, finely chopped
1 stick celery, finely chopped
1/3 cup (80 ml/2 3/4 fl oz) white wine
1/2 cup (125 ml/4 fl oz) tomato pasta sauce
4 gherkins, finely diced
2 tablespoons drained bottled capers, chopped
6 x 175 g (6 oz) pieces of skinless salmon fillet
   or ocean trout, boned
6 large dill sprigs
shredded rind of 2 lemons
30 g (1 oz) butter, cut into small cubes

1 Preheat the oven to moderate 180°C (350°F/Gas 4). Cook the pasta in a large pan of boiling water until *al dente*. Drain in a colander and run under cold water to cool. Transfer to a bowl.
2 Score a cross in the base of each tomato. Place in a heatproof bowl and cover with boiling water. Leave for 30 seconds, transfer to cold water, drain and peel away from the cross. Halve each tomato, scoop out the seeds and chop the flesh.
3 Heat the oil in a frying pan, add the spring onion and celery and stir for 2 minutes. Add the tomato and wine and bring to the boil. Boil for 3 minutes to reduce. Reduce the heat and stir in the pasta sauce, gherkins and capers. Season well with salt and black pepper. Mix thoroughly through the pasta.
4 To assemble, cut six 30 cm (12 inch) square sheets (depending on the shape of your fish) of baking paper and brush the outside edges with oil. Divide the pasta among the sheets, using a fork to curl the pasta. Place a piece of salmon on top of each, then top with dill and lemon rind. Divide the butter among the parcels.
5 Fold into parcels, turning over twice at the top to seal. Tuck the ends under and bake on a baking tray for 20 minutes. To serve, cut or pull open the parcel and serve in the paper, or if you prefer, slide off the paper onto serving plates.
NOTE: The parcels can be assembled a few hours ahead and refrigerated until required. If you do this, allow a couple of extra minutes cooking.

SEAFOOD SPAGHETTI PAPER PARCELS

Top each salmon fillet with dill, shredded lemon rind and a cube of butter.

Fold each parcel over twice at the top and tuck the ends under.

OPPOSITE PAGE:
Tagliatelle with prawns and cream (top); Seafood spaghetti paper parcels

JAMBALAYA

This Creole rice dish closely resembles Spanish Paella. It can include chicken, sausage, ham, prawns and other shellfish. Traditionally, it is served with Tabasco, a hot pepper sauce.

ABOVE: Prawn jambalaya

PRAWN JAMBALAYA

Preparation time: 20 minutes
Total cooking time: 1 hour 10 minutes
Serves 6

1 kg (2 lb) raw large prawns
1 small onion, chopped
2 sticks celery, chopped
1 cup (250 ml/8 fl oz) dry white wine
1/4 cup (60 ml/2 fl oz) vegetable oil
200 g (6 1/2 oz) chorizo or spicy sausage, chopped
1 onion, extra, chopped
1 red pepper (capsicum), chopped
425 g (14 oz) can crushed tomatoes
1/2 teaspoon cayenne pepper
1/2 teaspoon cracked black pepper
1/4 teaspoon dried thyme
1/4 teaspoon dried oregano
2 cups (400 g/13 oz) long-grain rice

1 Peel the prawns and pull out the dark vein from each prawn back, starting at the head end. Reserve the shells. Refrigerate the prawn meat. Put the heads, shells and tails in a pan with the small onion, 1 chopped stick celery, wine and 1 litre (32 fl oz) water. Bring to the boil, then reduce the heat and simmer for 20 minutes. Strain.
2 Heat the oil in a large heavy-based pan and cook the chopped sausage for 5 minutes, or until browned. Remove from the pan with a slotted spoon and set aside.
3 Add the extra onion, red pepper and remaining celery to the pan and cook, stirring occasionally, for 5 minutes. Add the tomato, cayenne, black pepper and dried herbs and bring to the boil. Reduce the heat and simmer, covered, for 10 minutes.
4 Return the sausage to the pan and add the rice and prawn stock. Bring back to the boil, reduce the heat and simmer, covered, for 25 minutes, until almost all the liquid has been absorbed and the rice is tender.
5 Add the prawns to the pan and stir through gently. Cover and cook for another 5 minutes. Serve immediately.

CRISPY FRIED NOODLES WITH PRAWNS

Preparation time: 30 minutes + 20 minutes drying
Total cooking time: 15 minutes
Serves 4

★ ★

100 g (3½ oz) dried rice vermicelli

oil, for shallow-frying

100 g (3½ oz) tofu, cut into strips

2 cloves garlic, finely chopped

4 cm (1½ inch) piece fresh ginger, finely grated

150 g (5 oz) chicken or pork mince, or a combination

100 g (3½ oz) raw prawn meat, roughly chopped

2 tablespoons fish sauce

1 tablespoon white vinegar

2 tablespoons soft brown sugar

2 tablespoons chilli sauce

1 teaspoon finely chopped red chilli

2 small pieces pickled garlic, chopped

40 g (1¼ oz) fresh garlic chives, chopped

30 g (1 oz) fresh coriander leaves

1 Place the rice vermicelli in a heatproof bowl, cover with boiling water and soak for 1 minute. Drain and allow to dry completely on crumpled paper towel for about 20 minutes.

2 Heat 2.5 cm (1 inch) oil in a wok or heavy-based frying pan to 180°C (350°F), or until a cube of bread dropped into the oil browns in 15 seconds. Cook the tofu in 2 batches for 1 minute each batch, or until crisp and golden brown all over. Remove with tongs and drain on crumpled paper towels.

3 Add the completely dry vermicelli to the wok in several batches, cooking for 10 seconds, or until puffed and crisp. Remove from the oil immediately to prevent the vermicelli absorbing too much oil. Drain on crumpled paper towels and allow to cool.

4 Carefully drain all but a tablespoon of the oil from the wok and reheat the wok over high heat. Add the garlic, ginger, chicken or pork mince, and the prawn meat. Stir-fry for 3 minutes. Add the fish sauce, vinegar, sugar, chilli sauce and red chilli to the wok and stir through until boiling.

5 Just before serving, return the noodles and tofu to the wok and mix in thoroughly. Add the pickled garlic, garlic chives and coriander leaves and toss well to combine. Serve immediately to prevent the noodles from becoming soggy.

NOTE: Pickled garlic is used as a flavour enhancer, relish, or garnish.

BELOW: Crispy fried noodles with prawns

THAI FRIED NOODLES WITH PRAWNS

Preparation time: 25 minutes + 8 minutes standing
Total cooking time: 10 minutes
Serves 4

200 g (6¹/₂ oz) dried thick rice stick noodles
1 tablespoon oil
2 cloves garlic, crushed
2 fresh red chillies, seeded and finely chopped
1 chicken breast fillet, thinly sliced
150 g (5 oz) raw prawn meat, chopped
¹/₄ cup (30 g/1 oz) chopped fresh garlic chives
2 tablespoons fish sauce
1 tablespoon soft brown sugar
2 tablespoons lemon juice
1 egg, lightly beaten
50 g (1³/₄ oz) deep-fried tofu, cut into strips
3 tablespoons fresh coriander leaves

¹/₄ cup (25 g/³/₄ oz) bean sprouts
¹/₄ cup (40 g/1¹/₄ oz) roasted peanuts, chopped
1 lemon, cut into wedges, for serving

1 Put the noodles in a heatproof bowl. Cover with boiling water and leave for 5–8 minutes, or until the noodles are soft and tender. Drain and set aside.
2 Heat the wok until very hot, add the oil and swirl it around to coat the side. Stir-fry the garlic, chilli and sliced chicken over high heat for 2–3 minutes, or until the chicken is browned.
3 Add the prawn meat to the wok and cook for 2 minutes, or until the prawn meat turns pink. Add the drained noodles and garlic chives, and toss until thoroughly combined.
4 Add the fish sauce, brown sugar, lemon juice, egg and tofu, and toss gently to combine, using a pair of tongs or two wooden spoons. Serve sprinkled with the coriander leaves, bean sprouts and peanuts. Serve with lemon wedges.
NOTE: Deep-fried tofu is available from Asian grocery stores and some supermarkets.

ABOVE: Thai fried noodles with prawns

NASI GORENG

Preparation time: 25 minutes
Total cooking time: 15 minutes
Serves 6

★★

350 g (11 oz) raw medium prawns
5–8 long red chillies, seeded and chopped
2 teaspoons shrimp paste
8 cloves garlic, finely chopped
4 tablespoons oil
2 eggs, lightly beaten
350 g (11 oz) chicken thigh fillets, cut into
   thin strips
8 cups (1.5 kg/3 lb) cold, cooked rice
1/3 cup (80 ml/2¾ fl oz) kecap manis
1/3 cup (80 ml/2¾ fl oz) soy sauce
2 small Lebanese cucumbers, finely chopped
1 large ripe tomato, seeded, finely chopped
lime halves, for serving

1 Peel the prawns and pull out the dark vein from each prawn back, starting at the head end.
2 Mix the chilli, shrimp paste and garlic in a food processor to form a paste.

3 Heat the wok until very hot, add 1 tablespoon of the oil and swirl it around to coat the side. Add the beaten eggs and, using a wok chan or metal egg flip, push the egg up the edges of the wok to form a large omelette. Cook for 1 minute over medium heat, or until the egg is set, then flip it over and cook the other side for 1 minute. Remove from the wok and cool before slicing into strips.
4 Reheat the wok, add 1 tablespoon of the oil and stir-fry the chicken and half the chilli paste over high heat until the chicken is just cooked. Remove the chicken from the wok.
5 Reheat the wok, add 1 tablespoon of the oil and stir-fry the prawns and the remaining chilli paste until the prawns are cooked. Remove from the wok and set aside.
6 Reheat the wok, add 1 tablespoon of oil and the cold cooked rice, and toss constantly over medium heat for 4–5 minutes, or until the rice is heated through. Add the kecap manis and soy sauce, and toss constantly until all the rice is coated in the sauces. Return the chicken and prawns to the wok, and toss until well combined and heated through. Season well with freshly cracked pepper and salt. Transfer to a large deep serving bowl and top with the omelette strips, chopped cucumber and tomato. Serve with the lime halves.

NASI GORENG

Remove the seeds from the red chillies and finely chop the flesh.

Process the chilli, shrimp paste and garlic until it forms a paste.

LEFT: Nasi goreng

253

PIES, CASSEROLES & BAKES

Although there may be a golden rule that seafood is at its best cooked quickly and simply, we all know some rules are meant to be broken. If we weren't allowed to simmer our seafood in a heady mix of Mediterranean herbs and wine, there would be no cioppino. If it was against the rules to cook prawns in a sauce of fragrant spices and coconut cream, we wouldn't have Thai prawn curry. And if we weren't allowed to bake flaked fish in a lemon and dill sauce, topped with creamy mash, there would be no such thing as fish pie. Unimaginable!

SEAFOOD QUICHE

Preparation time: 20 minutes + 20 minutes
    chilling
Total cooking time: 1 hour
Serves 4-6

2 sheets ready-rolled shortcrust pastry
100 g (3½ oz) scallops
30 g (1 oz) butter
100 g (3½ oz) raw prawn meat
100 g (3½ oz) canned, fresh or frozen
    crab meat
90 g (3 oz) Cheddar, grated
3 eggs
1 tablespoon plain flour
½ cup (125 ml/4 fl oz) cream
½ cup (125 ml/4 fl oz) milk
1 small fennel bulb, finely sliced
1 tablespoon grated Parmesan

1 Lightly grease a 22 cm (9 inch) diameter loose-based flan tin. Place the 2 sheets of pastry slightly overlapping, on a work bench, and roll out until large enough to fit the prepared tin. Press the pastry into the base and side of the tin and trim off any excess with a sharp knife. Refrigerate for 20 minutes.

2 Slice or pull off any vein, membrane or hard white muscle from the scallops, leaving any roe attached. Preheat the oven to moderately hot 190°C (375°F/Gas 5).

3 Cover the pastry with baking paper, fill evenly with baking beads or uncooked rice and bake for 10 minutes. Remove the paper and rice and bake for another 10 minutes, or until lightly golden. Cool on a wire rack. If the pastry puffs up, press down lightly with a tea towel.

4 Melt the butter in a frying pan and fry the prawns and scallops for 2–3 minutes, or until cooked. Allow to cool, then arrange all the seafood over the base of the pastry shell. Sprinkle with the Cheddar.

5 Beat the eggs in a small jug, whisk in the flour, cream and milk, and season with salt and pepper. Pour over the filling. Sprinkle with fennel and Parmesan. Bake for 30–35 minutes, or until set and golden brown. Cool slightly before serving.

RIGHT: Seafood quiche

COULIBIAC

Preparation time: 25 minutes + 30 minutes
  chilling
Total cooking time: 40 minutes
Serves 4-6

60 g (2 oz) butter
I onion, finely chopped
200 g (6¹/2 oz) button mushrooms, sliced
2 tablespoons lemon juice
220 g (7 oz) salmon fillet, boned, skinned,
  cut into 2 cm (³/4 inch) pieces
2 hard-boiled eggs, chopped
2 tablespoons chopped fresh dill
2 tablespoons chopped fresh parsley
I cup (185 g/6 oz) cold, cooked rice
¹/4 cup (60 ml/2 fl oz) cream
375 g (12 oz) block frozen puff pastry, thawed
I egg, lightly beaten

1 Lightly grease a baking tray. Melt half the butter in a frying pan. Add the onion and cook over medium heat for 5 minutes or until soft but not browned. Add the mushrooms and cook for 5 minutes. Add the lemon juice to the pan and stir to combine. Transfer the mixture to a bowl.
2 Melt the remaining butter in a pan, add the salmon and cook for 2 minutes. Transfer to a bowl, cool slightly and add the egg, dill, parsley and salt and pepper, to taste. Combine gently and set aside. Combine the rice and cream in a small bowl and season with salt and pepper.
3 Roll out half the pastry to a rectangle measuring 18 x 30 cm (7 x 12 inches) and place on the prepared tray. Spread half the rice mixture onto the pastry, leaving a 3 cm (1¹/4 inch) border all the way around. Top with the salmon mixture, then the mushroom mixture, and finish with the remaining rice.
4 Roll out the remaining pastry to 20 x 32 cm (8 x 13 inches) and place over the filling. Press the edges together, then crimp to seal. Decorate with pastry cut-outs if you like. Refrigerate for 30 minutes. Meanwhile, preheat the oven to hot 210°C (415°F/Gas 6–7). Brush the pastry with the beaten egg and bake for 15 minutes. Reduce the heat to moderate 180°C (350°F/Gas 4) and bake for another 15–20 minutes, until the top is golden brown.
NOTES: You can substitute ocean trout for the salmon. A can of red salmon can also be used.
  You will need ¹/3 cup (65 g/2¹/4 oz) raw rice.

BAKED POTATOES WITH PRAWNS AND YOGHURT

Wash and dry 4 large potatoes, then prick all over with a fork. Place on a baking tray and brush with oil. Bake in a hot 220°C (425°F/Gas 7) oven for 1–1¹/2 hours, until cooked through when tested with a skewer. Meanwhile, heat 300 g (10 oz) cooked and peeled small prawns in a lightly oiled pan with a crushed garlic clove. Stir in some chopped fresh chives and ¹/2 cup (125 g/4 oz) natural yoghurt. Cut a deep cross in the top of each potato and fill with prawn mixture. Serve with wedges of lemon. Makes 4.

ABOVE: Coulibiac

ZARZUELA

Preparation time: 40 minutes
Total cooking time: 1 hour 10 minutes
Serves 4

★★★

Sofrito sauce

1 tablespoon olive oil
2 onions, finely chopped
2 large tomatoes, peeled, seeded and chopped
1 tablespoon tomato paste (tomato purée)

Picada sauce

3 slices white bread, crusts removed
1 tablespoon almonds, toasted
3 cloves garlic
1 tablespoon olive oil

1 raw lobster tail (about 400 g/13 oz)
12–15 black mussels
750 g (1 1/2 lb) skinless white fish fillet (eg. flake, cod, warehou, monkfish), in bite-sized pieces
plain flour, seasoned with salt and pepper
2–3 tablespoons olive oil
125 g (4 oz) calamari rings

12 raw large prawns
1/2 cup (125 ml/4 fl oz) white wine
1/2 cup (125 ml/4 fl oz) brandy
3 tablespoons chopped fresh parsley

1 For the sofrito sauce, heat the oil in a pan over medium heat. Add the onion and stir for 5 minutes without browning. Add the tomato, tomato paste and 1/2 cup (125 ml/4 fl oz) water and stir over medium heat for 10 minutes. Stir in another 1/2 cup (125 ml/4 fl oz) water, season with salt and freshly ground pepper and set aside.

2 For the picada sauce, finely chop the bread, almonds and garlic in a food processor. With the motor running, gradually add the oil to form a paste, adding another 1/2 tablespoon of oil if necessary.

3 Preheat the oven to moderate 180°C (350°F/Gas 4). Cut the lobster tail into rounds through the membrane that separates the shell segments. Set the rounds aside.

4 Scrub the mussels with a stiff brush and pull out the hairy beards. Discard any broken mussels, or open ones that don't close when tapped on the bench. Rinse well.

5 Lightly coat the fish in flour. Heat the oil in a large pan and fry the fish in batches over medium heat for 2–3 minutes, or until cooked and golden

ZARZUELA

Zarzuela literally means 'operetta', an apt name for this dish from Catalonia. Zarzuela is a colourful concoction of all kinds of seafood, with different shellfish such as prawns, lobster, clams and mussels, baked in a casserole in a tomato-based sauce (sometimes with chopped red or green peppers included). The addition of wine helps moisten the seafood. Fried croutons are often sprinkled on top when serving.

ABOVE: Zarzuela

brown all over. Transfer to a large casserole dish.

6 Add a little oil to the pan if necessary, add the calamari and cook, stirring, for 1–2 minutes. Remove and add to the fish. Cook the lobster rounds and unshelled prawns for 2–3 minutes, or until just pink, then add to the casserole.

7 Add the wine to the pan and bring to the boil. Reduce the heat, add the mussels, cover and steam for 4–5 minutes. Add to the casserole, discarding any unopened mussels.

8 Ensuring nothing flammable is nearby, pour the brandy into one side of the pan and, when it has warmed, carefully ignite the brandy. Gently shake the pan until the flames have died down. Pour this mixture over the seafood in the casserole dish.

9 Pour the sofrito sauce over the top. Cover the casserole and bake for 20 minutes. Stir in the picada sauce and cook for another 10 minutes, or until warmed through—do not overcook, or the seafood will toughen. Sprinkle with the parsley.

TUNA AND WHITE BEAN CASSEROLE

Preparation time: 40 minutes + 8 hours soaking
Total cooking time: 3 hours
Serves 6

★★

2 cups (400 g/13 oz) dried cannellini beans
1/4 cup (60 ml/2 fl oz) olive oil
2 red onions, chopped
2 cloves garlic, crushed
1 teaspoon ground coriander
1 teaspoon finely grated lemon rind
2 teaspoons finely chopped fresh thyme
2 cups (500 ml/16 fl oz) white wine
2 cups (500 ml/16 fl oz) fish stock
475 g (15 oz) can tuna in oil, drained
60 g (2 oz) basil leaves
4 large very ripe tomatoes, cut in thick slices

Topping

1/2 cup (40 g/1 1/4 oz) fresh breadcrumbs
1 clove garlic, crushed
3 tablespoons finely chopped fresh parsley
30 g (1 oz) butter, melted

1 Put the beans in a large bowl and cover with cold water, allowing room for the beans to expand. Soak for 8 hours. Rinse well, then drain.

2 Heat the oil in a large frying pan, add the onion, garlic, coriander, rind and thyme, and cook over medium heat for 10 minutes, or until soft. Add the beans and cook for 10 minutes.

3 Add the wine and stock and bring to the boil. Reduce the heat to low, cover and cook for 2 hours, or until the beans are tender but not falling apart.

4 Preheat the oven to hot 210°C (415°F/ Gas 6-7). Transfer the bean mixture to a large casserole dish. Top with the tuna and basil leaves. Overlap the tomato slices over the basil.

5 For the topping, combine the breadcrumbs, garlic and parsley in a bowl and sprinkle over the tomato. Drizzle with the butter and bake for 30 minutes, or until the top is golden brown. Serve with crusty bread.

NOTE: This dish can be made a day in advance. Canned salmon can be used, but tuna is traditional with beans.

BELOW: Tuna and white bean casserole

FISH PIE

Mash the potatoes together with the milk or cream, egg and butter.

Put the pieces of fish in a frying pan and cover with the milk.

Spoon the mashed potato over the fish.

FISH PIE

Preparation time: 10 minutes
Total cooking time: 45 minutes
Serves 4

2 large potatoes (500 g/1 lb), chopped
1/4 cup (60 ml/2 fl oz) milk or cream
1 egg, lightly beaten
60 g (2 oz) butter
60 g (2 oz) Cheddar, grated
800 g (1 lb 10 oz) skinless white fish fillets
    (eg. ling, hake, snapper, monkfish), cut into
    large chunks
1 1/2 cups (375 ml/12 fl oz) milk
1 onion, finely chopped
1 clove garlic, crushed
2 tablespoons plain flour
2 tablespoons lemon juice
2 teaspoons lemon rind
1 tablespoon chopped fresh dill

1 Preheat the oven to moderate 180°C (350°F/ Gas 4). Boil or steam the potatoes until tender (pierce with the point of a small knife—if the potato comes away easily, it is ready) and mash well with the milk or cream, egg and half the butter. Mix in half the Cheddar, then set aside and keep warm.
2 Put the fish in a shallow frying pan and cover with the milk. Bring to the boil, then reduce the heat and simmer for 2–3 minutes, or until the fish is cooked. Drain the fish well, reserving the milk, and set aside.
3 Melt the rest of the butter in a pan and cook the onion and garlic over medium heat for 2 minutes. Stir in the flour and cook for 1 minute, or until pale and foaming. Remove from the heat and gradually stir in the reserved milk. Return to the heat and stir constantly until the sauce boils and thickens. Reduce the heat and simmer for 2 minutes. Add the lemon juice, lemon rind and dill, and season with plenty of salt and cracked black pepper.
4 Put the fish in a 1.5 litre (48 fl oz) capacity ovenproof dish and gently mix in the sauce. Spoon the mashed potato over the fish and top with the remaining Cheddar. Bake for 35 minutes, or until golden brown.

TUNA MORNAY

Preparation time: 20 minutes
Total cooking time: 25 minutes
Serves 4

60 g (2 oz) butter
2 tablespoons plain flour
2 cups (500 ml/16 fl oz) milk
1/2 teaspoon dry mustard
90 g (3 oz) Cheddar, grated
600 g (1 1/4 lb) canned tuna in brine, drained
2 tablespoons finely chopped fresh parsley
2 eggs, hard-boiled and chopped
1/3 cup (25 g/3/4 oz) fresh breadcrumbs
paprika, for dusting

1 Preheat the oven to moderate 180°C (350°F/ Gas 4). Melt the butter in a small pan. Add the flour and stir over low heat for 1 minute, or until pale and foaming. Remove the pan from the heat and gradually stir in the milk. Return the pan to the heat and stir constantly until the sauce boils and thickens. Reduce the heat and simmer for 2 minutes. Remove from the heat and whisk in the mustard and 60 g (2 oz) of the Cheddar, until melted and smooth.
2 Flake the tuna with a fork and mix into the sauce, with the parsley and egg. Season with salt and pepper, to taste. Spoon into four 1 cup (250 ml/8 fl oz) capacity ovenproof ramekins. Mix the breadcrumbs and remaining Cheddar and sprinkle over the mornay. Dust very lightly with paprika. Bake for 15–20 minutes, or until golden brown.
NOTES: For an interesting crunch to your tuna mornay, substitute roughly crushed potato crisps for some or all of the breadcrumbs in the topping. Choose plain, or salt-and-vinegar flavoured crisps.

Cans of salmon can be substituted for the tuna, using the same amount.

OPPOSITE PAGE: Fish pie (top); Tuna mornay

MUSSELS IN TWO SAUCES

Preparation time: 25 minutes
Total cooking time: 45 minutes
Serves 4

1.25 kg (2¹/₂ lb) black mussels
3 tablespoons olive oil
3 tablespoons grated mozzarella
2 tablespoons grated Parmesan

Tomato sauce

2 cloves garlic, crushed
¹/₂ cup (125 ml/4 fl oz) white wine
3 tablespoons tomato paste (tomato purée)

White sauce

25 g (³/₄ oz) butter
¹/₄ cup (30 g/1 oz) plain flour
1 cup (250 ml/8 fl oz) milk

*BELOW: Mussels
in two sauces*

1 Scrub the mussels with a stiff brush and pull out the hairy beards. Discard any broken mussels or open ones that don't close when tapped on the bench. Rinse well.
2 Heat half the oil in a large pan. Add the mussels and cook over high heat, shaking the pan, for 4–5 minutes until opened. Discard any unopened mussels. Strain the liquid and reserve. Allow the mussels to cool, then remove from their shells and discard the shells. Preheat the oven to moderately hot 190°C (375°F/Gas 5).
3 For the tomato sauce, heat the remaining oil in a pan. Add the garlic and fry over medium heat until golden. Add the wine and reserved mussel liquid, bring to the boil, reduce the heat and simmer gently for 4–5 minutes. Blend the tomato paste with 3 tablespoons water, then whisk into the simmering liquid. Simmer for another 10 minutes and season, to taste. Remove from the heat.
4 For the white sauce, melt the butter in a pan over low heat. Stir in the flour and cook for 1 minute, or until pale and foaming. Remove from the heat and gradually stir in the milk. Return to the heat and stir constantly until the sauce boils and thickens. Reduce the heat and simmer for 2 minutes. Season, to taste.
5 Combine the tomato sauce and mussels and spoon into four 1-cup (250 ml/8 fl oz) ovenproof ramekins. Carefully spoon the white sauce over the top and sprinkle with the combined cheeses. Bake for 20 minutes, or until the cheese has melted and the tops are golden brown. Serve with crusty bread.

BAKED LOBSTER

Preparation time: 15 minutes
Total cooking time: 20 minutes
Serves 4

2 raw large lobster tails
1 small clove garlic, crushed
¹/₂ cup (125 ml/4 fl oz) oil
¹/₄ cup (60 ml/2 fl oz) brandy
¹/₄ cup (60 ml/2 fl oz) lemon juice
salt and cayenne pepper
lemon wedges, for serving

1 Preheat the oven to moderately hot 200°C (400°F/Gas 6). Cut the lobster tails in half lengthways, with a sharp knife. Combine the garlic, oil, brandy and lemon juice in a bowl.

2 Season the lobster with salt and cayenne pepper and brush with the oil mixture. Place in a baking dish and bake for 15–20 minutes, or until cooked through—the flesh will turn white and the shell a deep orange. Baste several times during cooking. Serve with lemon wedges.

SEAFOOD, FENNEL AND POTATO STEW

Preparation time: 25 minutes
Total cooking time: 30 minutes
Serves 6

18–20 black mussels
6 baby octopus
16 raw medium prawns
1 large fennel bulb
2 tablespoons olive oil
2 leeks, white part only, thinly sliced
2 cloves garlic, crushed
1/2 teaspoon paprika
2 tablespoons Pernod or Ricard (see Note)
2/3 cup (170 ml/5 1/2 fl oz) dry white wine
1/4 teaspoon saffron threads
1/4 teaspoon fresh thyme leaves
500 g (1 lb) fish cutlets (eg. swordfish, kingfish, warehou, monkfish), cut into large chunks
400 g (13 oz) baby new potatoes
fennel greens, to garnish

1 Scrub the mussels with a stiff brush and pull out the hairy beards. Discard any broken mussels, or open ones that don't close when tapped on the bench. Rinse well.
2 Use a small sharp knife to cut off the octopus heads. Grasp the bodies and push the beaks out with your index finger; remove and discard. Slit the heads and remove the gut, then wash well.
3 Peel the prawns and pull out the dark vein from each prawn back, starting at the head end.
4 Trim off any discoloured parts and thinly slice the fennel. Heat the oil in a large pan over medium heat. Add the fennel, leek and garlic. Stir in the paprika, season lightly with salt and pepper and cook for 8 minutes, or until softened. Add the Pernod and wine and boil for 1 minute, or until reduced by a third.
5 Add the mussels to the pan, cover and cook, shaking the pan occasionally for 4–5 minutes, or until opened, discarding any unopened mussels.

Remove from the pan and allow to cool. Remove the mussel meat from the shells and set aside.
6 Add the saffron and thyme to the pan and cook, stirring over medium heat, for 1–2 minutes. Season if necessary, with salt and pepper, then transfer to a large, flameproof casserole dish.
7 Stir the octopus, prawns, fish and potatoes into the stew. Cover and cook gently for 10 minutes, or until the potatoes and seafood are tender. Add the mussels, cover and heat through. Garnish with fennel greens and serve.
NOTES: Pernod and Ricard are aniseed-flavoured liqueurs and complement the fennel.

Choose very small potatoes for this recipe. Sometimes they are called chat potatoes. Otherwise, cut larger ones in half.

ABOVE: Seafood, fennel and potato stew

263

1 Preheat the oven to moderate 180°C (350°F/ Gas 4). Wash the fish and pat dry inside and out with paper towels. Fill the fish cavities with the lime slices and some of the ginger, then place each fish on a large piece of lightly greased foil. Wrap the fish firmly to enclose and bake on a baking tray for 20–30 minutes, until the flesh flakes easily when tested with a fork. While the fish is cooking, prepare the syrup.

2 For the syrup, combine the sugar and lime juice with 1 cup (250 ml/8 fl oz) water in a small pan and stir without boiling until the sugar dissolves. Bring to the boil, reduce the heat and simmer for 10 minutes, or until syrupy. Stir in the remaining ginger and lime strips. Put the fish onto serving plates. Top with the coriander leaves and spoon the hot syrup over the top.

NOTES: Baby salmon can also be used.

This fish recipe is good for anyone on a low-fat diet.

CRAB AND SPRING ONION QUICHES

Preparation time: 25 minutes
Total cooking time: 20 minutes
Makes 15

6 sheets filo pastry
30 g (1 oz) butter, melted
2 x 170 g (5¹/2 oz) cans crab meat, drained
4 spring onions, chopped
2 eggs
³/4 cup (185 ml/6 fl oz) cream
1 tablespoon plain flour
90 g (3 oz) Gruyére or Cheddar cheese, grated
fresh thyme sprigs

1 Preheat the oven to moderate 180°C (350°F/ Gas 4). Layer the filo pastry together with the melted butter. Cut 15 rounds with an 8 cm (3 inch) plain cutter and place in round-based patty tins.

2 Drain the crab meat and squeeze the meat dry with your hands. Melt a little extra butter in a small pan and cook the spring onion until softened. Mix with the crab meat, eggs, cream, flour and 60 g (2 oz) of the cheese.

3 Fill each pastry case with crab filling and sprinkle with the remaining cheese. Place a sprig of thyme over the top. Bake for 20 minutes, or until puffed and golden brown.

TROUT WITH GINGER AND CORIANDER

Preparation time: 20 minutes
Total cooking time: 30 minutes
Serves 2

2 rainbow trout (about 330 g/11 oz each), cleaned and scaled
2 limes, thinly sliced
5 cm (2 inch) piece fresh ginger, julienned
¹/4 cup (60 g/2 oz) caster sugar
¹/4 cup (60 ml/2 fl oz) lime juice
rind of 1 lime, cut in thin strips
10 g (¹/4 oz) fresh coriander leaves

ABOVE: Trout with ginger and coriander

264

LEMON GRASS, CORIANDER AND FISH BAKE

Preparation time: 15 minutes
Total cooking time: 40 minutes
Serves 4

4 fish cutlets (eg. blue-eye, mahi mahi, snapper,
    jewfish, about 200 g/6 1/2 oz each)
plain flour, seasoned with salt and ground pepper
2–3 tablespoons peanut oil
2 onions, sliced
2 stems lemon grass, white part only,
    finely chopped
4 kaffir lime leaves, finely shredded
1 teaspoon ground cumin
1 teaspoon ground coriander
1 teaspoon finely chopped red chilli
3/4 cup (185 ml/6 fl oz) chicken stock
1 1/2 cups (375 ml/12 fl oz) coconut milk
3 tablespoons chopped fresh coriander
2 teaspoons fish sauce

1 Preheat the oven to moderate 180°C (350°F/ Gas 4). Toss the fish lightly in the flour. Heat half the oil in a large heavy-based frying pan and cook the fish, in batches if necessary, over medium heat until lightly browned on both sides. Transfer to a shallow ovenproof dish.
2 Heat the remaining oil in the pan. Add the onion and lemon grass and cook, stirring, for 5 minutes, or until the onion softens. Add the lime leaves, cumin, coriander and chilli and stir for about 2 minutes, or until fragrant.
3 Add the stock and coconut milk to the pan and bring to the boil. Pour over the fish, then cover and bake for 30 minutes, or until the fish is tender.
4 Transfer the fish to a serving plate. Stir the chopped coriander and the fish sauce into the remaining sauce, and season, to taste, with salt and freshly ground pepper. Pour over the fish.

LEFT: Lemon grass, coriander and fish bake

FISH WITH GARLIC BREADCRUMBS

Preparation time: 15 minutes
Total cooking time: 10–15 minutes
Serves 4

4 skinless white fish fillets (eg. John dory, ocean perch, snapper, bream, 200 g/6½ oz each)
75 g (2½ oz) butter, melted
3 cloves garlic, crushed
2 cups (160 g/5½ oz) fresh white breadcrumbs
1 tablespoon finely chopped fresh parsley
lemon wedges, for serving

1 Preheat the oven to moderately hot 200°C (400°F/Gas 6). Brush an ovenproof dish (large enough to hold the fish in a single layer) with olive oil and arrange the fish on the base.
2 Combine the butter and garlic in a bowl and set aside. Mix the breadcrumbs and parsley and scatter in a thick layer over the fish. Drizzle with the garlic butter.
3 Bake for 10–15 minutes, or until the fish is white and flakes easily and the crumbs are golden brown. If the crumbs are not golden but the fish is cooked, place under a hot grill for a couple of minutes. Don't take your eyes off it as it can burn very quickly. Serve with lemon wedges.

FISH EN PAPILLOTE

Preparation time: 20 minutes
Total cooking time: 20 minutes
Serves 4

4 skinless fish fillets (eg. John dory, orange roughy, snapper, bream, 200 g/6½ oz each)
1 leek, white part only, cut into julienne strips
4 spring onions, julienned
30 g (1 oz) butter, softened
1 lemon, cut into 12 very thin slices
2–3 tablespoons lemon juice

1 Preheat the oven to moderate 180°C (350°F/Gas 4). Place each fish fillet in the centre of a piece of baking paper large enough to enclose the fish.
2 Scatter with the leek and spring onion. Top each with a teaspoon of butter and 3 slices of lemon. Sprinkle with the extra lemon juice. Bring the paper together and fold over several times. Fold the ends under to form a parcel. Bake on a baking tray for 20 minutes (the steam will make the paper puff up). Check to see that the fish is cooked (it should be white and flake easily when tested with a fork) and then serve. You can serve as parcels or remove the fish from the parcels with a fish slice and serve on warm plates.

BAKED FISH AND CRACKED WHEAT

Preparation time: 25 minutes + 30 minutes standing
Total cooking time: 35 minutes
Serves 4

³/4 cup (130 g/4½ oz) cracked wheat (burghul)
1 onion, roughly chopped
250 g (8 oz) skinless fish fillets (eg. redfish, pike, cod, bream), cut into small pieces
½ teaspoon finely grated orange rind
2 teaspoons finely chopped fresh coriander
2 tablespoons oil
2 onions, sliced, extra
pinch of saffron threads

1 Soak the burghul in the 1½ cups (375 ml/12 fl oz) hot water for 30 minutes. Drain and press out the liquid between paper towel.
2 Meanwhile, blend the onion in a food processor for 30 seconds. Add the fish and process until the mixture is very smooth. Chill for 10 minutes.
3 Preheat the oven to moderately hot 200°C (400°F/Gas 6). Place the burghul, fish mixture, orange rind and coriander in a bowl. Season with salt and pepper, to taste. Mix thoroughly, then knead in a bowl for 5 minutes, or until quite smooth.
4 Heat 1 tablespoon of the oil and cook the extra onion until golden. Cover the saffron with a little boiling water and cool. Add the saffron and liquid to the onion and season, to taste.
5 Spread half the fish mixture in a small, lightly greased, round ovenproof dish. Top with the onion. Cover with the remaining fish and smooth the top. Score into a diamond pattern and sprinkle with the remaining oil. Bake for 25–30 minutes. Cool, then cut into serving pieces.

EN PAPILLOTE
When fish and other meats and vegetables are sealed and cooked in parchment or baking paper, the recipe is often referred to as en papillote. As the food cooks, it creates steam which is trapped in the paper, causing the paper to puff and rise into a tent or dome shape. The parcel can be served at the table and opened in front of your guests. Foil can be used to wrap the food but it won't puff as much as the paper.

OPPOSITE PAGE: Fish with garlic breadcrumbs (top); Fish en papillote

BRIK A L'OEUF

Carefully crack an egg into the centre of the tuna mixture.

Lay an extra 2 sheets of filo over the tuna and egg and fold in the sides.

Roll up the pastry into a neat firm package, keeping the egg intact.

BRIK A L'OEUF

Preparation time: 30 minutes
Total cooking time: 15 minutes
Serves 2

☆☆

6 sheets filo pastry

30 g (1 oz) butter, melted

1 small onion, finely chopped

200 g (6½ oz) can tuna in oil, drained

6 black olives, pitted and chopped

1 tablespoon finely chopped fresh parsley

2 eggs

1 Preheat the oven to moderately hot 200°C (400°F/Gas 6). Cut the filo pastry sheets in half widthways. Layer 4 sheets together with melted butter. Keep the remaining pastry covered with a damp tea towel. Combine the onion, tuna, olives and parsley in a bowl and spoon half the mixture onto one end of the buttered pastry, leaving a border. Make a well in the centre of the tuna mixture and break an egg into the well, being careful to leave it whole. Season with salt and freshly ground black pepper.

2 Layer 2 more sheets of filo together with melted butter and place on top of the tuna and egg. Fold in the pastry sides, then roll into a firm parcel, keeping the egg whole. Place on a lightly greased baking tray and brush with melted butter. Repeat with the remaining pastry, filling and egg.

3 Bake for 15 minutes, or until the pastry is golden brown. Serve warm.

NOTE: The yolk is still soft after 15 minutes. If you prefer a firmer egg, bake a little longer.

HADDOCK DUGLESE

Preparation time: 20 minutes
Total cooking time: 30 minutes
Serves 4

☆

500 g (1 lb) smoked haddock, or cod, fillets

1 cup (250 ml/4 fl oz) dry white wine

1 teaspoon whole black peppercorns

1 large onion, cut in 1 cm (½ inch) slices

30 g (1 oz) butter

2 tablespoons plain flour

2 tomatoes, peeled and chopped, seeds removed

¼ cup (60 ml/2 fl oz) cream

1 tablespoon chopped fresh parsley, to garnish

RIGHT: Brik a l'oeuf

1 Preheat the oven to moderate 180°C (350°F/ Gas 4). Thoroughly wash the haddock and place in a pan. Cover with water, bring slowly to the boil, reduce the heat and simmer, uncovered, for 5 minutes. Strain off the water.

2 Pour the wine and 1 cup (250 ml/8 fl oz) water over the haddock, scatter the peppercorns and onion on top. Cover and simmer gently for 5–8 minutes, or until just tender.

3 Remove the haddock with a slotted spoon and place in an ovenproof dish. Reserve 1 cup (250 ml/8 fl oz) of the liquid for the sauce.

4 For the sauce, melt the butter in a pan over low heat. Stir in the flour and cook for 1 minute, or until pale and foaming. Remove from the heat and gradually stir in the reserved stock. Return to the heat and stir until the sauce boils and thickens. Reduce the heat and simmer for 2 minutes. Add the tomato and the cream and stir until heated through.

5 Pour the sauce over the fish, sprinkle with parsley and bake for 15–20 minutes. Serve immediately with hot fluffy mashed potatoes and steamed vegetables.

FREEFORM PRAWN PIES

Preparation time: 30 minutes + 15 minutes chilling
Total cooking time: 30 minutes
Serves 4

2 cups (250 g/8 oz) plain flour
125 g (4 oz) chilled butter, cubed
1 kg (2 lb) raw medium prawns
1 tablespoon oil
5 cm (2 inch) piece fresh ginger, grated
3 cloves garlic, crushed
1/3 cup (80 ml/2¾ fl oz) sweet chilli sauce
1/3 cup (80 ml/2¾ fl oz) lime juice
1/3 cup (80 ml/2¾ fl oz) thick (double) cream
25 g (¾ oz) chopped fresh coriander
1 egg yolk, lightly beaten, to glaze
strips of lime rind, to garnish

1 Sift the flour into a large bowl, add the butter and rub into the flour with your fingertips until the mixture resembles fine breadcrumbs. Make a well, add 3 tablespoons water and mix with a flat-bladed knife, using a cutting action, until the mixture comes together in beads. Gather the dough together and lift out onto a lightly floured surface. Press into a ball and flatten into a disc.

(Alternatively, make in a food processor.) Wrap in plastic wrap and chill for 15 minutes.

2 Preheat the oven to moderately hot 200°C (400°F/Gas 6). Peel the prawns and gently pull out the dark vein from each prawn back, starting at the head end.

3 Heat the oil in a large frying pan and fry the ginger, garlic and prawns for 2–3 minutes. Remove the prawns and set aside. Add the chilli sauce, lime juice and cream to the pan and simmer over medium heat, until the sauce has reduced by about one third. Return the prawns to the pan and add the coriander; cool.

4 Grease 2 baking trays. Divide the pastry into 4 and roll out each portion, between sheets of baking paper, into a 20 cm (8 inch) circle. Divide the filling into 4 and place a portion in the centre of each pastry, leaving a wide border. Fold the edges loosely over the filling. Brush the pastry with egg yolk. Bake for 25 minutes, or until golden. Serve garnished with lime rind.

ABOVE: Freeform prawn pies

HERBED FISH TARTLETS

Preparation time: 40 minutes + 15 minutes
  chilling
Total cooking time: 45 minutes
Makes 8

1¼ cups (155 g/5 oz) plain flour
90 g (3 oz) butter, chopped
1 tablespoon chopped fresh thyme
1 tablespoon chopped fresh dill
2 tablespoons chopped fresh parsley
90 g (3 oz) Cheddar, finely grated
3–4 tablespoons iced water

Filling

400 g (13 oz) skinless white fish fillets
  (eg. blue-eye, warehou, cod, jewfish)
2 spring onions, finely chopped
2 tablespoons chopped fresh parsley
60 g (2 oz) Cheddar, finely grated
2 eggs
½ cup (125 ml/4 fl oz) cream

*ABOVE: Herbed
fish tartlets*

1 Lightly grease eight 10 cm (4 inch) round fluted flan tins. Sift the flour into a large bowl. Rub the butter into the flour with your fingertips until it resembles fine breadcrumbs. Stir in the herbs and cheese. Make a well in the centre. Add almost all the water and mix with a flat-bladed knife, using a cutting action, until the mixture comes together in beads. Gather together and form into a ball, adding more water if necessary. Wrap in plastic and refrigerate for 15 minutes.
2 Preheat the oven to hot 210°C (415°F/Gas 6–7). Divide the pastry into 8 portions. Roll each on a lightly floured surface, large enough to fit the tins. Ease into the tins, pressing into the sides. Trim the edges with a sharp knife or rolling pin. Place the tins on a baking tray. Cover each piece of pastry with a sheet of crumpled baking paper. Spread a single layer of dried beads or uncooked rice evenly over the base. Bake for 10 minutes. Remove the paper and beans and bake for 10 minutes, or until lightly browned. Cool.
3 Place the fish in a frying pan and add water to cover. Bring to the boil, reduce the heat and simmer gently for 3 minutes. Remove from the pan with a slotted spoon and drain on crumpled paper towel. Allow to cool, then flake with a fork. Divide among the cases and sprinkle with the combined spring onion, parsley and cheese. In a jug, whisk together the eggs and cream, then pour over the fish. Bake for 25 minutes, or until set and golden brown. Serve immediately.
NOTE: Smoked fish can be used. You can make the recipe in a 23 cm (9 inch) flan tin. Cooking time may be longer but check after 25 minutes.

SEAFOOD PARCELS

Preparation time: 25 minutes
Total cooking time: 35 minutes
Makes 20

★★

250 g (8 oz) skinless white fish fillets
  (eg. cod, snapper, coley, ocean perch)
100 g (3 1/2 oz) scallops
400 g (13 oz) cooked medium prawns
30 g (1 oz) butter
1 tablespoon lemon juice
1 tablespoon plain flour
1 cup (250 ml/8 fl oz) milk
60 g (2 oz) Cheddar, grated
1 tablespoon chopped fresh chives
1 tablespoon chopped fresh dill
10 sheets filo pastry
60 g (2 oz) butter, melted
2 teaspoons poppy seeds or sesame seeds

1 Preheat the oven to moderate 180°C (350°F/ Gas 4). Line a baking tray with baking paper.
2 Cut the fish into 1 cm (1/2 inch) wide strips. Wash the scallops and slice or pull off any vein, membrane or hard white muscle, leaving any roe attached. Peel the prawns and pull out the dark vein from each prawn back, starting at the head.
3 Melt the butter in a heavy-based pan. Add the fish, scallops and lemon juice. Cook over medium heat for 1 minute, or until tender. Remove from the pan with a slotted spoon, place in a bowl and keep warm.
4 Stir the flour into the butter and cook for 1 minute, or until pale and foaming. Remove from the heat and gradually stir in the milk. Return to the heat and stir constantly until the mixture boils and thickens. Reduce the heat and simmer for 2 minutes. Stir in the Cheddar, chives, dill, fish, scallops and prawns. Remove from the heat and season, to taste, with salt and pepper. Cover the surface with plastic wrap.
5 Layer 2 sheets of pastry together with melted butter, then cut into 4 equal strips. Cover unused pastry with a damp tea towel. Place 2 tablespoons of seafood mixture on one short end of each pastry strip. Fold in the edges and roll up. Repeat with the remaining pastry, seafood and some of the remaining butter. Place the parcels seam-side-down on the baking tray. Brush with the remaining melted butter, sprinkle with poppy seeds and bake for 20 minutes.
NOTE: You can make the sauce a day ahead and refrigerate until required.

LEFT: Seafood parcels

BAKED SPICED FISH CUTLETS

Preparation time: 15 minutes
Total cooking time: 15–20 minutes
Serves 4

1 tablespoon oil
1 onion, very finely chopped
2 cloves garlic, finely chopped
5 cm (2 inch) piece fresh ginger, finely grated
1 teaspoon ground coriander
1 stem lemon grass, white part only, finely
   chopped
2 teaspoons tamarind purée
2 teaspoons finely grated lemon rind
4 small fish cutlets (eg. blue-eye, snapper,
   kingfish, jewfish), tail end
lime wedges, to garnish

1 Preheat the oven to warm 160°C (315°F/
Gas 2–3). Line a baking dish or tray with foil and
lightly oil, to prevent the fish from sticking.
2 Heat the oil in a frying pan, add the onion,
garlic, ginger, coriander and lemon grass, and stir
over medium heat for 5 minutes, or until aromatic.
3 Stir in the tamarind, rind and some black
pepper. Remove from the heat. Allow to cool,
then spread over the fish. Arrange in the dish, in
a single layer. Bake for 10–15 minutes, or until
the flesh flakes easily when tested with a fork.
Don't overcook. Garnish with lime wedges.

BOMBAY FISH CURRY

Preparation time: 15–20 minutes
Total cooking time: 40 minutes
Serves 4-6

60 g (2 oz) ghee
1 small onion, finely chopped
1 clove garlic, crushed
2 dried red chillies, chopped, seeds removed
1/2 teaspoon grated fresh ginger
1 tablespoon ground coriander
1 teaspoon ground turmeric
1 teaspoon mustard powder
1/2 teaspoon chilli powder
1 1/4 cups (315 ml/10 fl oz) coconut milk

*BELOW: Baked
spiced fish cutlets*

2 tablespoons fresh lemon juice

1 kg (2 lb) whole fish (eg. snapper, bream),
cleaned and scaled

1 Melt the ghee in a frying pan. Add the onion,
garlic, chilli, ginger, coriander, turmeric, mustard
and chilli powder. Cook, stirring, for 3 minutes.
2 Add the coconut milk and lemon juice. Bring
to the boil, reduce the heat to low and simmer,
uncovered, until thickened.
3 Add the fish to the pan, cover and cook over
low heat for 20 minutes, or until tender. Turn
the fish once. Stir the sauce occasionally.

THAI-STYLE WHOLE SNAPPER

Preparation time: 10 minutes
Total cooking time: 30 minutes
Serves 4-6

2 cloves garlic, crushed

1 tablespoon fish sauce

2 tablespoons lemon juice

1 tablespoon grated fresh ginger

2 tablespoons sweet chilli sauce

2 tablespoons chopped fresh coriander

1 tablespoon rice wine vinegar

1 kg (2 lb) whole snapper, cleaned, scaled

2 spring onions, cut into julienne strips

1 Preheat the oven to moderately hot 190°C
(375°F/Gas 5). Place the garlic, fish sauce, lemon
juice, ginger, chilli sauce, coriander and rice
wine vinegar in a jug and mix well.
2 Place the snapper on a large piece of well
greased foil in a baking dish. Pour the marinade
over the fish and sprinkle with the spring onion.
3 Wrap the fish into a parcel and bake for
20–30 minutes, or until the flesh flakes easily.
Serve immediately with steamed rice.
NOTES: Make sure you grease the foil well or
the skin of the fish will stick to the foil and pull
away when the parcel is opened.

   You can also use a whole deep-sea bream,
murray cod or silver perch to make this recipe.

SNAPPER
Big snapper is often called
'old man snapper'. In
certain areas the older fish
develop a great bump over
the nape, while the snout
shows a prominent
swelling. The side view of
the head looks like that of
an old man.

*ABOVE: Thai-style
whole snapper*

MALAYSIAN FISH CURRY

Preparation time: 25 minutes
Total cooking time: 25 minutes
Serves 4

★ ★

500 g (1 lb) skinless white fish fillets
   (eg. ling, flake, hake, coley)
3–6 medium-sized fresh red chillies
1 onion, chopped
4 cloves garlic
3 stems lemon grass, white part only,
   sliced
4 cm (1 1/2 inch) piece fresh ginger, sliced
2 teaspoons shrimp paste
1/4 cup (60 ml/2 fl oz) oil
1 tablespoon fish curry powder (see Note)
1 cup (250 ml/8 fl oz) coconut milk
1 tablespoon tamarind concentrate
1 tablespoon kecap manis
2 ripe tomatoes, chopped
1 tablespoon lemon juice

ABOVE: Malaysian
fish curry

1 Cut the fish into cubes. Combine the chillies, onion, garlic, lemon grass, ginger and shrimp paste in a small food processor and process until roughly chopped. Add 2 tablespoons of the oil, to assist the blending, and process until the mixture forms a smooth paste, regularly scraping down the sides of the bowl with a spatula.
2 Heat the remaining oil in a wok or deep, heavy-based frying pan and add the paste. Cook for 3–4 minutes over low heat, stirring constantly until very fragrant. Add the curry powder and stir for another 2 minutes. Add the coconut milk, tamarind, kecap manis and 1 cup (250 ml/8 fl oz) water to the wok. Bring to the boil, stirring occasionally, then reduce the heat and simmer for 10 minutes.
3 Add the fish, tomato and lemon juice. Season, to taste, with salt and pepper. Simmer for 5 minutes, or until the fish is just cooked. The flesh will flake easily when tested with a fork. Serve immediately with steamed rice.
NOTE: Fish curry powder is a special blend of spices suited to seafood flavours. It is available from Asian food stores. Use chillies according to your taste. If you leave the seeds in, the curry will have a hotter taste.

THAI GREEN FISH CURRY

Preparation time: 40 minutes
Total cooking time: 20 minutes
Serves 4

4 fresh green chillies, seeded and chopped
4 spring onions, chopped
1 small onion, roughly chopped
2 cloves garlic, crushed
2 stems lemon grass, white part only, chopped
1 tablespoon chopped fresh coriander root
6 tablespoons fresh coriander leaves
6 whole black peppercorns
1 teaspoon ground coriander
2 teaspoons ground cumin
2 teaspoons finely grated lime rind
2 teaspoons shrimp paste
1 teaspoon ground turmeric
1 teaspoon salt
3 tablespoons oil
2¹/₂ cups (600 ml/20 fl oz) coconut milk

2 dried kaffir lime leaves
2 cm (³/₄ inch) piece dried galangal root
1 tablespoon fish sauce
750 g (1 ¹/₂ lb) skinless white fish fillet (eg. cod, coley, flake, ling), cut into cubes

1 Combine the chilli, spring onion, onion, garlic, lemon grass, coriander root and half the leaves, the peppercorns, ground coriander, cumin, lime rind, shrimp paste, turmeric, salt and 2 tablespoons of the oil in a small food processor. Blend to a smooth paste.

2 Heat the remaining oil in a pan, add half the curry paste and cook for 2 minutes, or until fragrant. Stir in the coconut milk, kaffir lime leaves, galangal and fish sauce and mix well.

3 Add the fish to the pan and simmer, uncovered, for 15 minutes, or until the fish is tender and the sauce has thickened slightly. Stir in the remaining coriander leaves. Serve with rice.

NOTE: This curry is even more delicious if made a day ahead. Refrigerate, covered. For a hotter dish, leave the chilli seeds in. Leftover paste can be sealed in an airtight container and refrigerated for up to 2 weeks, or frozen for up to 2 months.

GALANGAL
Fresh galangal is a rhyzome that looks like its close relative, ginger. It has a ginger-peppery flavour and is used as a seasoning. There are two types of galangal: white-fleshed *greater galangal* (also known as Siamese ginger, Laos ginger and Thai ginger) is the most common. *Lesser galangal*, which has orange-red flesh, is much hotter and stronger and is usually cooked as a vegetable.

ABOVE: Thai green fish curry

PRAWN GUMBO

Use a wooden spoon to stir the flour into the oil until the flour turns golden nutty brown.

Add the okra, bay leaf and tomato to the pan and bring to the boil.

Stir the peeled prawns and the roux into the mixture and season, to taste.

OPPOSITE PAGE:
Prawn gumbo (top);
Seafood burritos

PRAWN GUMBO

Preparation time: 30 minutes
Total cooking time: 50 minutes
Serves 4

 ✷ ✷

1 kg (2 lb) raw medium prawns
1/4 cup (60 ml/2 fl oz) oil
6 rashers bacon, finely chopped
2 1/2 tablespoons flour
2 tablespoons oil, extra
2 onions, finely chopped
1/2 teaspoon cayenne pepper
1 red pepper (capsicum), chopped
1 green pepper (capsicum), chopped
16 okra, ends trimmed, halved lengthways
1 bay leaf
2 x 400 g (13 oz) cans peeled tomatoes
1/2–1 teaspoon Tabasco sauce

1 Peel the prawns, leaving the tails intact. Gently pull out the dark vein from each prawn back, starting at the head end. Cover and set aside.
2 Heat the oil in a large saucepan, add the bacon and cook over medium heat for 5 minutes. Stir in the flour and cook, stirring until the flour turns nutty brown. Remove from the saucepan. This roux will be used to thicken and flavour the gumbo.
3 Heat the extra oil in the saucepan, add the onion, cayenne and peppers and cook, stirring over medium heat for 5 minutes, or until the onion is golden brown.
4 Add the okra, bay leaf and tomato to the saucepan and bring to the boil. Reduce the heat and simmer for 30 minutes. You may need to add up to 1 cup (250 ml/8 fl oz) water if the mixture is too thick.
5 Stir the prawns and the roux into the mixture and season, to taste, with salt and pepper, and Tabasco sauce. Cook for 5 minutes, or until the prawns are pink and cooked through.

SEAFOOD BURRITOS

Preparation time: 45 minutes
Total cooking time: 40 minutes
Serves 4

✷ ✷

250 g (8 oz) scallops
500 g (1 lb) raw medium prawns
500 g (1 lb) skinless salmon or ocean trout fillet
2 tablespoons oil
60 g (2 oz) butter
2 cloves garlic, crushed
3 small red chillies, seeded and finely chopped
4 large flour tortillas
2 1/2 tablespoons plain flour
1/2 cup (125 ml/4 fl oz) cream
3/4 cup (185 ml/6 fl oz) milk
1/2 cup (125 g/4 oz) sour cream
1/3 cup (35 g/1 1/4 oz) grated Parmesan
2 tablespoons chopped fresh parsley
125 g (4 oz) Cheddar, grated
chilli sauce, for serving

1 Slice or pull off any vein, membrane or white muscle from the scallops, leaving any roe attached. Peel the prawns and gently pull out the dark vein from each prawn back, starting at the head end. Cut the salmon into small pieces.
2 Preheat the oven to warm 160°C (315°F/ Gas 2–3). Heat the oil and half the butter in a frying pan. Add the garlic and chilli and cook for 1 minute. Add the scallops and cook for 2–3 minutes, then remove and drain on crumpled paper towels. Add the prawns and cook for 2–3 minutes; drain on paper towels. Add the salmon, cook for 3–4 minutes, then remove and drain on crumpled paper towels. Put all the seafood in a bowl.
3 Wrap the tortillas in foil and warm in the oven for 10 minutes. Melt the remaining butter in a pan over low heat, stir in the flour and cook for 1 minute, or until pale and foaming. Remove from the heat and gradually stir in the combined cream and milk. Return to the heat and stir constantly until the sauce boils and thickens. Stir in the sour cream (do not boil), Parmesan and parsley, pour over the seafood and mix well.
4 Fill each tortilla with some seafood and roll up to enclose. Place in a lightly greased ovenproof dish, sprinkle with the Cheddar and bake for 15–20 minutes, or until the tortillas are heated through and the cheese has melted. Serve with chilli sauce.

SARDINES WITH CHARGRILLED VEGETABLES

Preparation time: 25 minutes
Total cooking time: 35 minutes
Serves 4

2 large red peppers (capsicums)
4 finger eggplants (aubergines), cut into quarters lengthways

Dressing

1 tablespoon olive oil
1 tablespoon balsamic vinegar
1/2 teaspoon soft brown sugar
1 clove garlic, crushed
1 tablespoon chopped fresh chives

BELOW: Sardines with chargrilled vegetables

16 fresh sardines, butterflied (about 300 g/10 oz)
1 slice white bread, crusts removed
2 tablespoons fresh parsley
1 clove garlic, crushed
1 teaspoon grated lemon rind

1 Preheat the oven to moderate 180°C (350°F/Gas 4). Lightly grease a large baking dish with oil. Preheat the grill and line with foil.
2 Quarter and seed the peppers and grill until the skin is blistered and blackened. Cool in a plastic bag, peel and slice thickly lengthways. Lightly brush the eggplant with oil and grill each side for 3–5 minutes, until softened.
3 Combine the oil, vinegar, sugar, garlic and chives in a jar and shake well. Put the peppers and eggplant in a bowl, pour the dressing over, toss well and set aside.
4 Place the sardines on a baking tray in a single layer, well spaced. Finely chop the bread, parsley, garlic and lemon rind together in a food processor. Sprinkle over each sardine. Bake for 10–15 minutes, until cooked through. Serve the pepper and eggplant topped with the sardines.

ITALIAN FISH ROLLS

Preparation time: 25 minutes
Total cooking time: 20 minutes
Serves 4-6

1 large ripe tomato
1 tablespoon drained, bottled capers, chopped
45 g (1 1/4 oz) stuffed green olives, chopped
3 tablespoons finely chopped fresh lemon thyme
30 g (1 oz) Romano cheese, finely grated
2 teaspoons finely grated lemon rind
1/4 teaspoon freshly ground black pepper
8 thin white skinless fish fillets (eg. John dory, bream, perch, snapper, about 850 g/1 lb 11 oz)
1 cup (250 ml/8 fl oz) white wine
2 tablespoons lemon juice
3 tablespoons fresh lemon thyme leaves
2 bay leaves

1 Preheat the oven to warm 160°C (315°F/Gas 2–3). Score a cross in the base of the tomato. Place in a heatproof bowl and cover with boiling water. Leave for 30 seconds, then transfer to cold water and peel away the skin. Cut in half and

Remove the eyes by cutting a round of flesh from the base of the head.

Carefully slit open the head and remove the gut.

Use your fingers to push out the beak from the centre of the tentacles.

Cook the octopus in its own liquid over high heat until dry.

scoop out the seeds. Roughly chop the flesh and mix with the capers, olives, thyme, cheese, lemon rind and black pepper, in a small bowl.

2 Place the fillets skinned-side-up on a flat surface. Spread the tomato mixture evenly onto each fillet, then roll tightly and secure with a toothpick or skewer. Place in single layer in a shallow casserole dish.

3 Pour the combined wine, juice, thyme and bay leaves over the fish, cover and bake for 20 minutes, or until the fish is cooked and flakes easily when tested with a fork.

OCTOPUS IN RED WINE

Preparation time: 45 minutes
Total cooking time: 2 hours 20 minutes
Serves 4

1 kg (2 lb) baby octopus

2 tablespoons olive oil

180 g (6 oz) small brown pickling onions

1/3 cup (80 ml/2 3/4 fl oz) red wine vinegar

3/4 cup (185 ml/6 fl oz) dry red wine

1 ripe tomato, grated

1 bay leaf

1 teaspoon dried oregano leaves

1 To prepare the octopus, use a small sharp knife and remove the heads from the tentacles. Remove the eyes by cutting a round of flesh from the base of the heads. To clean the heads, carefully slit them open and remove the gut. Rinse thoroughly. Cut the heads in half. Push out the beaks from the centre of the tentacles from the cut side. Cut the tentacles into sets of four or two, depending on the size of the octopus. Pull away the skin from the heads and tentacles if it comes away easily.

2 Place the octopus in a large pan and cook over high heat in their own liquid for 15–20 minutes, or until dry. Add the oil and the onions, and toss over heat until well coated. Add the vinegar, wine, tomato, bay leaf, oregano, 1 cup (250 ml/8 fl oz) water and 1/2 teaspoon cracked black pepper, and bring to the boil. Reduce the heat to low and simmer for 1 1/2–2 hours, or until the flesh is tender. If not yet tender, add a little more water and continue cooking. The liquid remaining in the pan should just coat the octopus like a sauce.

NOTE: Young, small octopus are more tender than large ones. The octopus is closely related to squid and cuttlefish, so if you are unable to buy small octopus, you can use either of these.

ABOVE: Octopus in red wine

SEAFOOD MORNAY

Preparation time: 35 minutes
Total cooking time: 35 minutes
Serves 8–10

80 g (2³/4 oz) butter
¹/2 cup (60 g/2 oz) plain flour
¹/2 cup (125 ml/4 fl oz) dry white wine
1 cup (250 ml/8 fl oz) thick (double) cream
1 cup (250 ml/8 fl oz) milk
125 g (4 oz) Cheddar, grated
2 tablespoons wholegrain mustard
1 tablespoon horseradish cream
6 spring onions, chopped
1 cup (80 g/2³/4 oz) fresh breadcrumbs
1 kg (2 lb) skinless white fish fillets
    (eg. monkfish, coley, snapper, flathead),
    cut into cubes
450 g (14 oz) scallops, cleaned
400 g (13 oz) cooked peeled small prawns

Topping

3 cups (240 g/7¹/2 oz) fresh breadcrumbs
3 tablespoons chopped fresh parsley
60 g (2 oz) butter, melted
125 g (4 oz) Cheddar, grated

1 Preheat the oven to moderate 180°C (350°F/ Gas 4). Lightly grease a 2 litre (64 fl oz) capacity ovenproof dish.
2 Melt 60 g (2 oz) of the butter in a pan over low heat. Stir in the flour until pale and foaming. Remove from the heat and gradually stir in the wine, cream and milk. Return to the heat and stir over high heat until the sauce boils and thickens. Season with salt and pepper, to taste. Add the Cheddar, mustard, horseradish, spring onion and breadcrumbs. Mix well and set aside.
3 Melt the remaining butter in a large pan and add the fish and scallops in batches. Stir over low heat until the seafood starts to change colour. Drain the seafood, add to the sauce with the prawns, then transfer to the greased dish.
4 For the topping, mix all the ingredients and spread over the seafood. Bake for 35 minutes, or until the top is golden and the sauce bubbling.

ABOVE: Seafood mornay

CIOPPINO

Preparation time: 30 minutes + 30 minutes
    soaking
Total cooking time: 1 hour
Serves 4

2 dried Chinese mushrooms
1 kg (2 lb) skinless white fish fillets (eg. hake,
    snapper, ocean perch, red mullet)
375 g (12 oz) raw large prawns
1 raw lobster tail (about 400 g/13 oz)
12–15 black mussels
1/4 cup (60 ml/2 fl oz) olive oil
1 large onion, finely chopped
1 green pepper (capsicum), finely chopped
2–3 cloves garlic, crushed
425 g (14 oz) can crushed tomatoes
1 cup (250 ml/8 fl oz) white wine
1 cup (250 ml/8 fl oz) tomato juice
1 cup (250 ml/8 fl oz) fish stock
1 bay leaf
2 sprigs of fresh parsley
2 teaspoons chopped fresh basil
1 tablespoon chopped fresh parsley, extra

1 Place the mushrooms in a small bowl, cover
with boiling water and soak for 20 minutes. Cut
the fish into bite-size pieces, removing bones.
2 Peel the prawns, leaving the tails intact. Gently
pull out the dark vein from each prawn back,
starting at the head end.
3 Starting at the end where the head was, cut
down the sides of the lobster shell on the
underside of the lobster with kitchen scissors.
Pull back the flap, remove the meat from the
shell and cut into small pieces.
4 Scrub the mussels with a stiff brush and pull
out the hairy beards. Discard any broken
mussels, or open ones that don't close when
tapped on the bench. Rinse well.
5 Drain the mushrooms, squeeze dry and chop
finely. Heat the oil in a heavy-based pan, add the
onion, pepper and garlic and stir over medium
heat for about 5 minutes, or until the onion is
soft. Add the mushrooms, tomato, wine, tomato
juice, stock, bay leaf, parsley sprigs and basil.
Bring to the boil, reduce the heat, then cover
and simmer for 30 minutes.
6 Layer the fish and prawns in a large pan. Add
the sauce, then cover and leave on low heat for
10 minutes, or until the prawns are pink and the
fish is cooked. Add the lobster and mussels and
simmer for another 4–5 minutes. Season. Discard
any unopened mussels. Sprinkle with parsley.

SALMON CRUMBLE

Peel and quarter 1 kg (2 lb) floury potatoes,
(russet or pontiac). Boil until tender, drain and
mash. Melt 60 g (2 oz) butter in a pan and fry
10 finely chopped spring onions and 2 cloves
crushed garlic until soft. Stir into the potato
with 4 tablespoons milk and a 415 g (13 oz)
can of drained, flaked salmon. Spread into a
shallow casserole dish. Combine 60 g (2 oz)
melted butter, 2 cups (160 g/5$^{1}/_2$ oz) fresh
breadcrumbs, 3 tablespoons grated Cheddar
and some chopped parsley in a bowl. Sprinkle
over the top. Bake in a moderately hot 200°C
(400°F/Gas 6) oven for 20 minutes, or until
golden and crisp. Serves 4–6.

BELOW: Cioppino

INDIAN PRAWN CURRY

Preparation time: 25 minutes
Total cooking time: 20 minutes
Serves 4

★

1 kg (2 lb) raw medium prawns
25 g (³⁄₄ oz) ghee or butter
1 onion, finely chopped
3 cloves garlic, crushed
1 teaspoon grated fresh ginger
¹⁄₂ teaspoon cayenne pepper
2 teaspoons ground cumin
1 teaspoon garam masala
¹⁄₂ teaspoon ground turmeric
425 g (14 oz) can chopped tomatoes,
    undrained
¹⁄₃ cup (80 ml/2³⁄₄ fl oz) coconut cream
2 teaspoons finely chopped green chilli
2 tablespoons chopped fresh coriander

1 Peel the prawns, leaving the tails intact. Gently pull out the dark vein from each prawn back, starting at the head end.
2 Heat the ghee or butter in a large, deep frying pan. Add the onion and cook over medium heat until soft and golden. Add the garlic and ginger and cook for 1 minute. Add the cayenne pepper, cumin, garam masala and turmeric and cook for another minute, or until fragrant.
3 Add the prawns and tomato to the pan and simmer for 10–15 minutes, or until the prawns are cooked and the liquid has reduced.
4 Stir in the coconut cream. Add the chilli a little at a time until the mixture is as hot as you like. Season, to taste, with salt, and serve scattered with the coriander.
NOTE: You can substitute white fish fillets for half or all the prawns.

ABOVE: Indian prawn curry

Peel away the shells from the prawns, but leave the tails intact.

Process the onion, garlic, chillies, salt, oil, rind, herbs and spices until the mixture forms a smooth paste.

Add the fish sauce, galangal, coconut cream and lime leaves to the pan.

Add the prawns and simmer until the prawns turn pink and the sauce has thickened slightly.

THAI PRAWN CURRY

Preparation time: 30 minutes
Total cooking time: 10 minutes
Serves 4

★

1 kg (2 lb) raw medium prawns
1 small onion, roughly chopped
3 cloves garlic
4 dried red chillies
4 whole black peppercorns
2 tablespoons chopped fresh lemon grass
1 tablespoon chopped fresh coriander root
2 teaspoons grated lime rind
2 teaspoons cumin seeds
1 teaspoon sweet paprika
1 teaspoon ground coriander
1 teaspoon salt
3 tablespoons oil
2 tablespoons fish sauce
2 cm (³/4 inch) piece fresh galangal, thinly sliced
2 kaffir lime leaves
2 cups (500 ml/16 fl oz) coconut cream

1 Peel the prawns, leaving the tails intact. Gently pull out the dark vein from each prawn back, starting at the head end.
2 Put the onion, garlic, chillies, peppercorns, lemon grass, coriander root, lime rind, cumin seeds, paprika, coriander, salt and 2 tablespoons of the oil in a small food processor. Chop until the mixture forms a smooth paste.
3 Heat the remaining oil in a pan. Add half the curry paste and stir over low heat for 30 seconds. Add the fish sauce, galangal, kaffir lime leaves and coconut cream to the pan, and stir until well combined.
4 Add the prawns to the pan and simmer, uncovered, for 10 minutes, or until the prawns are cooked and the sauce has thickened slightly. Serve with steamed rice.
NOTE: Any unused curry paste can be refrigerated in an airtight container for 2 weeks, or frozen for up to 2 months.

ABOVE: Thai prawn curry

FISH BAKED IN SALT

Preparation time: 20 minutes
Total cooking time: 30–40 minutes
Serves 6

1.8 kg (3 lb 10 oz) whole fish (eg. blue-eye,
    jewfish, sea bass, groper), scaled and cleaned
2 lemons, sliced
4 sprigs of fresh thyme
1 fennel bulb, thinly sliced
3 kg (6 lb) rock salt
100 g (3½ oz) plain flour

1 Preheat the oven to moderately hot 200°C
(400°F/Gas 6). Rinse the fish and pat dry inside
and out with paper towel. Place the lemon,
thyme and fennel inside the cavity.
2 Pack half the salt into a large baking dish and
place the fish on top.
3 Cover with the remaining salt, pressing down
until the salt is packed firmly around the fish.
4 Combine the flour with enough water to form
a smooth paste, then brush, spreading carefully
and evenly, over the surface of the salt. Be
careful not to disturb the salt.
5 Bake the fish for 30–40 minutes, or until a
skewer inserted into the centre of the fish comes
out hot. Carefully crack open the salt crust with
the back of a spoon and gently remove the skin
from the fish, ensuring that no salt remains on
the flesh. Serve with Montpellier butter (see
page 129).

CURRIED PRAWNS

Preparation time: 20 minutes
Total cooking time: 10 minutes
Serves 4

1 kg (2 lb) raw medium prawns
30 g (1 oz) butter
1 onion, chopped
1 clove garlic, crushed
1 tablespoon curry powder
¼ cup (60 g/2 oz) plain flour
2 cups (500 ml/16 fl oz) milk
¼ teaspoon ground nutmeg
¼ teaspoon paprika

1 Peel the prawns, leaving the tails intact. Gently
pull out the dark vein from each prawn back,
starting at the head end.
2 Melt the butter in a pan over low heat, add
the onion and cook until soft. Stir in the garlic,
curry powder and flour and cook for 1 minute,
until the onion is coated in flour.
3 Remove from the heat and gradually stir in
the milk, nutmeg, and paprika. Return to the
heat and stir until the sauce boils and thickens.
4 Add the prawns and stir over medium heat for
2–3 minutes, or until the prawns are pink and
cooked through.

STUFFED FISH

Preparation time: 30–40 minutes
Total cooking time: 45 minutes
Serves 4

1 kg (2 lb) whole fish (eg. snapper, murray cod,
    sea bass), scaled and cleaned
¼ cup (60 ml/2 fl oz) lemon juice
30 g (1 oz) butter, chopped

Stuffing

2 tablespoons olive oil
1 small onion, finely chopped
3 tablespoons chopped celery leaves
2 tablespoons chopped fresh parsley
1 cup (80 g/2¾ oz) fresh breadcrumbs
1½ tablespoons lemon juice
1 egg, lightly beaten

1 Preheat the oven to moderate 180°C (350°F/
Gas 4). Pat the fish dry and sprinkle with salt and
the lemon juice. Set aside.
2 For the stuffing, heat the oil in a pan, add
the onion and cook over medium heat for
2 minutes, or until softened. Add the celery
leaves and parsley and cook, stirring, for another
2 minutes. Spoon into a bowl, add the
breadcrumbs, lemon juice and salt, to taste, then
mix well. Cool slightly, then stir in the egg.
3 Place the stuffing in the fish cavity and secure
the opening with skewers. Place the fish in a
large greased baking dish and dot with butter.
Bake for 30–35 minutes, or until the fish is
cooked and flakes easily when tested with a fork.
The thickness of the fish will determine the
cooking time. Transfer to a serving dish. Can be
garnished with lemon slices and fresh dill sprigs.

FISH BAKED IN SALT
When whole fish is baked
in layers of salt, the flesh
stays very moist, without
being too salty. When the
skin is peeled back, a
delightful, succulent flesh
is revealed. The salt helps
retain the moisture as well
as adding flavour. Since
ancient times, salt has
been used in food
preparation as both a
preservative and flavouring.

OPPOSITE PAGE:
Fish baked in salt (top);
Stuffed fish

ABOVE: Seafood terrine

SEAFOOD TERRINE

Preparation time: 1 hour
Total cooking time: 35 minutes + cooling + chilling
Serves 8

★ ★ ★

First layer

500 g (1 lb) raw medium prawns, chilled
2 egg whites, chilled
pinch of freshly grated nutmeg
1 cup (250 ml/8 fl oz) cream, chilled
150 g (5 oz) baby green beans

Second layer

250 g (8 oz) skinless salmon or ocean trout fillet, chopped
2 egg whites, chilled
2 tablespoons chopped fresh chives
1 cup (250 ml/8 fl oz) cream, chilled

Tomato coulis

750 g (1 1/2 lb) very ripe Roma (egg) tomatoes
2 tablespoons extra virgin olive oil
1 onion, very finely chopped
2 tablespoons Grand Marnier (optional)

1 Preheat the oven to moderate 180°C (350°F/ Gas 4). Brush a 1.5 litre (48 fl oz) capacity loaf tin, measuring 22 x 12 cm (9 x 5 inches), with oil and line the base with baking paper.
2 For the first layer, peel the prawns and gently pull out the dark vein from each prawn back, starting at the head end. Finely chop the prawns in a food processor. Add the egg whites one at a time, processing until smooth. Season with salt, pepper and nutmeg. Gradually add the cream. Don't over-process or it will curdle. Spoon into the prepared loaf tin, cover and refrigerate.
3 Cook the beans in boiling water until tender, then drain and plunge into cold water. Drain and dry with paper towels. Arrange lengthways over the prawn mixture.
4 For the second layer, process the fish until finely chopped. Add the egg whites one at a time and process until smooth. Add the chives. Gradually add the cream. Do not over-process or it may curdle. Spread evenly over the beans.
5 Cover the terrine tightly with foil brushed with oil and place in a baking dish. Pour cold water into the dish to come halfway up the side of the tin. Bake for 35 minutes, or until lightly set in the centre. Cool before removing the foil. Cover with plastic wrap and refrigerate until firm. Serve at room temperature.
6 For the tomato coulis, score a cross in the base of each tomato. Place in a heatproof bowl and cover with boiling water. Leave for 30 seconds, transfer to cold water, drain and peel away from the cross. Cut the tomatoes in half, scoop out the seeds with a teaspoon and chop the flesh. Heat the oil, add the onion and stir for 2–3 minutes, or until tender. Add the tomato and cook over medium heat, stirring often, for 8 minutes, or until reduced and thickened slightly. Stir in the Grand Marnier and cook for 1 minute. Cool, then process until smooth. Season, to taste, and serve with slices of terrine.

BREAM WITH TOMATO CHEESE CRUST

Preparation time: 40 minutes
Total cooking time: 15 minutes
Serves 4

2 ripe tomatoes
1 small onion, finely chopped
1 tablespoon tomato paste (tomato purée)
1/2 teaspoon ground cumin
1/2 teaspoon ground coriander
Tabasco, to taste
1/4 teaspoon ground pepper
1 tablespoon lemon juice
20 g (3/4 oz) butter, melted
4 medium skinless bream fillets
90 g (3 oz) Cheddar, grated
1/2 cup (40 g/1 1/4 oz) fresh breadcrumbs
lemon wedges, for serving

1 Score a cross in the base of each tomato, place in a heatproof bowl and cover with boiling water. Leave for 30 seconds, then plunge briefly in cold water. Peel away from the cross. Cut each tomato in half, remove the core and scoop out the seeds with a teaspoon. Finely chop the tomato flesh.

2 Preheat the oven to moderate 180°C (350°F/ Gas 4). Lightly grease a baking tray. Put the tomato in a small bowl and mix with the onion, tomato paste, cumin, coriander and Tabasco.

3 Combine the pepper, lemon juice and butter in a small bowl. Put the bream fillets on the prepared tray. Brush each fillet with the pepper mixture and top with tomato. Sprinkle with the combined Cheddar and breadcrumbs and bake for 15 minutes, or until tender and the fish flakes easily when tested with a fork. Serve with lemon wedges.

NOTE: Instead of bream, you can use snapper, John dory or ocean perch.

BREAM

Bream is a mild, sweet-tasting, popular variety of round fish. Its name is derived from the Old English for 'glitter', because of its shiny skin. Bream is available all year round. It can be grilled or baked whole, or filleted and fried or poached.

BELOW: Bream with tomato cheese crust

STUFFED CRABS

Preparation time: 30 minutes
Total cooking time: 25 minutes
Serves 6

★★

6 cooked medium blue swimmer crabs
60 g (2 oz) butter
2 cloves garlic, finely chopped
1/2 red pepper (capsicum), finely chopped
1/2 small green pepper (capsicum), finely
    chopped
1 small onion, finely chopped
1 stick celery, finely chopped
1/2 fresh red chilli, chopped
1/4 teaspoon celery salt
1/4 teaspoon dried thyme
2/3 cup (170 ml/5 1/2 fl oz) canned condensed
    seafood bisque
1 cup (80 g/2 3/4 oz) fine fresh breadcrumbs

BELOW: Stuffed crabs

1 Pull away the crab legs and claws, crack open and extract the meat from the legs. Reserve 2 front claws on each crab. Lift the flap on the underside of each crab and prise off the top shell. Remove the soft organs and pull off the gills. Scrub the crab back shells and set aside. Shred the crab meat, picking out the shell fragments.
2 Melt the butter in a pan and add the chopped garlic, pepper, onion, celery and chilli. Cook, stirring over medium heat, for about 5 minutes.
3 Add the celery salt, thyme and bisque and cook for 3 minutes. Add the crab meat with half the breadcrumbs. Stir until combined and season, to taste, with salt and pepper if necessary.
4 Preheat the oven to moderately hot 200°C (400°F/Gas 6). Spoon the mixture into the crab shells, smooth the tops and press the remaining crumbs over the surface. Bake the crabs on a baking tray for about 15 minutes, or until heated through and golden, adding the extra claws close to the end of cooking, to warm through.
NOTE: This can be made with frozen crab meat and baked in small ramekins. Oyster or cream of chicken soup can be substituted for bisque.

SEAFOOD CREPES

Preparation time: 25 minutes + 1 hour standing
Total cooking time: 30 minutes
Serves 6

★★

2/3 cup (85 g/3 oz) plain flour
1 cup (250 ml/8 fl oz) milk
1 egg
15 g (1/2 oz) butter, melted
1 teaspoon sugar

Seafood filling

300 g (10 oz) raw prawns
60 g (2 oz) unsalted butter
4 spring onions, finely chopped, white and
    green chopped separately
1 teaspoon Cajun spice mix (see Note)
1/2 teaspoon sweet paprika
1 large tomato, chopped
1/2 cup (125 ml/4 fl oz) dry white wine
170 g (5 1/2 oz) canned crab meat, drained, flaked
1/2 cup (125 ml/4 fl oz) cream
1 tablespoon plain flour
24 fresh oysters
2 tablespoons grated Cheddar

CREPES
Crepes are thin pancakes made from eggs, flour and milk and can include the addition of a little melted butter. Sugar is often added to crepes and herbs and spices can be used to flavour savoury crepes. Unfilled cooked crepes can be frozen for up to 3 months. To freeze, separate each crepe with a square of baking paper. When cold, wrap in plastic wrap, then foil, or store in an airtight container and freeze. When you want to use the crepes, it is best to thaw them in the fridge.

1 Sift the flour into a large bowl and make a well in the centre. Combine the milk, egg, butter and sugar in a bowl. Gradually add to the flour and whisk to make a smooth batter. Cover and stand for 1 hour.

2 For the filling, peel the prawns and gently pull out the dark vein from each prawn back, starting at the head end. Chop the prawns. Melt the butter in a pan, add the white parts of the spring onion and cook, stirring over medium heat for 2 minutes. Add the Cajun spice mix, paprika and tomato, and cook, stirring, for 3–4 minutes. Add the wine and cook, stirring until the sauce has thickened.

3 Stir the prawns and crab meat into the sauce and simmer for 2–3 minutes. Blend the cream and flour together in a small bowl and add to the pan. Cook, stirring, until the mixture boils and thickens. Add the oysters and green onion tops. Remove from the heat and set aside.

4 Preheat the oven to moderate 180°C (350°F/ Gas 4). Rub a crepe pan or small (16 cm/ 6½ inch) non-stick pan with paper towel dipped in butter or oil, then heat over moderate heat.

Pour in a small quantity of the batter and tip the pan so the batter spreads to cover the base. Cook until bubbles form on the surface, then turn and cook the other side until light golden. Remove from the pan. Repeat the process until all the batter is used. Stack the cooked crepes on top of each other and cover with a clean cloth.

5 Spoon some seafood mixture into each crepe and roll up to enclose. Arrange in a single layer in a lightly greased ovenproof dish. Sprinkle with the cheese and bake for 10 minutes, or until heated through. Can be served with lemon or lime wedges or slices and garnished with watercress sprigs.

NOTE: Cajun spice mix is available in some supermarkets and speciality food stores. Alternatively, see page 143 if you prefer to make your own spice mix.

ABOVE: Seafood crepes

SMOKED COD FLAN

Preparation time: 30 minutes + 20 minutes
  chilling
Total cooking time: 55 minutes
Serves 6

Pastry

1 cup (125 g/4 oz) plain flour

60 g (2 oz) butter, chopped

1 egg, lightly beaten

1 tablespoon lemon juice

Filling

300 g (10 oz) smoked cod or haddock fillets

3 eggs, lightly beaten

1/2 cup (125 ml/4 fl oz) cream

60 g (2 oz) Cheddar, grated

1 tablespoon chopped fresh dill

1 Preheat the oven to hot 210°C (415°F/Gas 6–7).
Lightly grease a 22 cm (9 inch) diameter loose-
bottomed fluted flan tin.
2 Sift the flour into a large bowl and rub in the
butter with your fingertips until it resembles fine
breadcrumbs. Make a well in the centre and add

the egg, lemon juice and up to 1–2 tablespoons
of water. Mix with a flat-bladed knife until the
mixture comes together in beads. Gently gather
the dough together into a ball, flatten into a disc
and wrap in plastic. Refrigerate for 20 minutes.
3 Roll the dough out, between 2 sheets of
baking paper, until large enough to cover the
base and side of the tin. Remove the top sheet of
paper and put the pastry in the tin, pressing into
the sides. Line with crumpled baking paper large
enough to cover the base and sides and spread a
layer of uncooked rice or baking beads over the
top. Bake for 10 minutes. Remove from the
oven and discard the paper and rice or beads.
Bake for another 5 minutes, or until golden.
Remove and cool slightly. Reduce the oven to
moderate 180°C (350°F/Gas 4).
4 Put the cod in a frying pan and cover with
water. Bring to the boil, reduce the heat and
simmer for 10–15 minutes, or until the cod flakes
easily when tested with a fork. Drain on
crumpled paper towels, then allow to cool.
5 For the filling, flake the cod into small pieces,
using a fork. Combine the eggs, cream, cheese
and dill in a bowl, add the cod and mix well.
Spoon into the pastry shell and bake for
40 minutes, or until set. Serve the flan hot
or cold with wedges of lemon or lime and
a green salad.

ABOVE: Smoked cod flan

FISH WELLINGTON

Preparation time: 30 minutes
Total cooking time: 1 hour 15 minutes
Serves 6

40 g (1¼ oz) butter

3 onions, thinly sliced

2 x 300 g (10 oz) skinless fish fillets (eg. monkfish, flake, hake, ling, each 30 cm/12 inches long)

½ teaspoon sweet paprika

2 red peppers (capsicums)

1 large (320 g/11 oz) eggplant (aubergine), cut into 1 cm (½ inch) thick slices

375 g (12 oz) frozen block puff pastry, thawed

⅓ cup (35 g/1¼ oz) dry breadcrumbs

1 egg, lightly beaten

1 cup (250 g/8 oz) natural yoghurt

1–2 tablespoons chopped fresh dill

1 Melt the butter in a saucepan, add the sliced onion and stir to coat. Cover and cook over low heat, stirring occasionally, for 15 minutes. Uncover and cook, stirring, for 15 minutes, or until the onion is very soft and lightly browned.

Cool, then season with salt and pepper, to taste.
2 Rub one side of each fillet with paprika. Place one on top of the other, with the paprika on the outside. If the fillets have a thin and a thick end, sandwich together so the thickness is even along the length (thin ends on top of thick ends).
3 Cut the red peppers into quarters, remove the seeds and membrane and cook, skin-side-up, under a hot grill until the skin blackens and blisters. Cool in a plastic bag, then peel. Place the eggplant on a greased baking tray and brush with oil. Sprinkle with salt and pepper. Grill until golden, then turn to brown the other side.
4 Preheat the oven to hot 220°C (425°F/Gas 7). Roll the pastry out on a floured surface until large enough to enclose the fish, about 35 x 25 cm (14 x 10 inches). The pastry size and shape will be determined by the fish. Sprinkle the breadcrumbs lengthways along the centre of the pastry and place the fish over the breadcrumbs. Top with the onion, then an overlapping layer of red pepper, followed by an overlapping layer of eggplant.
5 Brush the pastry edges with egg. Fold the pastry over, pinching firmly together to seal. Use any trimmings to decorate. Brush with egg, then bake for 30 minutes. Cover loosely with foil if the pastry is overbrowning. Slice to serve.
6 Stir the yoghurt and dill with a little salt and pepper in a bowl. Serve with the Wellington.

BELOW: Fish Wellington

SPICY BAKED FISH WITH VEGETABLES

Preparation time: 15 minutes + 30 minutes marinating
Total cooking time: 45 minutes
Serves 4

1 tablespoon cumin seeds
4 cloves garlic
1 small fresh red chilli
1 small bunch of coriander, leaves, stems and roots, roughly chopped
1 teaspoon salt
1 tablespoon lemon juice
5 tablespoons olive oil
1.5 kg (3 lb), or 2 x 750 g (1 1/2 lb) whole fish, (eg. snapper, red emperor, ocean perch, monkfish), scaled and cleaned
2–3 ripe tomatoes
450 g (14 oz) new potatoes, sliced
100 g (3 1/2 oz) pitted green olives, cut in halves

BELOW: Spicy baked fish with vegetables

1 Toast the cumin seeds in a dry pan over medium heat for 2–3 minutes, or until fragrant. Grind the seeds to a fine powder in a mortar and pestle, or in a spice grinder.

2 Mix the ground cumin, garlic, chilli, coriander, salt and lemon juice in a food processor, to form a smooth paste. With the motor running, add 2 tablespoons of the olive oil, in a thin steady stream.

3 Rinse the fish and pat dry with paper towels. Make 3–4 diagonal slits on both sides of the fish, then rub the spice mixture over the fish. Cover with plastic wrap and marinate in the refrigerator for 30 minutes.

4 Preheat the oven to very hot 240°C (475°F/Gas 9). Thickly slice the tomatoes and cut the slices in half. Place the fish in the centre of a large baking dish. Scatter the tomato, potato and green olives around the fish. Pour 1/4 cup (60 ml/2 fl oz) water and the remaining olive oil over the fish and vegetables. Bake, basting often, for 40 minutes, or until the fish is cooked through. When cooked, the fish will flake easily when tested with a fork.

GREEK-STYLE CALAMARI

Preparation time: 30 minutes
Total cooking time: 35 minutes
Serves 4-6

Stuffing

1 tablespoon olive oil

2 spring onions, chopped

1 1/2 cups (280 g/9 oz) cold, cooked rice

60 g (2 oz) pine nuts

75 g (2 1/2 oz) currants

2 tablespoons chopped fresh parsley

2 teaspoons finely grated lemon rind

1 egg, lightly beaten

1 kg (2 lb) medium squid hoods

Sauce

4 large ripe tomatoes

1 tablespoon olive oil

1 onion, finely chopped

1 clove garlic, crushed

1/4 cup (60 ml/2 fl oz) good-quality red wine

1 tablespoon chopped fresh oregano

1 Preheat the oven to warm 160°C (315°F/ Gas 2–3). For the stuffing, mix the oil, spring onion, rice, pine nuts, currants, parsley and lemon rind in a bowl. Add enough egg to moisten all the ingredients.

2 Wash the squid hoods and pat dry inside and out with paper towels. Three-quarters fill each hood with the stuffing. Secure the ends with toothpicks or skewers. Place in a single layer in a casserole dish.

3 For the sauce, score a cross in the base of each tomato, put in a bowl of boiling water for 30 seconds, then plunge into cold water and peel away from the cross. Chop the flesh. Heat the oil in a pan. Add the onion and garlic and cook over low heat for 2 minutes, or until the onion is soft. Add the tomato, wine and oregano and bring to the boil. Reduce the heat, cover and cook over low heat for 10 minutes.

4 Pour the hot sauce over the squid, cover and bake for 20 minutes, or until the squid is tender. Remove the toothpicks before cutting into thick slices for serving. Spoon the sauce over just before serving.

NOTE: You will need to cook 1/2 cup (100 g/ 3 1/2 oz) rice for this recipe.

ABOVE: Greek-style calamari

ABOVE: Baked salmon

BAKED SALMON

Preparation time: 10 minutes
Total cooking time: 35 minutes + 45 minutes
   standing
Serves 8

2 kg (4 lb) whole salmon, cleaned and gutted
2 spring onions, roughly chopped
3 sprigs of fresh dill
1/2 lemon, thinly sliced
6 black peppercorns
1/4 cup (60 ml/2 fl oz) dry white wine
3 bay leaves

1 Preheat the oven to moderate 180°C (350°F/
Gas 4). Rinse the salmon under cold running
water and pat dry inside and out with paper
towels. Stuff the cavity with the spring onion,
dill, lemon and peppercorns.
2 Brush a large double-layered piece of foil with

oil and lay the salmon on the foil. Sprinkle with
wine and arrange the bay leaves over the top.
Fold the foil over and wrap up, enclosing the
salmon tightly.
3 Place in a shallow baking dish and bake for
30 minutes. Turn the oven off and leave the
salmon in the oven for 45 minutes with the
door closed.
4 Undo the foil and carefully peel away the skin
of the salmon on the top side. Carefully flip the
salmon onto the serving plate and remove the
skin from the other side. Pull out the fins and
any visible bones. Serve at room temperature.
The baked salmon can be served with a sauce of
your choice.
NOTES: Do not open the foil during the cooking
or standing time. Remove the fish head if
necessary. You can also use ocean trout.

A simple cucumber sauce for serving with
the salmon can be made by mixing some
chopped Lebanese cucumbers with chopped
fresh chives and 2 tablespoons of whole-egg
mayonnaise and a little French mustard.

SNAPPER PIES

Preparation time: 25 minutes
Total cooking time: 1 hour 10 minutes
Serves 4

★ ★

2 tablespoons olive oil

4 onions, thinly sliced

1¹/₂ cups (375 ml/12 fl oz) fish stock

3¹/₂ cups (875 ml/28 fl oz) cream

1 kg (2 lb) skinless snapper fillets,
  cut into large pieces

2 sheets ready-rolled puff pastry, thawed

1 egg, lightly beaten

 Preheat the oven to hot 220°C (425°F/
Gas 7). Heat the oil in a large deep-sided frying
pan, add the onion and stir over medium heat
for 20 minutes, or until the onion is golden
brown and slightly caramelized.

2 Add the fish stock, bring to the boil and cook
for 10 minutes, or until the liquid is nearly
evaporated. Stir in the cream and bring to the
boil. Reduce the heat and simmer for about
20 minutes, until the liquid is reduced by half, or
until it coats the back of a spoon.

3 Divide half the sauce among four 2-cup
(500 ml/16 fl oz) capacity, deep ramekins. Put
some fish in each ramekin, then top each with
some of the remaining sauce.

4 Cut the pastry sheets into rounds slightly larger
than the tops of the ramekins. Brush the edges of
the pastry with a little of the egg. Press onto the
ramekins. Brush lightly with the remaining
beaten egg. Bake for 30 minutes, or until crisp,
golden and puffed.

NOTE: You can substitute bream, sea perch or
garfish for the snapper fillets.

ABOVE: Snapper pie

INDEX

page numbers in *italics* refer to photographs. Page numbers in **bold** type refer to margin notes.

ACKNOWLEDGEMENTS

HOME ECONOMISTS: Miles Beaufort, Anna Beaumont, Anna Boyd, Wendy Brodhurst, Kerrie Carr, Rebecca Clancy, Bronwyn Clark, Michelle Earl, Maria Gargas, Wendy Goggin, Kathy Knudsen, Michelle Lawton, Melanie McDermott, Beth Mitchell, Kerrie Mullins, Briget Palmer, Maria Papadopoulos; Justine Poole, Tracey Port, Kerrie Ray, Jo Richardson, Maria Sampsonis, Christine Sheppard, Dimitra Stais, Alison Turner, Jody Vassallo

RECIPE DEVELOPMENT: Roslyn Anderson, Anna Beaumont, Wendy Berecry, Janelle Bloom, Wendy Brodhurst, Janene Brooks, Rosey Bryan, Rebecca Clancy, Amanda Cooper, Anne Creber, Michelle Earl, Jenny Grainger, Lulu Grimes, Eva Katz, Coral Kingston, Kathy Knudsen, Michelle Lawton, Barbara Lowery, Rachel Mackey, Voula Mantzouridis, Rosemary Mellish, Kerrie Mullins, Sally Parker, Jacki Passmore, Rosemary Penman, Tracey Port, Jennene Plummer, Justine Poole, Wendy Quisambing, Kerrie Ray, Jo Richardson, Tracy Rutherford, Stephanie Souvilis, Dimitra Stais, Beverly Sutherland Smith, Alison Turner, Jody Vassallo

PHOTOGRAPHY: Jon Bader, Paul Clarke, Tim Cole, Joe Filshie, Andrew Furlong, Chris Jones, Andre Martin, Luis Martin, Reg Morrison, Andy Payne, Lindsay Ross, Hans Sclupp, Peter Scott

STYLISTS: Marie-Hélène Clauzon, Georgina Dolling, Kay Francis, Mary Harris, Donna Hay, Vicki Liley, Rosemary Mellish, Lucy Mortensen, Sylvia Seiff, Suzi Smith

The publisher wishes to thank the following for their assistance in the photography for this book:
The Bay Tree Kitchen Shop, NSW;
Bertoli Olive Oil;
Breville Holdings Pty Ltd, NSW;
Chief Australia;
CSIRO Marine Research, Australia;
MEC-Kambrook Pty Ltd, NSW;
Orson & Blake Collectables, NSW;
Royal Doulton Australia Pty Ltd, NSW;
Ruby Star Traders Pty Ltd, NSW;
Southcorp Appliances;
Sydney Fish Market Pty Ltd (Fish Line), NSW;
Villery & Boch Australia Pty Ltd, NSW;
Waterford Wedgwood Australia Ltd, NSW.